P9-BAU-381

EXTREME
GRANDPARENTING

Other Books by Dr. Tim Kimmel

Little House on the Freeway
Raising Kids Who Turn Out Right
Home Grown Heroes
The High Cost of High Control
Basic Training for a Few Good Men
Grace Based Parenting
Why Christian Kids Rebel
50 Ways to Really Love Your Kids
Raising Kids for True Greatness

"Tim and Darcy Kimmel speak from experience to provide a framework for the new era in grandparenting. Filled with their passion for building the family, this book is a call to action and a guide for grandparents striving to glorify God by building relationships."

—Dr. Dennis Rainey
President of FamilyLife

"Sometimes they come for a visit, and sometimes they come to live with you, but grandchildren always offer an opportunity for positive impact. For grandparents who take their role seriously, *Extreme Grandparenting* will give you the tools. As a grandparent, I highly recommend it."

—Gary D. Chapman, Ph.D.
Author of *The Five Love Languages,*
and *The Five Languages of Apology*

"In *Extreme Grandparenting* my good friends Tim and Darcy Kimmel have given me, and others who are and will be grandparents, an invaluable resource for understanding and executing the unique God-given role of passing on a godly legacy to our grandchildren."

—Dr. Tony Evans
Senior Pastor of Oak Cliff Bible Fellowship

"I love being a grandpa! It almost makes growing older worthwhile! And thanks to Tim and Darcy Kimmel's insights in *Extreme Grandparenting,* I now know how to do a much better job of loving my grandkids and blessing them in ways that will have eternal significance. Every grandparent needs to read this book."

—Gary Smalley
Best-selling author and proud grandpa

"The ultimate reward of having kids is having grandkids! But with the reward comes an amazing opportunity. Wide-eyed, grandkids love their grandparents, and no one has the opportunity to impact their lives quite like their parents' parents. Our friends Darcy and Tim will help you capture the moment."

—Joe and Martie Stowell
Teaching Pastor, Harvest Bible Chapel
Former President, Moody Bible Institute

"*Extreme Grandparenting* is the very best book we've read about understanding why it's imperative to invest our lives in our grandkids. Don't miss out. Grab a copy for yourself and buy one for each of your kids—that way they won't think you've gone crazy. (Just tell them you're crazy over being a grandparent!) And as Tim and Darcy would tell you, 'Get going on the ride of your life!' Tim and Darcy are leading the pack, and we are extremely proud to be following their footsteps in grandparenting with a purpose!"

—Dr. Gary and Barb Rosberg
America's Family Coaches and authors
of *The Five Sex Needs of Men and Women*

EXTREME GRANDPARENTING

the ride of your life!

DR. TIM & DARCY KIMMEL

TYNDALE HOUSE PUBLISHERS, INC., CAROL STREAM, ILLINOIS

Extreme Grandparenting

A Focus on the Family book published by
Tyndale House Publishers, Inc., Carol Stream, Illinois 60188

People's names and certain details of their stories have been changed to protect the privacy of the individuals involved.

Editor: Mary Ann Jeffreys
Cover design by: Jessie McGrath
Cover photograph of boy and grandfather, copyright © by Maria Teijeiro/Getty Images. All rights reserved.
Cover photograph of biker jumping, copyright © by Nick White/Getty Images. All rights reserved.

Library of Congress Cataloging-in-Publication Data
Kimmel, Tim.
Extreme grandparenting : the ride of your life! / Tim and Darcy Kimmel.
p. cm.
Includes bibliographical references.
ISBN-13: 978-1-58997-460-9
ISBN-10: 1-58997-460-3
1. Grandparents. 2. Grandparents—Conduct of life. 3. Grandparenting. I. Kimmel, Darcy, 1951- II. Title.
HQ759.9.K56 2007
248.8'45—dc22

2007005380

Printed in the United States of America
1 2 3 4 5 6 7 8 9 / 12 11 10 09 08 07

contents

Dedicated to all of those who come behind us:
Our children and their children.
May they find us faithful.

introduction

Starbucks Grandparents

Hi! I'm Tim Kimmel, but you can call me Grandpa.

And I'm Darcy Kimmel, and you can call me Darcy.

As you know, parents get the naming rights on their children, but grandchildren seem to get naming rights for their grandparents. Grandchildren get to call us whatever they come up with when they start to talk. Before it's over, we could end up being called any one of a bunch of names: Nana, Mimi, or Gramma; Papa, Granddad, or Pap. And we'll answer to any of them.

We relish our title of grandparents and, just like you, are desirous to know all we can about the grand role that we have the privilege of playing. Over the past three decades, we have been studying family relationships, writing about them, speaking about them, and encouraging others to fulfill their commitments and keep their promises.

Although we have dedicated our lives to educate, equip, and encourage families for every age and stage of life, we do not consider ourselves experts. We're just veterans. We each grew up in a family with six children. We have been doing constant research on the dynamics within families since we started Family Matters back in 1982. So far, we have published 10 books on how to let grace flourish within families. We've spoken to literally millions of people along the way about how to make the most of the unique relationships within marriage and the extended family.

God was wise to give us four children of our own to keep us in touch with reality. And realizing that a day would come when we would enter the holy of holies of parenting—grandparenting—we have been focusing on this wonderful role and taking detailed notes along the way. We have learned from the experiences of other grandparents and from the examples of our own parents (our children's grandparents) and grandparents, and we have learned from being grandparents ourselves. We are very excited to share with you what we have learned from our research, our observations, our interactions, our biblical study, and our own personal adventure down the back roads of grandparenthood. As you shift gears into this new thrill of grandparenthood, you are in for the ride of your life!

Twenty-First-Century Grandparenthood

There was a time when grandparents looked like their houses often smelled: old, musty, out of date, and out of touch. Some still do. Most don't.

You may not have heard the rumor going around, but the word on the street is that 60 is the new 40!

And it's not just a physical thing we're talking about. Grandparents not only look younger, they often act younger and *think* younger than the grandparents who came alongside them when they were children.

It's not out of the question to see a grandmother stop by Starbucks on her way home from the gym. She orders a Frappuccino ("nonfat milk, please"), pulls out her BlackBerry to check her email, and then text messages a business contact in Australia followed by another to her son at a university three states away. She may have five or six decades of living in her rearview mirror, but she is as contemporary as the *New York Times* sitting on the rack in the corner of the coffee shop.

A generation before, this woman's husband was more likely to have worn a blue collar to work than a white one. He would have been a tradesman or a man who worked with the land. His commute home from work was seldom more than a few miles. He was one of those grandfathers who still washed his own car and shingled his own roof. And there was a day on the calendar when he knew he would be able to walk away from his work for good and live on his Social Security.

Not anymore.

Most likely, the man married to this Starbucks grandmother has a college education, a passport with several stamps in it, and more money in his retirement accounts than his grandparents made in their entire lives. He doesn't make major repairs on his car or house. It's not that he's incapable of doing these things, but they simply don't make economic sense for him. Besides, his crowded schedule doesn't afford him the necessary time those chores of the past required.

Word on the street is that 60 is the new 40!

And if you want to see any recent pictures of the grandkids who fill these people's hearts with so much pride, they can make them appear on the screens of their cell phones in about the time it takes you to ask them if they'd mind.

The one thing today's grandparents have in common with their predecessors in past generations is that they carry in their hearts an innate and overwhelming love for their grandchildren. We call it a "Grand Love." We're convinced it's a *God* thing. Since the time Adam and Eve became the first grandparents, people in this role have always been inclined to spill over with pride when they think or talk of their grandkids.

But that is about as far as the comparison to our predecessors goes.

New Complexities

Today's grandparents have to process far more complex dynamics with the children whose photographs cover the doors of their refrigerators. For starters, grandchildren are more likely to be scattered all over the map of the Northern Hemisphere with multiple time zones separating them from their grandparents. This makes it far more difficult to enjoy the hands-on influence for which grandparenthood is known.

Because of the impact of divorce that haunts this new crop of grandparents, it's not uncommon that a breakup has occurred—either in the grandparents' marriage or in the marriage of one of their children. Besides the stress this puts on the kids and the "yours, mine, and ours" pressure this puts on the parents, grandparents are having to figure out where they fit into the lives of the kids within these blended families that often grow on one or more limbs of their family trees.

When it comes to finances, decades of a growing economy and rising property values have created grandparents who come to their position with far more discretionary resources than their successful counterparts in former generations. And there are a lot more of these types of grandparents. We're not suggesting that the average grandparents are wealthy. They aren't. And there are still many who come to their position with tight margins in their finances. But more and more, this generation of grandparents clearly has greater financial options going for them. This is both a blessing and a curse.

Money often complicates the relationships between grandparents and their offspring. When it comes to the financial holes children can dig for themselves, many of today's young families are deeper in debt than were parents raising their kids in the closing decades of the twentieth century. These financial challenges often create an economic connection between grandparents and their children that fogs up the bigger family picture. Where is the boundary line between being involved too much or too little in our children's financial lives?

And what about the challenges facing parents trying to raise their children within today's moral climate? Reality may not always be the bearer of good news, but it nonetheless must be embraced. The fact is that today's parents come to their jobs with far more cultural competition against their moral values and far less understanding of how to raise truly great kids. Today's grandchildren process enormous challenges to their concept of personal identity, their sense of confidence, their view of success, and their ability to figure out where they fit in the bigger world that surrounds them. All this simply means that grandparents can't assume they can ever come close to carrying out their God-given responsibilities if they are only giving accidental attention to their job.

Grand Help and Grand Hope

On the contrary, if grandparents want to make a positive difference in their grandchildren's lives, they must have a plan.

We've got one for you. We didn't make it up. God did. As always, the God who dreamed up intergenerational societies based on healthy families left a schematic in His Word for how to be an effective grandparent. As it turns out, God saw fit to give us grandparents four basic roles to play in our grandchildren's lives. We'll show you exactly what they are. And when we carry out these roles, we get a chance to not only help our grandchildren live far more fulfilling lives, but also increase their chances of making a significant impact on eternity.

Even with a plan, there are factors that complicate our ability to play these roles. Perhaps you didn't do as effective a job of raising your kids as you would have liked. The sins of commission and omission stalk your relationship with your kids. Perhaps this has left some heavy chips on your children's shoulders and some serious distance between their hearts and yours. These emotional distances often make it difficult for grandparents to play a significant part in their grandchildren's lives. We're going to help you with this.

We're going to learn about grandparenting up close as well as from a distance. We'll talk about the money issues, the time issues, and the discipline issues. And we're going to deal with the problem that millions of grandparents are contending with—playing the role of parent to their grandchildren. We'll show you how to make the most of this often-difficult situation.

We'll look at the problems that develop and the kind of position you can play in your grandchildren's lives when your own children go through a divorce.

It's not uncommon for our children to take themselves and their families in a different spiritual direction than our convictions would prefer. We'll learn how to walk the delicate balance this scenario requires.

And there's the issue of spoiling and favoritism. How do you spoil "properly" and avoid favoritism altogether? We'll show you how.

Grandparenthood is not just another phase of your life; it's a sacred calling. You have the opportunity to influence another generation of children; you play an eternal role in their lives. It's not often that we get such a significant second chance.

Grandparenthood is a sacred calling.

It doesn't matter whether you prefer listening to your music on a cassette or an iPod, whether you drop your checks in the mail or pay your bills online, whether you've been around the world or barely cleared the county line, you can play a profound and contemporary role as a grandparent. And you can have a blast in the process, having more fun than you ever did as a parent. Not only that, but you can help other grandparents be better equipped too.

You hold in your hands the big picture of grandparenting. Having the bigger picture in your mind and eternity in your heart turns inconvenience into opportunity, sacrifice into significance, and more of your time and energy into profound ministry in your grandchildren's lives. Knowing your clearly defined roles keeps the end product in mind.

Just like with parenting, the days may seem long, but the years are even shorter. That's why we must not only step up to the opportunity before us, but do so in a way that has the most lasting impact for good.

A great precept we ran across early in our lives that has helped us make wise choices about the things that matter most is this: Never sacrifice the permanent on the altar of the immediate. When it comes to our role as grandparents, there are a lot of low priorities that masquerade as urgent ones. There are a lot of myths and lies that masquerade as conventional wisdom. We're going to help you separate the wheat from the chaff. When you are done reading this book, you will understand the amazing opportunity you have been given and will have learned the priorities that will keep you from allowing the immediate to hold you hostage.

This book not only develops the overarching principles and the practical ways you can bring the best out of your grandchildren, but it contains tools that will show you how to use its principles until they become second nature. And the coolest thing is that it provides all you need to study it with others in your church or neighborhood who want to be better grandparents too.

Whether you're new to the role or a seasoned veteran, your confidence and stock value are going to go up by the time you get to the end of this book. In the process, you are going to gain a better grip on the joy that can be found in loving your children's children.

For Further Thought and Discussion

One generation will commend your works to another;
    they will tell of your mighty acts.
They will speak of the glorious splendor of your majesty,
    and I will meditate on your wonderful works.

They will tell of the power of your awesome works,
    and I will proclaim your great deeds.
They will celebrate your abundant goodness
    and joyfully sing of your righteousness. (Psalm 145:4-7)

1. What are some of the differences you see in the grandparents today and your parents or grandparents?
2. Based on those differences, what advantages did your parents or grandparents have? What advantages do you have in your role of grandparenthood today?
3. What are you hoping to learn or gain as a result of reading this book?

Heavenly Father,
Thank You for this blessing of grandchildren. As I read this book, please speak to my heart and help me to be open to the conviction of the Holy Spirit as I seek to grow in my role. I want to be the best grandparent I can be and I can only do that with Your help. Please show me how I can celebrate Your abundant goodness and commend Your works to my grandchildren. Amen.

part one

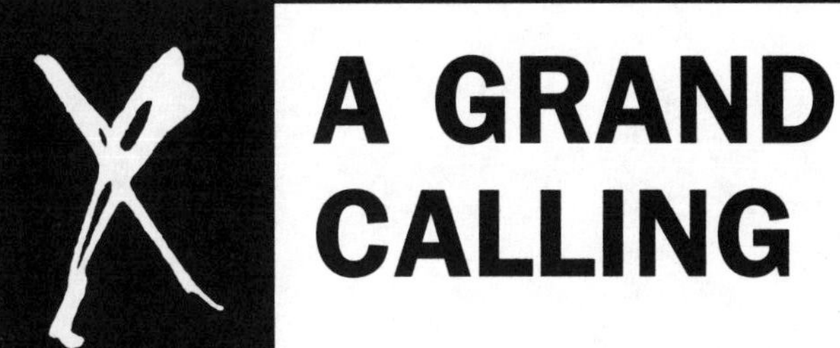

A GRAND CALLING

1 Putting the *Grand* Back in Grandparenting

Most grandparents would agree they have a role to play in their grandchildren's lives, but many aren't sure what that role is. They think they're doing well to send a card on a special occasion, offer a well-thought-through blessing at Thanksgiving, and occasionally take in a ball game together. But too many grandparents fail to realize the huge influence for good they could be in the lives of their grandchildren.

A gentleman in a field-test group for our DVD study that complements this book told us, after finishing just the first session, that even though he knew he had certain responsibilities as a grandparent, he never thought his sphere of influence was as great as it is.[1] By the end of the field test a paradigm shift had occurred for all the participants. They had a uniform desire to "step up their game" as grandparents. They also had a newfound excitement about what this role of grandparent could mean for them personally as they finished out their time here on earth.

It used to be that grandparents were nearby extensions to the greater family. Some even assumed they would finish the last couple of decades of life living in the same home as their grandkids. This was often anticipated and welcomed by everyone in the group picture. Some still enjoy this configuration, but as a twenty-first-century game plan, it is the exception rather than the rule.

And that's okay. Often, the configurations of the past were based on economics or convenience rather than some well-planned design. But, even if planned, the current alternatives aren't necessarily an improvement.

A lot of people who wear the mantle of grandparent still have kids of their own at home and are holding down full-time jobs. They have many years before they will either choose to or be *invited* to join the ranks of retirees. However, when you put the total years the average person is a grandparent in perspective, most of them will be spent in those retirement years. If they aren't careful, these grandparents could find themselves duped into embracing some of the cultural misinformation going around about how we are to view the last part of our lives. Will they misunderstand the term *empty nest* to mean freedom from any responsibility for their offspring? Will a warped view of what retirement is supposed to look like unwittingly encourage them to squander their greater role as grandparents?

Living Legends

If we could hand you anything that serves as a fitting symbol of your role as a grandparent, we'd hand you a golfer's glove. And it's not because we are suggesting you spend all of your free time on the golf course (though for at least one of the persons writing this book it would be fun to see what that feels like for a month or two!). It's just that golf is one of the great synonyms for life.

On those occasions when people who golf actually get to hit a round, they are often reminded of how much practice they need. Golf is a game that requires incredible skill within an environment of relaxed but focused concentration. Most people aren't born with the natural talent needed to be good at it. When you're a hacker, you have to do your best to develop your skill as you go along. That's what we often feel like when we take on our first major role in life—parenthood. But golf also offers some great parallels when it comes to this subject of grandparenting.

For instance, in professional golf, one of the finest tours in the PGA is the Champions Tour. This is a collection of the best golfers over 50 years of age—the crème de la crème, so to speak, who show a new generation of golfers how they got to be so good. These are the legends of golf who have endured the grueling demands of the PGA Tour and still have an immense love for the game. Grandparenting can be like that. It's a chance for parents who have fought a good fight and charted a good course to mentor a new generation of moms and dads.

Grandparenting offers us a chance to help groom a generation for greatness.

But there's another great parallel that golf offers to the subject of grandparenting. Often you hit the golf ball, and it doesn't go where you thought you were aiming it. You shank one into the woods or drop one in the lake. Unfortunately, because of the way the game is scored, those shots end up costing you dearly. But it's nice when the folks you're playing with give you a touch of grace. Someone says, "Hey, man, why don't you play a mulligan?"

For those of you who haven't taken up the game of golf, let us explain what that expression is all about. When someone grants you a mulligan, you get to take the shot over again and not have the original one count against your score. It's a chance to redeem yourself from the trouble you got yourself into. In a way, it describes what it's like to be a grandparent. It's like a second chance to make a profound and positive impression on a child's life—even if you struggled to do so with your own children.

Some people are given a greater amount of natural ability when it comes to golf. It's the same with parenting. Some of you—perhaps thanks to God-given insight or growing up in a certain type of family—have done a terrific job of raising your children. Others of you wish you had known more at the time or been able to dedicate more of your waking hours being the kind of parent your child needed. Here's what's great about grandparenting. It's like God whispers in your ear, *Why don't you play a mulligan. How about if I give you another chance to leave a powerful impression on a member of your immediate family?* Whether or not we were as effective as we wanted to be as parents, grandparenting offers each of us a chance to once again help groom a generation for greatness.

Welcome to the Best Years of Your Life

Most parents don't think much about their future role as grandparents when they welcome their first newborn into their hearts. They are too preoccupied to look that far ahead. But it is the logical and next step to our role as parents. And just like parents should have a strategy and a vision for their role, grandparents need one too.

Until recent years, most grandparents would say, "What's the big deal about being grandparents? We don't need a book to tell us how to take a kid fishing or show one how to bake cookies or read a grandchild a story in the rocker." But grandparenthood is more than rocking chairs—especially in this culture of fractured families and overloaded schedules. Grandparents can fill in the gaps and bolster the effectiveness of parents.

Rabbits and Storks

Some parents have to wait a long time before their married children bring them home some grandchildren. They drop subtle hints, such as wrapping a birthday present in a disposable diaper, or not-so-subtle hints, like ambushing their kids at Thanksgiving with questions such as, "What's taking you two so long? Haven't you figured out how this whole baby thing works?"

Other parents find themselves caught a bit off guard by the news that they are going to be grandparents. That's what happened to us with our first grandchild. We were just getting used to having a married daughter and a son-in-law. On Christmas Eve, seven months after our daughter's wedding, we were entertaining a houseful of family and friends, including our son-in-law's parents. It was there that our children chose to pull the four of us aside and present us with their Christmas present in private. When our son-in-law's mom and Darcy saw the small rectangular box containing their gift, they assumed it was the completed wedding video we had been anxiously awaiting. We would soon discover that the wedding was in the distant past and new adventures were about eight months away. Our son-in-law's mom opened the box, screamed, immediately shut it, and then threw it to Darcy.

Darcy couldn't imagine the reason for her reaction, so she cautiously removed the cover of the box only to discover two positive home pregnancy tests.

We are extremely grateful they don't do that test with rabbits anymore.

It took about 30 seconds for the news to register with the moms. It took a bit longer for the dads to figure out what all the screaming was about.

But it didn't take long for any of us to decipher what it all meant. For Darcy and me, grandparenting is something we had been thinking about and studying for years. Because of our work with families, we have been keenly aware—sometimes painfully—of the strategic role grandparents play or fail to play in their grandchildren's lives. Our children were offering us a chance to come alongside them and cheer them on as they assisted God in a miracle. They were in the process of creating new life, and we were given the opportunity to help them give that new life great meaning. Grandparenting is a sacred trust, a chance to imprint a child for true greatness. And just like parents have a God-given bond with their children, so grandparents have a natural affinity to their grandchildren. Grandparents and grandchildren represent a marvelous love affair between the generations.

It's true! There's something unique about the natural connection grandparents have with their grandchildren. And vice versa. There are few things that compare to the uninhibited shriek of a grandchild running through the open front door, ignoring everyone else in her path, until she flies into the arms of gramma or grampa. The smothering affection of a grandchild who couldn't care less about how old you are or how you look makes you feel like you live a gilded life. And there's something hauntingly attractive about the calm connection of a teenager to his grandparent, especially when that teenager is going through a period where he's convinced his parents have lost their minds.

Grandkids have an innate desire to love and be loved by their grandparents.

Grandkids have an innate desire to love and be loved by their grandparents. In fact, sometimes they actually develop a more peaceful relationship with their grandparents than they have with their own parents. As we mentioned in the introduction, that's what we like to call "Grand Love." This wonderful connection between the hearts of grandchildren and grandparents can sometimes annoy the parents caught between the generations. They wonder why their parents get along better with their children than they do. Someone has suggested the reason grandparents get along so well with their grandchildren is that they both share a common enemy!

A lot of you know exactly what that means. You've been conspiring with your grandkids to even up a few scores! But regardless of whether your relationship with your own children went smoothly or had a lot of bumps, you want to make sure you don't miss this divine opportunity to help your children raise a person who can stand strong and make a significant difference in the world.

A New Type of Grandparent

Let's take a look at how this present generation of grandparents compares to past generations. Presently, there are close to 80 million of us in the United States alone. The National Survey of American Households indicates average age of a first-time grandparent is now 47. They're the best educated, most active, and youngest "older" generation that has ever lived. Almost all of us have graduated from high school, and 7 out of 10 have attended college or technical school. In spite of the pressures on us financially, we still have more discretionary income than our parents or our grandparents could have ever imagined. We continue to work or earn income years longer than our counterparts of the past generation. We're not into rocking chairs and Metamucil as much as our grandparents were. We compute more and crochet less. We buy more and bake less. Our hand-painted Volkswagen van has been replaced by an SUV or a motor home. The more vigorous among us have exchanged tie-dye for t'ai chi. And almost all of us have exchanged love beads for love handles.

The bulk of this generation of grandparents tends to shy away from thinking they are old. They're more street-smart, financially savvy, and sexually active than their predecessors. And when it comes to energy and how much activity we are used to cramming into a typical day, the new challenge is not whether we can keep up with our grandchildren, but whether they can keep up with us! It brings to mind something Peggy Noonan said. Peggy is not only a presidential speechwriter, author, and columnist; she is a careful student of our culture. She is also a member of this current generation of grandparents. She wonders, as so many do, just what kind of impact we will have. Listen to how she framed the issue. Ms. Noonan says, "We are and have been the most significant demographic fact of American life in all of American history. We changed, in our youth, the culture of a great nation, sweeping it with our music, our movies, our art and styles and tastes in entertainment. Our assumptions about sex changed the sexual landscape. We altered our country's political climate when we decided to oppose a war, changing American attitudes about our government in the process."[2]

A question needs to be asked: Based on all that our generation has done, will we proceed to redefine grandparenthood too? Well, in response to this question, not only do we think we will redefine grandparenthood, but we're convinced we already have. But to follow up that question: Is what we're coming up with an improvement, or is it a digression from what God expects of us? Many of the things this generation has going for it—better health, economic flexibility, and affordable mobility—can also work against it when it comes to making a commitment to remain a vital part of the nuclear family. We have so many more options for where we live, where and when we travel, how long we remain in the marketplace, and how we can spend our discretionary time. Unlike our own parents or grandparents, we are not tied down to our hometown or a job that ends at age 65. We have the world before us! We want to challenge you to make sure your children and their children are always a huge part of that world.

You've no doubt heard the running joke among grandparents that goes something like, "If I had known grandchildren were going to be this much fun, I would have had them first." It gets a polite laugh, but we all know why God never meant for it to be that way. God placed a strategic order into a family's timeline. Grandparenting is an earned privilege that fits right into God's perfect plan. There are reasons why He wanted us to be parents first. Obviously, He wanted us to raise the kids to whom we give birth. But He also wanted to use this time to groom us to be loving, effective grandparents once our children started giving birth to the next generation. God wanted us to experience those 20-year-long wake-up calls called *children*, so when the time came, we would be able to come alongside our own grown children with a more seasoned and tempered view of life as they try to raise their own kids.

The Words of a Seasoned Grandfather

We have some favorite passages of Scripture that encourage us as grandparents, but there is one that really stands out like a theme for our lives as mentors to a new generation. It's Psalm 71:17-18. The Bible doesn't say who the author of this psalm is. But we can take a fairly good guess. We can assume the writer is someone who has lived a long life and has taken careful notes along the way. And because Psalm 71 references six other psalms—some are quoted verbatim—and all six of those psalms were written by David, there is a good chance this psalm was penned by him too, most likely toward the end of his life. That would make it a psalm written by a man who made a lot of mistakes as a father. And yet, as he moved into the twilight of his life, he wanted to use what opportunities he had to imprint a new batch of young people with truths he'd learned along the way. This passage presents words of wisdom from a person who knows how to turn the lessons of life—even the regrettable ones—into practical help for those who follow behind.

Listen to how he summarizes the essence of a person who uses the end of his life to touch the people just starting theirs: "Since my youth, O God, you have taught me, and to this day I declare your marvelous deeds. Even when I am old and gray, do not forsake me, O God, till I declare your power to the next generation, your might to all who are to come."

The writer of this psalm is reminding all of us that during these years when we get to sit on the top limbs of the family tree, we have more than an opportunity—we have a responsibility—to use our position to make a difference in the lives of the people closest to us. We need to be committed grandparents. We need to see this as one of the best opportunities we will ever be offered—outside of raising our own children—to do something that lives on long after we are gone.

Much of the media coverage regarding senior adults talks about the search for significance apart from the marketplace. Someone shared something with us about life, and it fits perfectly as we close out this chapter: "Rather than filling your life with things to make you feel significant, fill your life with significant things." Your grandchildren are very significant. They are the best reasons in the world to be proud God chose to put the word *grand* in front of your title.

Starting Out on the Right Foot[3]

1. Don't nag your kids until they produce grandchildren.
2. Let them make the announcement to your family and their friends.
3. Don't play the name game. Let them come up with the names of their children, and then smile.
4. Resist the temptation to tell about all your pregnancies and births.
5. Accept the fact that they are going to do things differently than you would and did.
6. Offer your assistance, and then back off until called upon.
7. Make an effort to get to know the other set of grandparents. You are going to be co-conspirators with them.
8. Don't start going wild with your purchases. Ask permission or advice before you go crazy in the baby department.
9. Build up their confidence by affirming their ability to be good parents.
10. Pray, pray, pray for your kids, for the baby, for the other grandparents, for the siblings, and for yourselves.

For Further Thought and Discussion

Since my youth, O God, you have taught me,
 and to this day I declare your marvelous deeds.
Even when I am old and gray,
do not forsake me, O God,
till I declare your power to the next generation,
 your might to all who are to come. (Psalm 71:17-18)

1. During your lifetime, what are some of the ways God has taught you about Himself?
2. What do you want to tell your children about God's power and might when it comes to raising their children?
3. How are you personally continuing to grow in your faith so you can tell your grandchildren about God's work in your life in the present tense?
4. Knowing what you know now, has your philosophy of parenting changed much since you were raising your children? How does this affect your view of your children's philosophy of parenting?

Heavenly Father,
Thank You for all You have taken me through in my life. Thank You for the things You have taught me about Yourself and myself. Now Lord, please help me use my life to pass on Your love to my grandchildren. Thank You for this second chance to be used by You for Your kingdom. Amen.

2 Grand Assets

In a Western culture with boundless opportunities and thriving economies, it's easy to get sucked into the "success lie"—a view that limits the people we consider successful to the ones who have an abundance of money, are easy to look at, can push their weight around, or are well-known. If you can corner the market in all four categories, the success lie says you're in a league of your own. It's the "wealth, beauty, power, and fame" mantra that drones from the pages and programs devoted to the lifestyles of the high and mighty.

This delusional view of what really matters can set a trap for our children. Our culture loves to dispense generous doses of the poison pill known as "comparison." Unfortunately, many young couples take it like it's their daily vitamin. They look around at what conventional wisdom says is important, and the next thing you know, they're working with a madness to get their piece of the wealth, beauty, power, and fame pie.

The logical next step is for them to push their children toward these same goals. Parents get preoccupied with how their children look, the status of their children's friends, the elite nature of their children's schools, and the performance behind their children's efforts. Their kids know they are being evaluated by how they stack up next to other kids.

Wealth, beauty, power, and fame become the invisible yardsticks with which parents measure their children's success. Grandchildren are pushed toward stellar grades, exclusive friendships, and the need to outperform the people with whom they compete. They are pushed to be on the best teams, get into the best colleges, marry people of status, and corner the career market.

In too many families, the commitment of parents to the success fantasy isn't even subtle. Everything they do testifies to their goal and passes it on to their children: If you want to be *somebody* and have an enviable position among those considered wealthy, beautiful, powerful, or well-known, you've got to start in childhood to work toward that goal.

This is a bankrupt view of life, self-possessed in its focus and extremely limiting in its positive influence. But it is embraced by so many of our up-and-coming families. What these parents don't realize is how debilitating the success illusion is on their children's ability to grow up and actually live lives that matter. Nor do they see that they are actually inviting tremendous tension into their homes.

The success lie is the ultimate joy stealer when it comes to raising kids. Aiming children at the empty targets of success increases sibling rivalry, disrespect toward parents, disenchantment with themselves, and teenage rebellion. And when kids can't make the superficial grade, the success lie can lead toward frightening self-destructive behavior. Too many choose drugs, alcohol, promiscuity, and self-annihilation in their reaction to difficult and meaningless goals.

Probably the worst problem with the success illusion is that kids are pushed toward a future that is a direct contradiction of what God has called parents to be building into their children's lives. This explains why so many kids brought up in homes that try to push both a relationship with God and superficial success goals end up with kids who have no heart for God. The success lie is a recipe for spiritual indifference.

Here's the saddest commentary on this issue: Many of these young parents were taught this faulty view of life . . . by us.

A Truly Great Life

I (Tim) wrote a book about this toxic kind of parenting titled *Raising Kids for True Greatness.*[1] In it I put the success illusion on trial and show parents how to ignore the one-dimensional mantra of culture and instead aim their children at something far more exciting and fulfilling than a future as shallow as "success." Instead, we need to aim our children at *true greatness.*

And what is that? True greatness is a commitment to live their personal lives and inspire *their* children's lives with a passionate love for God that shows itself in an unquenchable love and concern for others.

True greatness is about aiming our kids at a future that puts God and others ahead of themselves. It's about living lives for something bigger than life. It's about investing their futures in ways that will outlive them.

A commitment to instilling true greatness into children puts a priority on building qualities into their hearts that set them up to live lives that matter in profound and eternal ways. It's about building them up to be valuable resources to God, to society, and to the people close to them. Whereas the success lie pushes the priorities of wealth, beauty, power, and fame, true greatness lifts up the priorities of humility, gratefulness, generosity, and a servant spirit. *Raising Kids for True Greatness* outlines exactly how to build these wonderful qualities into a grandchild's life as well. It also demonstrates how these wonderful qualities can set them up to be . . . truly *successful in God's eyes.* True greatness—that passionate love for God that shows itself in an unquenchable love and concern for others—prepares children to answer the three biggest questions in life:

- What is my mission in life going to be?
- Who is my mate going to be?
- Who is my Master going to be?

Ironically, studies and statistics demonstrate that people formatted with a commitment to living truly great lives are more attractive to the marketplace. These are the very people who are being handed the keys to the most significant offices and the most strategic positions in the corporate world. Studies and statistics also demonstrate that people with a commitment to live truly great lives have happier marriages, have more satisfying sexual lives, raise more contented children, and experience a lot less divorce. For Christians it's all because they've made a decision to make the Lord the Master of their lives. They want to live their lives for the things He says are important—things that last forever.

It's about investing their futures in ways that will outlive them.

Obviously, there is nothing wrong with being wealthy or beautiful or powerful or famous. The problem is when a person *needs* these things in order to feel complete. When parents aim their children at true greatness, often worldly success follows. Except now they are in a position to enjoy it and steward it well. Why? Simple—they don't need it to feel complete.

We grandparents have a chance to play a huge role in helping instill this priority into our grandchildren's lives.

Sobered by Reality

We mentioned above that sometimes the reasons our children are pushing our grandchildren toward the emptiness of one-dimensional success is because we taught them how to do it. Let's be honest. Many people moving into the ranks of grandparenthood swallowed the hook of the success lie too. Many sold their souls to it. But by now we should be able to see through the empty nature of success for success' sake. By now we should know that people are more important than things, love is more important than time, and God is more important than everything. If we don't realize at this point in our lives that wealth doesn't determine happiness, beauty is indeed only skin deep, power is a two-edged sword, and fame isn't nearly what it's cracked up to be, then obviously, we haven't been paying attention.

Unfortunately, the track record of many grandparents indicates that far too many of us haven't paid attention. If you're not convinced about the long-term damage the success lie brings or of the overwhelming value of choosing a life of true greatness, you might want to mark your spot in this book, go read *Raising Kids for True Greatness*, and then come back and pick up where you left off. You will be a far better grandparent if you do. You can't afford to squander the opportunity before you. Furthermore, you don't need to. God wants to use these next years of your life to do something that is truly extraordinary. You can be the grandparent who has infused true greatness into your DNA. And you are the best person to show your children and grandchildren how they can do the same. Your commitment to embody and model a "truly great" life will put you in the best position ever to share the amazing assets you bring to your role.

More Than Meets the Eye

The average grandparent has little concept of the assets he or she brings to bear on the role. It's too bad. If they fully grasped this, they might be more inclined to invest their lives in their children's children and use the wisdom they've gained to set them up for better lives.

No doubt the inordinate priority our culture puts on the shallow measurements of one-dimensional success contributes to some grandparents missing the incredible value they bring to the equation. If we get to the golden years of our lives without much gold to show for our years spent getting there, it's easy to think we don't have much to offer our grandchildren. This false notion is accentuated when the grandparents on the other branch of the family tree score higher marks in the wealth, beauty, power, and fame categories than we do. This is a good time to remind ourselves that these symbols of success have no bearing on whether a person is good or decent or noble. Having a lot to offer our grandchildren has nothing to do with our commercial status in society.

Taking an Inventory of Your Assets

When it comes to grandparenting, you don't have to be financially rich to be wealthy. You don't have to have youthful lines and be easy to look at to be beautiful. You don't have to be the bull of the block to wield enormous influence. And you don't have to be widely known outside your family circle to be a celebrity. We'll throw in one more: You don't have to have a postgraduate degree to be wise.

There's something to be said for having been around the block several times. There's something to be said for the worry lines around our eyes and the gray hair that clusters at our temples. God brings us to our role as mentors to our adult children and our grandchildren with the weathered experience of a veteran parent. We know what it's like to feel alone, to feel inadequate, and to feel unqualified.

That's why some of the key contributions we bring to our calling as grandparents are the assets we've accumulated from living life and hopefully paying attention along the way.

Handing Down Life's Lessons

When our first child was born, Darcy's mom had been with us for two weeks waiting for the baby to arrive. She had determined her airline schedule based on Darcy's due date. Unfortunately, our firstborn took her time, arriving ten days after that due date. When she finally made her entrance into our lives, by C-section, it was another five days before Darcy and the baby could come home from the hospital. That was the day Darcy's mom had to get back to her home in Florida. I (Tim) remember hugging my mother-in-law good-bye just before putting her on the plane and thinking, *What are we going to do now? We have no idea what to do with a new baby.* The presence of a seasoned veteran like Darcy's mother—a woman who birthed and raised six kids—would have eased the anxiety we felt as we processed that first month as parents.

You don't have to be financially rich to be wealthy.

Somehow we survived and ultimately thrived as we learned parenting lessons together. We know what it's like to be overwhelmed with responsibilities. We've struggled through the challenges of expensive demands and limited resources. We understand that parenting can push you to the limits of joy and frustration in the same moment.

Many years later, when that same daughter we brought home from the hospital was giving birth to our first grandchild, we were standing outside the door of the delivery room. The door was deliberately left ajar, and we were able to listen as she and our son-in-law, the doctor, and the attendants all played their parts in the wonderful symphony called "birth." As we listened to our granddaughter gasp for her first breaths and then let out that beautiful first wail of life, we knew that God was calling us all to step up to new roles.

It wasn't that our parenting days were over. Rather, it was the expansion of that role into the lives of a new generation—but on a far "grander" scale. We were now going to get to love our children in an entirely new way, by loving their children and walking alongside them as they experienced the good, the bad, and the ugly that crowd the continuum of parenthood.

Royal Grandparents

Over the last few decades, God has been graciously grooming us through life experiences that—when coupled with our relationship with Him—have created a treasure chest of relational assets. The time has arrived for us to apply this godly wisdom to our relationships with our grown children and grandchildren. Consider it a *royal* opportunity. There's a biblical reason you might want to do this.

The Bible mentions several types of crowns we can end up wearing as a result of our pilgrimage with God. But there are two crowns in particular that are great additions to our wardrobe as grandparents. The first type of crown can be found in Proverbs 17:6. It says, "Children's children are a crown to the aged, and parents are the pride of their children." Our grandchildren are like jewels set in gold that God rests on our heads. They are supposed to be a reward for making it this far and not strangling them in the process. But we have to keep in mind that many people have worn crowns but didn't live up to the responsibilities the crown represented. A crown says we have been put in a position of privilege. But it's a position that has loyal (or disloyal) subjects whom we are responsible to lead with wisdom.

Our children and grandchildren need to be able to trust us to walk worthy of our calling as people who have been appointed by God for a sacred purpose. We need to wear our crowns responsibly. It starts by reeling in our egos and rolling out God's grace.

This first crown is the best precursor to another type of crown God mentions in His Word. Except this one isn't figurative. When it comes to this crown, some grandparents (mothers!) get by with a little help from their friends at L'Oréal. But for most of us, it's for real. We're told all about this crown in Proverbs 16:31: "Gray hair is a crown of splendor; it is attained by a righteous life."

Our Five Greatest Assets

Our gray hair says we've put some miles on our hearts. It's a mantle of wisdom that puts us in a position to invest some great assets into our grand calling. We'd like to list a handful of our most strategic assets. These are the assets our children and grandchildren desperately need from us. And when invested wisely, these are the assets that multiply the odds that the generations following behind us can have the best chance at living meaningful and significant lives.

Asset #1—Maturity

Don't choke as you read that word. One of the first assets we bring to the forefront of our role as grandparents is *maturity.* At least it should be. Maturity is the result of a deliberate decision on our part to learn from life.

- It's letting our victories and defeats be our teachers.
- It's viewing what we've been through against the backdrop of God's eternal truth.
- It helps us draw better conclusions, more careful assumptions, and more tempered suppositions when we're facing the future.

Our children and grandchildren desperately need us to consider it a mandate that we act like grown-ups. That doesn't mean we can't be fun loving, youthful, and even occasionally silly within our role as grandparents. But they need to know that when life is trying to get the best of them, they can look to us and see people they can count on to process everything through years of experiencing God's grace.

They don't need to see us being petty, throwing tantrums, acting selfish, or being ruled by our egos. One of the best ways to make sure we bring maturity to the picture is by feasting on a regular diet of God's Word.

If you have not been a student of the Scriptures up to this point in your life, it's not too late to become one. One of the wisest things Darcy and I have done as individuals is commit to reading the Bible daily. This ongoing exposure to what God says about life and how He relates to us both at our best and at our worst has had a calming effect on our lives over time. It has given us an ability to view life from God's vantage point and try to make more mature choices. Our mentioning this could easily be misinterpreted as boasting. We're certainly not looking for applause. If anything, we're merely a couple of beggars telling other people who could use a good meal where to go for food.

It's simple. The best way to turn our years of life into maturity is to allow God to teach us as we go. The best way to know what He thinks about all we are experiencing is to weigh everything against the truth found in His Word. As the wise sage said, "The fear of the LORD is the beginning of wisdom, and knowledge of the Holy One is understanding. For through me your days will be many, and years will be added to your life" (Proverbs 9:10-11).

Asset #2—Experience

You've run your fair share of laps around the infield of life. By this time, you've just about seen it all (and perhaps done it all). Because of your life experiences:

- You know that you can raise a family on a shoestring.
- You know that no matter how crazy the children may act, eventually, they calm down and fall asleep.
- You know from experience that you can endure more than you think you can.

Your experiences provide clout when you offer advice. They help you maintain a sense of calm in the face of the most frightening dilemmas your children might encounter with your grandchildren.

They enable you to whisper a *wiser* encouragement into a grandchild's ear when life seems to be getting the best of him. Hopefully, because of the many things you've been through, you can confidently say to your child or grandchild, "You are going to get through this. I know because we have too."

We know a wonderful grandmother who had cared for her elderly mother for many years. Her mother had very demanding emotional and physical needs as her mind and body deteriorated in the last two decades of her life. This grandmother was able to encourage her daughter when her child was diagnosed with autism. The grandmother knew how important a support system was, how necessary it was to redefine "normal," and how to keep expectations realistic. She also knew the pain, disappointment, and discouragement her daughter and son-in-law might face. She understood how this could take a toll on their marriage if they didn't guard against it. She was able to be there with encouragement as well as hands-on help because of what she had been through with her own mother.

We come alongside to help them carry their heavy burden of parenting.

Which brings up another vital asset we can offer to the next generation.

Asset #3—Perspective

If you don't live near your grandchildren, it's easier to distance yourself from some of their urgent demands. Because your grandchildren's problems aren't your personal problems, you can be more objective. But even if your grandchildren live with you, your head start in the marathon of life gives you a more tempered view of its demands.

Perspective not only helps us see a problem more clearly, it also lends an eye through retrospection. We can evaluate our grandchildren's challenges under a less-biased and longer-view microscope. Our seasoned perspective helps us see through academic setbacks, sibling competition, and teenage rebellion to a bigger view. How many times have you looked back on your parenting days and realized that what you thought was a big deal at the time was really minor compared to the big picture? Grandparents have the vantage point of being above tree line whereas parents are still in the woods. Our perspective doesn't cause us to trivialize serious matters, but it can help keep us from overreacting. It can also help lessen our children's anxiety by our calm approach and response to problems.

Permit us to recite a litany of experiences that have won us our current perspective: I (Tim) once sank my dad's boat. During my junior-high years the cops picked me up and took me down to the local precinct on the occasion of my being an idiot. I was suspended from high school twice. Darcy and I spent a lot of time and money in emergency rooms. We've done our share of waiting up for a kid who was out past curfew. We know how lonely and frightening an all-night bedside vigil can be. Our kids have broken bones during mission trips in Spain while we were back in Arizona. We've had kids knocked unconscious. We've had kids on the receiving end of broken hearts. We've had an ATV flip over on one of our sons and smash the helmet he was wearing (fortunately his head was spared the fate of the helmet). Darcy and I know what it feels like to have a child chosen last or to watch a couple of seasons where our boy played on a team that didn't win a single game.

Chances are you also faced these same types of events in your home. And it's the calm response and hope-laden advice you offer to your children and grandchildren when the sky is falling on them that will help them weather life's setbacks. Perspective helps us use the past to evaluate the present so that we can make more sober choices in the future.

A relationship with God can give us His perspective when it comes to helping our children and grandchildren make sense out of their lives. Scripture says, "God is our refuge and strength, an ever-present help in trouble. Therefore we will not fear, though the earth give way and the mountains fall into the heart of the sea" (Psalm 46:1-2). What we learned about God's presence and power in the past can equip us to be phenomenal assets to our children as well as their children.

Obviously, an adult can get to the position of grandparent and yet not have developed a very advanced level of maturity, experience, or perspective. Even if that's the situation, grandparents still have a responsibility toward their families. We all need to concentrate on our development as grandparents. We hope this book will encourage you to grow in these areas. These first three assets create the context in which we can give the last two assets to our children and grandchildren. These are the assets that come covered with sweat.

Asset #4—Assistance

It is a sobering thought to realize that the child who could not remember to brush her teeth and couldn't find the homework she was holding in her right hand is now in charge of our grandchildren. Realizing what a huge assignment that is, we know how important it is to be available to help our children out.

There are four key ways we can offer assistance. The first is by giving them our *time.* Not that we are sitting around with nothing to do, but one of our roles as a grandparent is to make time for our kids and grandkids. The apostle Paul says in Philippians 2:3-4, "Do nothing out of selfish ambition or vain conceit, but in humility consider others better than yourselves. Each of you should look not only to your own interests, but also to the interests of others." Measured against the backdrop of these powerful words, it would be hard to justify not having time for our grandchildren.

Do you remember the old Rolaids commercial where they asked,

"How do you spell relief?" and then they spelled out "Rolaids"? Well, *grandparent* has an alternative spelling too: it's T-I-M-E. Grandparenthood and time are two sides of the same coin. Whether our children live next door or across the country, they need us to devote time to assist them when they become parents. Our older daughter was married and had two little girls while our youngest two children were still in high school. Just when the demands of parenting were supposed to be winding down and the nest clearing out, we found ourselves with two other children who needed our time and attention. Though we often have to balance spending our little bit of discretionary time between parenting and grandparenting, it's an investment that can pay off forever. And it's a lot of fun to boot!

It's an investment that can pay off forever.

Our willingness to offer assistance through the investment of our time naturally parlays into a second key way we can assist our children, and that's by offering them *relief.* True, we might need to buy Rolaids in Costco portions in order to bring this relief to our children, but it is a vital assistance. We can come alongside them when they're discouraged, exhausted, or sick to help them carry their heavy burden of parenting.

When a friend lost his wife during the birth of their first child, it was his mother, slipping into the middle of his grief, who helped calm his anxiety and allay his fears. She brought continuity and hope into his life until he remarried a couple of years later.

A wonderful grandma in our office took care of her granddaughter so her son-in-law could take her daughter to a nice resort over a weekend to celebrate her birthday. It was a welcome relief that allowed them to invest in the greatest part of their role as parents—their marriage.

We take our grandchildren with us each summer for the week we speak at a wonderful family conference center in Texas. That week gives their parents a much-needed respite from the daily grind. It also gives our grandchildren a great adventure they look forward to each year.

All of these are standard ways grandparents can ease the burden their children have to carry, providing time for parents to get recharged before going back on duty.

A third way we can be of assistance to our children is by being a *sounding board* that lets them try out ideas regarding their role as parents. Obviously, we can do more harm than good if we offer unsolicited advice, or cross the border and become a controlling, manipulative parent, but those grandparents who humbly seek God for wisdom—when approached by their children for help with a dilemma—can have a phenomenal impact on their lives.

One way we have been used as a sounding board is through hosting and facilitating a young-couples study at our home. Actually, it was our older daughter's idea. She pointed out that many of her friends were finding themselves overwhelmed by the pressures of marriage and parenting. When we first approached these young couples with the idea of getting together, they were excited about the opportunity to have mentors who had time and experience to share with them. Though we are only official grandparents to two of the children represented by this group, we have had the joy of patiently listening to these wonderful young moms and dads and encouraging them as they raise their children. Without a seasoned and godly sounding board, it is too easy for our children to listen to the wrong voices when it comes to their marriages and their children.

There is a fourth way we can be of assistance to our children. But it is the one that holds the greatest potential for harm if we don't manage it carefully. It's when we assist them with *money*. There is a right way and a wrong way to offer financial assistance. To do this well, a grandparent needs wisdom to discern when, why, and how much to offer. Because of the tricky nature of this type of assistance, we are going to address it in depth later on in the book. But in this overview of our grand calling, we at least wanted to give it honorable mention.

Asset #5—Love

How could we make a list of assets we need to bring to our position as grandparents and not mention *love*? Love is what motivates us to offer all of our other assets. I suppose it's assumed that grandparents would certainly offer love to their children and grandchildren. But the relationship allows for a special type of love—a *grand* love, one that has been seasoned and tempered with years of the previously mentioned assets: maturity, experience, and perspective. We are now able to love our children in grander ways and offer a love to our grandchildren that may be closer to what we wished we could have given our children. When our children become parents:

- They need a love that comes with fewer strings attached than perhaps they got when they were growing up in our homes.
- They need a love that is unclouded with regrets and mistakes of the past.
- They need a love tempered with forgiveness.
- They may even need a love that asks us to give up much in order to give *their* children a chance for rewarding lives.

Jesus summed it up when He said, "Greater love has no one than this, that he lay down his life for his friends" (John 15:13). The great thing about a grandparent's love is that it comes with fewer selfish motives. Another bonus is that by now we should have more patience than we had as parents.

Many times, grandparenting love is as close to unconditional love as a human love can get. We've had years of experience at turning the qualities of love listed in 1 Corinthians 13 from nice poetic words into real life. If anyone should embody the type of love expounded in this key passage of Scripture, it should be grandfathers and grandmothers. Grand love should be a love that "is patient, is kind, does not envy, does not boast, is not haughty, is not rude, is not self-seeking, is not easily angered, keeps no record of wrongs, does not delight in evil but rather rejoices with the truth, always protects, always trusts, always hopes, always perseveres, and never fails" (1 Corinthians 13:4-8, author paraphrase).

As grandparents, we're more likely to love our grandchildren with less need for them to meet an unrealistic performance standard. There are two reasons for this: First, our grandchildren's behavior is more of a reflection on their parents than on us. We can see past many of their shortcomings, hang in with them, and touch them with love at the core of their hearts. The second reason is that by this time in our lives we should be able to see how hollow and dysfunctional it is to attach their performance (either good or bad) to the level of love we offer. We should be mature enough to love without conditions.

We've learned over the years that many things masquerade as love, but they are actually cheap knockoffs. When we're young and inexperienced about the ways of life and love, we have some excuse for offering up a half-baked love. But when we get to this point in our lives, when our love has been tested, it's time for us to offer a love our kids and grandkids can count on. And if you carefully define what you mean when you say "love," you're more likely to offer the genuine article.

For many years we have been sharing a definition of love with couples, parents, and grandparents all over the country. It covers every scenario you may encounter in relationships and defines the type of love a grandparent needs to have for a grandchild. It is this: "Love is the commitment of my will to your needs and best interests, regardless of the cost."

Our grandchildren's needs and best interests may not always align with their wants. And meeting their needs may not always be convenient for us. If we use this definition of love as a starting point, we're in a better position to let God "selfish-proof" our love into something that can really make a difference in the lives of our children and grandchildren.

So as a grandparent who has the benefit of seasoned wisdom, you have the opportunity to come alongside your children and grandchildren with maturity, experience, perspective, assistance, and a love they profoundly need.

Meanwhile, Back at the Church

We'd like to close this chapter with a special message to the people who oversee our churches: the pastors, priests, elders, and deacons.

Today's families are in an intense cultural struggle, facing many and formidable contrary forces. Many families are overwhelmed with the stresses that push them to the limits of their energy and resources. Now more than ever, grandparents are necessary to a family's success, providing the extra strength and endurance young parents need to face the challenges of raising truly great children. Grandparents can bring the valuable assets of maturity, experience, perspective, hands-on assistance, and love that their grand calling requires. But they can do this a lot more effectively if the church is willing to come alongside and offer encouragement along the way.

And there's the rub. Grandparenting as a valuable spiritual role is seldom given ongoing focus by the church. What's more, most church leaders are unaware of the relational gold mine they have in grandparents, instead viewing them as relics with little to offer the present generation. Grandparenthood is acknowledged as a title and a privilege, but grandparents get little, if any, formal training in churches.

This is why we've written this book as well as created the *Extreme Grandparenting: The Ride of Your Life* DVD curriculum for churches.[2] We want to show churches how they can mine the depths of the riches of grandparents and thereby equip them to mentor both their married children and *their* children. Also, it's a way for the church to encourage and empower their grandparents as they carry out their sacred calling and role.

When churches make a commitment to equipping grandparents, the church gains much in return. All the assets grandparents bring to their families can also be brought to bear on the greater church family. Creating an environment that places high value on the position of grandparent gives the seasoned population within a church a higher sense of purpose. They are more engaged in the greater work of the church. They are more inclined to bring their maturity, experience, perspective, hands-on assistance, and love to church and to spread it around.

If value is given to grandparents within a congregation, they give value back. A church is only as healthy as the health of the families showing up each Sunday. Grandparents who are equipped and trained to bring the best out of their children and grandchildren improve the moral, emotional, and spiritual health of their churches.

Today, grandparents matter more than ever before. Yet even though they play a vital part in the success of today's families, many grandparents feel irrelevant, undervalued, disconnected, or even unsure of their roles or boundaries. A well-thought-through curriculum and an outspoken enthusiasm for the role of grandparents can make an earthly and eternal difference to the youngsters who gather in the church's nurseries, children's ministries, and youth groups.

We've built discussion tools into this book as an asset to help churches meet this vital need. To learn more about the DVD curriculum *Extreme Grandparenting: The Ride of Your Life* that complements this book, go to www.grandparenthood.net. You can view a promotional video where we introduce the study, as well as view samples of each session.

Grandparenthood is supposed to be the dividend years of our life. It can be if we accept our grand calling and turn our relational assets into investments that will last forever.

For Further Thought and Discussion

The fear of the LORD is the beginning of wisdom,
and knowledge of the Holy One is understanding.
For through me your days will be many,
and years will be added to your life. (Proverbs 9:10-11)

1. Which of the five assets (maturity, experience, perspective, assistance, and love) do you feel most qualified to offer?
2. What are some of the experiences you have been through that give you a more realistic view of parenting and that you could use to encourage your children in raising your grandchildren?
3. Using the definition "Love is the commitment of my will to your needs and best interests, regardless of the cost," list several needs and best interests of your children or grandchildren that you as a grandparent can offer to meet with the assets discussed in this chapter.

Heavenly Father,
Please remind me of the struggles of parenthood, and give me a patient empathy for my children as they are raising my grandchildren. Lord, may I love them the way You love me—with grace. Impress upon me the best ways I can come alongside them with the maturity, experience, perspective, assistance, and love with which You have gifted me. Show me how I can help meet their needs and best interests and give me the strength to make the sacrifices necessary. Thank You for the sacrificial love You have shown for me. Amen.

3 Sacred-Cow Tipping

There are some stunts from the past that this new generation of kids will simply never get to try. Cow tipping is one of them—as in pushing a cow onto its side. For one thing, if you want to see a cow, most kids have to go to the zoo. Today, most cows live in nice, rural, bovine-type "country clubs" designed for efficiency and maximum output. Cows don't graze much anymore.

But we'd like to bring back the tradition for a few pages and tip over some cows in this chapter—some *sacred* cows, defined as anything exempt from questioning. They've been trampling down a lot of the better pasture for effective grandparenthood for too long. It's time we did something about them.

Sacred Cow #1: The Empty Nest

The first sacred cow we want to tip over is the one called the *empty nest.* But first we need to agree on the meaning. It's not just when the baby of the family heads off for college. When this happens, our nest isn't really empty; it's just temporarily vacated. Until they make that final move over the horizon for good, they'll be back every few months to download and refuel. For our discussion, we're not talking about this temporary configuration but rather that time in our lives when our last child moves out to create his or her own life somewhere else.

From an emotional standpoint an empty nest is either a time for grieving or a time for celebrating, or both. Sometimes one spouse grieves while the other one pops the champagne. Like any major change in life, the transition into an empty nest configuration requires some internal and external adjustments. But once the reality sets in that you can actually listen to *your* music all the time, don't have to play tug-of-war with a teenager over the TV remote, and are actually free to chase each other around the house wearing as little as you want, the empty nest usually finds itself well received by the two people left behind.

It's easy to fall prey to interpreting empty bedrooms and empty chairs at the dinner table as a license to abdicate our ongoing role as parents. The feeling you get when you finally see the last child up and running in his or her own life is much like the feeling you get when you cross the finish line of a marathon. I (Tim) know of what I speak. I've crossed several marathon finish lines. The primary thing you want to do once you've finished running 26 miles and 325 yards is sit down, or maybe lie down, or better yet go to sleep for a couple of weeks. After such a major physical and mental challenge, you need a break.

It's the same with the empty nest. You've invested 20-plus years of your life, spent tons of money, lost years of sleep, and put some rough miles on your body for each of your children. It was time, money, and tears well spent, but you're older now and a little slower than you were the day you brought the first child home from the hospital. It's natural to relish the thought that most of the sweat, labor, and heavy lifting is behind you.

After running a marathon, it's tempting to turn a temporary rest break into a way of life. That's why runners magazines advise us to decide in advance that within three to four days after you've run your marathon, you'll slip into your running shoes and put a few miles on them. The same works for the empty nest. If you find the quietness, the slower pace of life, and the lack of daily hassles intoxicating, beware of the danger of your empty nest changing from a living configuration to a syndrome.

That would be a huge mistake.

Here's the good news: Most parents don't fall into this trap. When their last child drives away, their hearts go with that child. That son or daughter may be out of sight, but he or she is still very much on their minds. And if that son or daughter has a child, most empty nesting parents are ready to make a strong heart connection to that grandchild.

However, there are two debilitating attitudes that can take root in the heart of a parent who is enjoying the new life of empty nesting too much. One diminishes the returns on our calling as grandparents. The other dismisses the calling altogether.

Loving Our Comfort = Diminishing Returns

The first attitude is being too enamored with our personal *comfort.* We're willing to be grandparents as long as it doesn't require much. We'll go to events at school, show up for a soccer game, have the kids over, and even watch the grandkids as long as it isn't often and doesn't require much time or energy on our part.

Here's the problem with this attitude: Just about anything our kids would want us to do with or for the grandkids is going to be inconvenient. It takes time, physical energy, money, and a lot of flexing of our emotional muscles to be good grandparents. If we let ourselves get too attached to our new leisure, we will undermine the relationship God meant for us to have with our grandkids.

Our children and grandchildren know when we view them as inconveniences. They know when we'd rather be elsewhere. It says to them, "You're not that important to me."

While I was visiting some friends back east, sitting in their kitchen with their three children, one set of grandparents stopped by, announcing their arrival as they came through the front door. As they did, the three kids scrambled out through the back hallway and upstairs to their bedrooms. Their parents forced them to come back downstairs to say hello to their grandparents. In less than 15 minutes, the grandparents were gone.

After waving good-bye at the door, the mother turned to her husband, rolled her eyes, and shook her head.

"What's wrong?" I asked.

In response, they volunteered how frustrated they were with this particular set of grandparents, the mom's. I inquired about the kids' hasty exit when their grandparents arrived.

"Oh, it goes way back to when they were little. It was obviously a hassle for Mom and Dad to come to birthday parties and family gatherings. They've been no-shows at a couple of very important events in our kids' lives, even after they had told us they would be there. They've left some birthday parties before the candles were blown out. Once they called at the last minute to tell us they had planned to go to a movie at that time. A movie! The kids went out of their way to invite their grandparents to things like Grandparents Day at school, ball games, and church programs. Though they sometimes came, it was obvious to the kids as well as to us that they'd rather have been somewhere else."

Our grandchildren know when we view them as inconveniences.

She went on to describe one incident that seemed to define the relationship. "Our oldest son needed help with his math. His grandfather is a superb mathematician. Our son called him and asked if he'd be willing to come over to work with him for an hour each Saturday morning. More than anything, he just wanted to spend time with his grandfather. He was told that Saturday morning was when Granddad liked to read the newspaper and putter in his workshop.

Our son asked if it would be better if he met him over at his own house, so they could study and then tinker together. That didn't fly. When our son suggested an alternative time later that day, there was another lame excuse.

"The kids don't respect their grandparents because they don't feel their grandparents have much regard for them. You know what really gets me? These are the last people I thought would wimp out on the whole grandparenting thing. They were fine parents, but it seems that once all of us kids moved out, they reconfigured their life to one that didn't put a high priority on us. They don't call us; we have to call them. It hurts us that they have so little enthusiasm for us as a family."

"But they just now came by without being invited," I said. "Doesn't that indicate anything?"

"I'm always glad when they stop by like that," my friend's wife said. "I love seeing them, but it only happens when it fits into their schedule."

Loving Our Freedom = Devastating Returns

If getting too attached to our comfortable empty-nest life gives diminishing returns, this second attitude completely devastates our high and holy calling to grandparenthood. We're talking about falling too much in love with our *freedom.*

Parents who have a difficult time getting their children through to adulthood are at high risk of letting this attitude get a grip on their hearts. Other candidates are those parents who, for whatever reasons, view their years of parenting as a time when they had no life. They always felt strapped by the responsibilities of raising their children. When the last one leaves, they redefine their life by focusing on doing all the things they couldn't do while raising kids.

Along come grandchildren.

It's hard to get parents who are too enamored with their freedom to engage in a meaningful relationship with their grandchildren. It's not that they *reluctantly* agree to watch the grandchildren; they almost *never* agree. They make it clear they don't do diapers, field trips, Disneyland, or intergenerational vacations. As far as their role as grandparents, they aren't inclined toward anything that interferes with their personal agenda. It's not uncommon for these types of grandparents to traffic in high control, manipulation, and guilt to justify their lack of involvement in their grandchildren's lives.

Darcy and I know a young couple with some extremely tough times on the front end of their marriage. The husband held down two jobs for several years, and his wife had serious medical problems. One set of grandparents lives within three miles of them—a support, you'd think.

On one occasion, the couple wanted to go to a three-day marriage conference their church was sponsoring. It was several months away. They really needed to spend some focused time working on their marriage. The set of grandparents that lived farther away (hers) were more than happy to watch the kids for the weekend. They not only viewed it as a great chance to be with their grandchildren but were glad to help their children improve their marriage. But work demands dictated they could only be there the second and third day of the event.

The son called his parents who lived nearby. First he asked if they were doing anything on the particular weekend of the marriage conference. When the grandparents said they didn't have anything planned, the son asked if they'd be willing to help that first day by staying with the kids overnight. The grandparents said they'd get back to them.

After two weeks and no answer, our young friend called to see if his parents were going to help. That's when they announced they had decided to go on a four-day cruise over that weekend; they had just bought the tickets. When the son asked if they had been considering this trip when he called earlier, he was informed that they just made the decision on the spur of the moment. "You know, Dad, that same ship leaves every five days from the same dock to the same ports of call. Why that weekend?" That's when the father made his true colors clear.

He said, "Son, we're not going to plan our lives around your needs for a babysitter."

His son shot back, "Dad, it wasn't a babysitter we were looking for. I can hire a babysitter. We wanted the kids to spend some time with their grandparents. They love you."

"And we love them, too. But we're not going to have our plans held hostage by our children or our grandchildren. We've waited a long time to have our weekends to ourselves, and nothing is going to get in our way. It's just not going to happen."

In a balanced life, there's plenty of room for the things that are important.

We could go on for many pages with examples like this. Whether it's something as demanding as keeping an eye on the grandchildren or something as incidental as occasionally calling to see how they are doing, some grandparents simply aren't inclined to do much of anything. They aren't willing to do anything substantive that might help their kids carry the heavy load of parenting. They aren't willing to do anything that requires them to submit their personal agenda to the best interests of their grandchildren.

Sometimes, only one of the grandparents is wired this way. But the selfish attitude of the one automatically puts limitations on the spouse's ability to be involved in the grandchildren's lives.

Let's make sure we keep this era of the empty nest in perspective. When our last child slips over the horizon into her own adult life, there are many comforts and freedoms we can start to enjoy. But our job as parents is not finished; it's just redefined. Though things might slow down enough to make life more enjoyable and less hectic, an empty nest is not a free ticket to indulge ourselves to the exclusion of our families. Our strategic calling as grandparents requires that we stay connected, emotionally engaged, and personally involved in our children's and grandchildren's lives.

Nothing we've said here denies grandparents the benefits that come with finally getting full control over the house and personal time. And we certainly aren't implying that just because you're connected, emotionally engaged, and personally involved, your children can take advantage of you. In a balanced life, there's plenty of room for all the things that are important. We just need to be careful not to let comfort and freedom trump our great calling as grandparents.

Sacred Cow #2: Retirement

A second sacred cow that has proven itself capable of rendering grandparents nonentities in their grandchildren's lives is the misguided view of *retirement.*

If an empty nest occurs when we are relieved of our daily responsibilities of raising our children, retirement occurs when we are relieved of our daily responsibility of making a living. Retirement is like the empty nest on steroids.

It's hard for some people to realize that retirement was never meant to be part of the equation for how we spend the last third of our lives. Retirement literally means, "backing away." That's the last thing God ever had in mind when it comes to how we finish off our time here on earth.

In the Bible, parents stayed involved in the bigger family picture until the day they died. As parents got older, the younger generation took over the physically demanding work and invited their older parents to move into the roles of patriarch and matriarch. They were to bring their years of wisdom to bear on the life of the family. And because these older parents remained engaged in the ongoing struggles of life, they received enormous respect. In return, these older members of the family tree expressed enormous pride in the grandchildren who surrounded them. The respect for the patriarchs is seen in the willingness of the Bible's 12 sons of Jacob to comply with Jacob's dying wish to have his body carried from Egypt all the way back to Israel for burial. You can see this kind of respect for elders even more in how the offspring of Joseph complied with his wish to have his descendants take his body with them when they all left Egypt. That didn't happen until four hundred years later. But because of the overwhelming respect for Joseph, the nation of Israel not only took his mummified remains with them, but they carried them around for the 40 years they wandered in the wilderness until they finally entered the Promised Land, where they buried Joseph.

Even with their many flaws, these biblical elders had a profound impact on the generations that came after them. Unfortunately, the concept of retirement in today's culture has a tendency to undermine this respect for elders if we aren't careful.

Government Conspiracy

Retirement (as we know it today) is an invention of the twentieth century. It's a by-product of our tax laws and our Social Security system. The arbitrary retirement age of 65 (now gradually moving up to 67) was determined by actuarial tables from the 1920s. Back then, the average person only lived to his late sixties. The assumption was that you would cease from your labor at 65, live a few years, and then die.

Almost a hundred years later the average person lives much longer. In fact, millions of people in North America will live several decades past their 65th birthdays. Most people, as they move into their retirement years, do so with the traditional view that developed from its inception—they quit working and get to enjoy an excused absence from responsibilities. This is the classic view of retirement.

It's also the view that has caused the older generation to lose a great deal of status in the eyes of the younger.

But there are new winds blowing, especially among the ranks of the baby-boomer generation. Millions within this generation are demonstrating they aren't interested in retiring even though they can.

I (Tim) fall into this last category. Our contemporary concept of working to a point on the calendar and then spending the rest of our days on cruise control does not come from God's playbook. That's why I want to stay involved in proclaiming truth and investing my life in my family till the day I die. Darcy teases me that some day she expects to get a call saying the late Dr. Kimmel passed away in the middle of delivering his third message of the morning in some church. She pictures them taking the pulpit I was standing behind, laying it down on its face, putting me inside of it, and then shipping me home. It's a running joke between us that reminds us we need to stay focused on the real finish line—when we take our last breath.

Sadly, this twentieth-century legacy of viewing the retirement years as ones where people back away from shouldering much responsibility or making much of a difference in society has branded itself into many people's minds. They embrace the comfort and freedom of retirement and in the process buy into the deception that retirement means we have the *right* to relegate our children and grandchildren to the status of footnotes in our daily lives. "We're retired! Let's party 'til we drop!"

Living at Luby's Cafeteria

With more discretionary time and funds at their disposal, today's grandparents often view their retirement years as a recess from family responsibility with one big, universal road trip tagged on for fun. Magazines that cater to the senior members of our society have been known to portray this time as retirees' pig-out with periodic re-entries into the greater-family solar system to check in and get their mail.

And, as the argument goes, "Why not?" After all, these people have worked hard over the years and clearly deserve a break from the daily grind of their careers. We Kimmels couldn't agree more about the well-deserved rest from labors. But there is nothing in the Bible that says this is a time to abdicate our roles as parents and grandparents.

What too many grandparents never figure out is that their most productive years for the kingdom of God may be ahead of them once they retire. And the people who could define their extraordinary impact are the little kids whose faces adorn their refrigerators. We desperately need to have a clear picture of the potential of our relational and spiritual role as grandparents within the context of a balanced view of retirement.

Heaven! I'm in Heaven!

I was watching television when an advertisement came on for one of the retirement communities in our area. The voice-over promised a leisurely lifestyle, surrounded by all the amenities guaranteeing a relaxing and carefree life. The voice talked of playing all day, enjoying your hobbies, and not being badgered by any tedious responsibilities (like grandchildren). As I listened, I thought, *To some people, that place sounds like heaven on earth!* The problem is, heaven is a place that God has waiting for us *when we die.* While we're still here on earth, we have precious lives to touch and a difference to make.

Let's make sure we're getting the big picture. No doubt retirement affords us a chance to enjoy many of the things we had to put off because we were still working. There's nothing necessarily wrong with living in a community that takes into consideration many of the unique needs we have as we get older. Yet it grieves our hearts when we see the kind of deed restrictions that are often built into many of these retirement communities. We have some retirement communities in our area that house tens of thousands of retirees who can have just about anything they want—except their kids and grandkids.

Family members under 50 years of age can only stay for a few days. If your child loses a spouse through death or divorce and needs to move in with you, that's not allowed. If your son or daughter is in the military and deploying to the front lines of the war, you can't have the family live with you for the duration. If one of your teenage grandchildren is going through a tough time and needs to come live with you, sorry—against the rules.

Many of these retirement-community grandparents might desire involvement in their grandchildren's lives, but their choice of address does not encourage a substantive one. And, being retired, they feel somewhat justified. But they're showing a level of rejection toward their children and grandchildren that can do incredible harm.

One couple who filled out a survey for us shared this sad observation: "Our parents would rather be RVing with total strangers than spending the holidays with their own flesh and blood." Without question, choosing to live disconnected or distant from our grandchildren undermines our ability to have a significant impact on their lives.

There is a shift happening regarding how retirement is being viewed.

Research verifies the importance of geographic proximity to the closeness that grandparents experience with their grandchildren. Obviously, grandparents who live closer to their grandchildren have greater opportunities to spend face-to-face time with them, undoubtedly leading to emotional closeness. There may be extenuating circumstances that mandate we move away from our grandchildren or that they move away from us. We'll address ways to make the most of this configuration in a later chapter. But if it's just a choice on our part to move to a more pleasurable place that puts great distance between our families and us, then we may be sacrificing the permanent on the altar of the immediate.

Fortunately, this new generation of grandparents just moving into position is resisting the status quo. Once boomer grandparents retire, many are choosing to move closer to their children rather than farther away. "According to the 2003 census data, 28 percent of people who moved said family was the reason for doing so. That's more than the percentage of people who moved for job-related reasons."[1]

Developers are recognizing that there is a shift happening regarding how retirement is being viewed. They are responding with intergenerational master-planned communities that don't have age restrictions. These are all-encompassing projects that have day-care centers on one end of the spectrum, nursing homes on the other, and something for everyone else in between. It's like Mayberry meets Starbucks.

When Noble Causes Get Out of Balance

Not all retirees view the free time at the end of their lives as an excuse to indulge their selfish appetites. Many see these years as an opportunity to turn their attention toward doing things that make the world a better place. They might volunteer on a full-time basis or start a second career as a key player in an urgent social or ministry cause. We can't applaud these people enough. You get a standing ovation from us. We think this is one of the best ways to finish out our time here on earth.

But these noble ways of investing our retirement years must be done in subordination to our greater calling as grandparents. It's just like when we were parents: We may have wanted to use a great deal of our time trying to serve others through our churches, mission outreaches, or social organizations, but we were never supposed to do that to the neglect of our children. These things we might have done were important but not more important than our responsibilities to our children. The same goes for grandparenthood.

We recently had a couple remark about this issue. In this case, it was the husband's parents who were dedicating their retirement years to serving others—just not their grandchildren. As this young man explained, his father and mother were phenomenal people, awesome parents, and fabulous spiritual examples for him as he was growing up. When he got married, both he and his wife looked forward to the wonderful ways in which these two people would rub off on their children.

But once these terrific parents retired, they decided to give their resources, talents, and time to a mission cause in Colombia, South America. There is absolutely nothing wrong with that. But their decision ended up pulling them completely away from their grandchildren's lives. They decided to permanently move to Colombia. They come home for one week every Christmas. Other than that, the grandchildren never see them. And because of the demands of the work they are doing, they seldom hear from them either.

This young couple was hurt by the choice of these two retired people. They were saddened, knowing their children were missing not being more exposed to these two senior members of the faith. Because of the noble cause their parents had chosen, they felt they had no place saying anything to them about it. But based on the way the senior parents had lived their lives, the young couple had expected more from them.

Just this past weekend, we met a couple on par with those grandparents who had moved lock, stock, and barrel to Colombia. They too had retired. They had decided to spend their retirement years bringing their decades of experience to a vibrant ministry that works with the poor in their hometown. But several years into this, their son and his wife had their first child. Without hesitation, the retired grandparents sold their house, moved away from the town they had called home since they were first married, and relocated in the same town as their grandchild. Since then, their son and daughter-in-law have had several children.

We asked them if they regretted the move. "Are you kidding? It was the best choice we could ever make. Plus, we still are able to give our time to the needs of the poor here. There are vibrant ministry opportunities anywhere you live." That's so true. And that's why, when it comes to using our retirement years to serve in ministry and also be effective grandparents, it isn't necessarily a case of either/or.

Obviously, we can't live near all of our grandchildren. And just because we're grandparents doesn't mean we shouldn't serve in other noble endeavors. It's just that when we weigh the two options, our role as grandparents is the one that offers us the chance to have the most effective long-term impact for ministry. Our ministry to our grandchildren should get more weight. They should matter most.

When they don't, it's not surprising that we don't get the kind of recognition from the younger generations we think we deserve for our position in life.

R-e-s-p-e-c-t

Is it any wonder that the respect seniors once enjoyed in the eyes of the younger generation evaporated in wholesale ways over the last half of the twentieth century? And is it any wonder that many of the older generation now look on the younger generation with indifference or wholesale disdain? When we move into the fourth quarter of our lives with a distorted view of retirement that says we've earned the right to shift our focus from others to ourselves, a lack of respect coming up and condescension going down is what you get.

Our churches have become the unfortunate battlefields for these intergenerational tensions. "Worship wars" over music styles and budget priorities plague many of our churches. At its bottom line, the question is whether or not a church is going to configure itself to reach the new generation of families. What's sad about this conflict is that most of the resistance to change comes from the generation that should know better.

When we were young and raising our children, many of us sought out churches that were formatted to our family's needs as well as aligned with where we were culturally. The music and the presentation of the truth reflected our tastes as well as our passions. It made it easier for us to connect ourselves and our children to the God behind the music and the message.

A new generation of families is coming to our churches, looking for the same help and hope. When they find a church poised to leap into the 1980s, they realize they've come to a church that is stuck in the past, a church committed to irrelevancy. Either the church has lost touch or has no desire to reach this generation. When they observe that the resistance against adapting to a new generation of families is coming from the ranks of the grandparents in the congregation, they realize it is a church held hostage by a group of people that place little value on youth. Most of the time, these young families simply leave and keep looking for a church that understands their needs.

How tragic.

With all due respect, we of the older generation had our turn to have our churches formatted to our needs and tastes. Now it's the younger generation's turn. What's more, as we grow older in our relationship with God, we should be becoming more graceful rather than legalistic, more mature rather than childish, more ingratiating rather than selfish, more magnanimous rather than territorial, more desirous of reaching the next generation of families rather than being wrapped up in silly spiritual turf wars. We grandparents are the ones who should be leading the parade in formatting our churches to reach the generation that represents our grandchildren. We should especially be outspoken in our desire to see the style of worship adapted to connect to the younger families.

It's called *grace.*

Personally speaking, we Kimmels would gladly spend the rest of our lives listening to music that is foreign to our personal tastes if it empowers our church to touch the lives of the younger generation with God's truth. Our advice is: Wear earplugs to help you deal with the volume, get in the middle of these young people, and pick up the rhythm of the worship. If we have truly matured in our faith, this shouldn't even be an issue with us. Life is not about us. Church is not about us. Retirement is not about us. All these things are supposed to be about God. And when God is dominating our attitudes, He leads us to focus on other people's best interests over our own.

Don't let the world system define what your retirement years look like.

As we said, this shouldn't even be an issue, but it's a huge one. One of the main reasons we have grown into a world with so much disconnect between the older and younger generations is the older generation's "stepping back" from playing an ongoing and relevant role in their retirement years.

Mandatory retirement has created a parenthesis for many retirees where they stop growing and stop contributing. How could we ever expect our grandchildren to want to lean on us for guidance when a warped view of retirement presents us as people who have willingly chosen to lose touch with the greater world around us?

The primary point we're trying to make here is that we've all got to be careful that we don't let the world system define what our retirement years look like. We should let God make that call for us.

God never meant for us to see our twilight years as a time to put our lives on cruise control and not be involved in making life significant to the people who matter most to us. He never meant for us to view the last few decades of our lives as a time to hit the pause button and stop the upward climb toward emotional maturity and spiritual responsibility. It would be a shame to do that. It robs you, it robs your children and grandchildren, and it robs God. If anything, retirement is a time to step up to the greater responsibility of being a patriarch and a matriarch—wisdom hunters who set a great example and offer unfettered love and a humble, winsome character to their larger family.

All the Lonely People, Where Do They All Come From?

We have a dear friend who works in a nursing home. The number one issue among the residents of her home is loneliness. They are sad because their children and grandchildren rarely, if ever, come to visit. Sometimes they spend years in this state of great disappointment. I realize there might be other reasons why the kids and grandkids aren't stopping by, but often it's the by-product of grandparents who checked out of substantive involvement with their children and grandchildren during their years in the empty nest and retirement. They spent two to three decades of their lives living primarily for themselves.

Now, sadly, they die alone.

Here's reality: If we don't have time for our kids when they need us most, they won't have time for us when we need them most. If our grandchildren are an afterthought to us when we're enjoying the healthy years of empty nest and retirement, we shouldn't be surprised that they don't go out of their way to stop by when we are facing our last days on earth.

When deciding what the last laps of our lives will look like, it is critical that we don't view these years as a time to ditch our families. Rather, we need to see them as a divine opportunity to play a role in our children's and grandchildren's lives that can be enjoyed down to the moment when we say our final good-byes.

Taps

President George H. W. Bush was bringing his 1990 State of the Union message to a close when he gave this challenge:

> The anchor in our world today is freedom, holding us steady in times of change, a symbol of hope to all the world. And freedom is at the very heart of the idea that is *America.* Giving life to that idea depends on every one of us. Our anchor has always been faith and family.
>
> In the last few days of this past momentous year, our family was blessed once more, celebrating the joy of life when a little boy became our twelfth grandchild. When I held the little guy for the first time, the troubles at home and abroad seemed manageable and totally in perspective.
>
> Now, I know you're probably thinking, *Well, that's just a grandfather talking.* Well, maybe you're right. But I've met a lot of children this past year across this country, as all of you have, everywhere from the Far East to Eastern Europe. And all kids are unique, and yet all kids are alike—the budding young environmentalists I met this month who joined me in exploring the Florida Everglades; the Little Leaguers I played catch with in Poland, ready to go from Warsaw to the World Series; and even the kids who are ill or alone—and God bless those boarder babies, born addicted to drugs and AIDS and coping with problems no child should have to face. But you know, when it comes to hope and the future, every kid is the same—full of dreams, ready to take on the world—all special, because they are the very future of freedom. And to them belongs this new world I've been speaking about.
>
> And so, tonight I'm going to ask something of every one of you. Now, let me start with my generation, with the grand-

parents out there. You are our living link to the past. Tell your grandchildren the story of struggles waged at home and abroad, of sacrifices freely made for freedom's sake. And tell them your own story as well, because every American has a story to tell.

And, parents, your children look to you for direction and guidance. Tell them of faith and family. Tell them we are one nation under God. Teach them that of all the many gifts they can receive, liberty is their most precious legacy; and of all the gifts they can give, the greatest is helping others.

And to the children and young people out there tonight: With you rests our hope, all that America will mean in the years and decades ahead. Fix your vision on a new century—your century, on dreams we cannot see, on the destiny that is yours and yours alone.

And finally, let all Americans—all of us together here in this Chamber, the symbolic center of democracy—affirm our allegiance to this idea we call America. And let us remember that the state of the union depends on each and every one of us.

Here, here!

For Further Thought and Discussion

Do nothing out of selfish ambition or vain conceit, but in humility consider others better than yourselves. Each of you should look not only to your own interests, but also to the interests of others. (Philippians 2:3-4)

1. How do you think our culture's view of the empty nest and the retirement years can undermine the opportunity we have to impact our grandchildren's lives?

2. What are some ways to still enjoy the benefits of the empty nest and retirement years without missing out on the regular interaction with and influence on our grandchildren?
3. List some practical ways you can use these dividend years to step up to your role of a patriarch or matriarch in your family.

Heavenly Father,
Thank You for bringing me to this point in my life. Thank You for those You have given me to love. Please give me direction, stamina, and a heart for remaining engaged and proactive in my grandchildren's lives. Help me to view these coming years as a gift from You that I can give to those I love so much. Amen.

part two

A GRAND ROLE

4 A Grand Job Description

Imagine you're taking a walk down a quiet, secluded trail. There's a nice bite to the air, and the easy breeze that washes over you gives your ears and nose an invigorating sense of comfortable cold. Suddenly, a voice slips through the stillness and grabs your attention.

It's God.

He has a question for you. He asks, *Would you like to have a strategic influence on the people I consider greatest in My kingdom?* Being the type of person you are—a person who wants to make a difference, who wants your life to count for something and leave a positive mark on society—I imagine you, like us, would be inclined to say, "Yes, I sure would." And then because you are a person who is trying to do things right, you'd probably start to create a plan for making an impact on these very important people.

No doubt you've figured out where this is going. It's about children. But when you look at the way our culture tends to view children, you realize that too many people aren't aware of the incredible value God places on the next generation. They aren't quick to assume it's children that God would be talking about in an encounter like this.

It's true. If the average person were offered an opportunity to play a key role in the lives of people God considers greatest in His kingdom, he'd typically assume He's talking about "dignitaries" or "celebrities." And the further assumption of what it would take to influence these "greatest" people demonstrates how warped our view is of what really matters to God. If you're thinking "the greatest" has to be someone at the top of the financial food chain, a mover or shaker of society, or a card-carrying member of the "beautiful people," it would be easy to imagine that reaching them would require getting more education, upgrading our looks and wardrobes, maybe increasing our grasp of theology, and coming up the learning curve on current events. But because of our subject matter, you know the punch line to this scenario.

It's the same scenario Jesus' disciples were wrestling with in Matthew 18 when they asked, "Who is the greatest in the kingdom of heaven?" (verse 1). To answer their question, Jesus could have grabbed one of them; He could have conjured up a rabbi or a ruler—maybe even some Roman dignitary. But that's not what He did. He called a child over and sat him on His lap. And this is what Jesus said: "Truly I say to you, unless you are converted and become like children, you will not enter the kingdom of heaven. Whoever then humbles himself as this child, he is the greatest in the kingdom of heaven. And whoever receives one such child, in My name, receives Me" (verses 3-5, NASB).

When a child is born, he is the closest he will ever be to the image of God.

You see, when a child is born, he is the closest he will ever be to the image of God. Although he has a nature that has been corrupted because of the sin that plagues all members of the human race, he has yet to sin personally. True, it doesn't take him long to figure out the drill, but he is born far more aligned with the heart of God than is the typical adult who gave him birth. Children also have the capacity to accept and understand spiritual truth—by faith—more than they do as they move into adult life. That explains why (according to

George Barna's research) about 85 percent of all people who put their faith in God through Christ do so before the age of 18.

Because of the childlike faith of our grandchildren, we grandparents have a wonderful opportunity to influence these little people who operate with the attitude that God considers greatest to Him. You probably heard the anecdote about the little girl in elementary school learning about whales. The teacher had just explained that though some whales are huge, a whale couldn't swallow a man because its throat is too narrow. But the little girl had learned the story of Jonah from the Bible and was certain her teacher was mistaken. When she pointed this out, the teacher reiterated that it is impossible for a whale to swallow a man.

Finally, the girl said, "Well, when I get to heaven, I'll just ask Jonah if that's the way it happened."

The teacher said, "What if Jonah isn't in heaven?" to which the child replied, "Well, then you'll have to ask him!"

There's something about kids that seems to give them a huge capacity to trust and to believe . . . and sometimes to be a bit precocious.

A child's huge capacity to exercise faith spills over to their ability to love and trust their grandparents. God has built a natural heart connection between grandparents and their grandchildren that gives us a great platform to affect their beliefs about Him and their views about themselves.

Jabba the Baby

I saw the blunt reality of this natural heart connection the night our first child was born. Darcy had had an emergency C-section at about one o'clock in the morning. She was resting in recovery, so I slipped into the nursery to study our brand-new little girl. I had on surgical scrubs and could have easily been mistaken for hospital staff. Our daughter was lying in the middle of the large nursery, surrounded by empty bassinets. Her feet were turned toward me with her head toward the visitors' window. She was wrapped like a burrito. Her plumbing was obviously concealed. The name tag on her bassinet was also facing me.

All of a sudden, two older folks came rushing down the hallway, exploded through the doors of the visitors' room, and raced up to the window that separated them from the new babies. They were obviously proud grandparents who had come to the hospital in the middle of the night to see their new grandchild. I did not recognize them.

What was amazing to me was how these two people, assuming our little girl was their grandchild, made an immediate heart connection to her. You could see them jabbering away, going on and on about her. Both were laughing and crying as they studied her little head and her face and her tiny hands. Finally they both stopped talking and just stood there in silence, smiling. The grandmother put her hand on her heart and then placed it on the window. Streams of tears rolled down her cheeks.

One other baby, a boy, had been born that night about half an hour before our daughter was born. He weighed in at over 12 pounds!

He was huge!

He weighed twice as much as our daughter but looked like he was four times her size. He was lying in a bigger bed over by the wall across the room. I realized that because he was so far out of sight, and there were no other babies in the room, these two people logically assumed our child was their grandchild.

I waved to them, then pointed to the junior-high-size baby boy in the bed by the wall and mouthed the words, "He's yours!" When they looked over at him, their countenances immediately fell. Looks of sheer horror crossed their faces. They looked back at our child, then to the boy. Back one more time to our daughter, then over to the boy by the wall. And then, something extraordinary happened. When they realized this robust baby boy was *their* grandson, they immediately disconnected from our child and connected with him. I went over and pushed his bed next to the glass as they leaned in to the window, overcome with incredible joy.

This grandparent/grandchild connection is a God thing. That's how God designed it to be. God knew these children would need someone, in addition to their parents, who was fully committed to their best interests; no matter how big or small they were, whether they were fast or slow, clever or careful, cute as a button or just another face in the crowd.

Because of the way He designed it, family is one of the most effective conduits for God's blessings. Perhaps that's why in the Bible *family* is the metaphor God most often uses to describe His relationship with us. He is our Father; we are His children, joint heirs, sons and daughters of the grace of life. We are to model our relationship with our grandchildren after God's relationship with us.

Treating Your Family the Way God Treats His

The wonderful word that defines the way God deals with His children is *grace.* God shows kindness, love, patience, and acceptance of us that has nothing to do with our behavior. If anything, it's in spite of it. His grace cannot be bought or earned. He makes the unilateral decision to love us whether or not we are lovely.

One of the best ways we can carry out the four roles of grandparents (which this part of the book addresses) is treating our grandchildren the same way God treats His children—by being grace-based grandparents.

We realize it's a mouthful. But when you understand what it is, it's worth saying, and it's also the only logical way to carry out our sacred responsibilities to our grandchildren. Grace brings out the best in people. It sustains relationships when life happens to throw a series of curve balls at everyone involved.

Treating our grandchildren with the same grace with which God treats us increases the impact and effectiveness of the four roles we're called to play. Grace is not so much what we do, but how we do what we do.

Let me use an illustration to give context to this point. By this time in your life, you should have matured to a point in your relationship with God that you desire to do and say the right things to the people in the inner circle of your life. You are a follower of Jesus, so you want to be biblically correct in the advice you give. You want to be spiritually discerning as you handle dilemmas that come your way. It's like what the people who plan a worship service at your church set out to do. From the selection of music, to the quality of the worship, to the application of the Bible in the sermon, great forethought is put into doing everything and saying everything *right.*

> ***Our liberty in Christ is not a license to do whatever we want to do.***

But let's say you are sitting in your church service as usual, wearing what you usually wear, and everything that is being done is being done properly, except the temperature in the room is 20 degrees Fahrenheit. Everything is being done right, but the atmosphere is keeping you from being able to concentrate or appreciate all the good things that are happening. To continue the analogy, let's turn the thermostat up a hundred degrees. Once again, everything is being done right, with forethought, and with a desire to glorify God, but you can't appreciate it because you are so uncomfortably hot.

Many families of faith are trying hard to do the right things, but the response of the children in them isn't what the parents and grandparents think it should be. Maybe the grandchildren are annoyed, indifferent, or even hostile to the spiritual priorities that are embraced by their parents or grandparents. Regardless, it's discouraging how ineffective the spiritual efforts of the leaders involved seem to be.

It could well be that the missing ingredient is grace. Grace creates an optimum room temperature for God's influence through parents and grandparents. When we display an attitude of grace to our grandchildren, they are more inclined to *want* to favorably respond to the spiritual influences around them. This is how grace-based grandparenting empowers the greater roles we play. It takes the natural heart connection that God has created between our grandchildren and us, then moves it to a level of incredible impact.

Grace Is About Freedom

When we carry out our God-given roles in an atmosphere of grace, we set our grandchildren free to grow to a much greater spiritual potential. But lest we get misunderstood on this issue, let's deal with a common myth when it comes to grace.

A lot of people dismiss the concept of grace because they assume that when people like us are talking about it, we are saying that grace lets grandchildren do whatever they want to do. Nothing could be further from the truth. Our liberty in Christ is not a license to do whatever we want to do. And anyone who would assume that license is the essence of grace clearly doesn't know what God's grace is all about. If grace is anything, it's a call to a higher holiness, not a lower one. Freedom in the Bible isn't the option to do what we *want* to do; rather, it's freedom to do what we *ought* to do.

Grace-based grandparenting is a commitment to grant the same freedoms to our grandchildren that God grants to us. When we do this, we create a comfortable affinity between our hearts and theirs. It raises their respect for us. It also makes them more inclined toward our advice and more responsive toward our correction.

There are four freedoms that grandparents want to give their grandchildren. We need to offer these on an around-the-clock basis.

When these are the defining features of our relationship with our grandchildren, our greater roles will be far easier for us to play.

The First Freedom: Being Different

Grace-based grandparents give their grandchildren the freedom to *be different.* It might help to throw in a few synonyms for "different" so that you understand exactly what this freedom means. How about these words: *weird, bizarre, strange, goofy, quirky.* Grace-based grandparents have a huge place in their hearts for grandkids described by these words. We need to be people who don't react to the silly things that may come out of their mouths, the benign but bizarre clothing they may wear, or the astonishing experiments they may perform with their hair. God is a God of variety. He hasn't made two people alike yet. We shouldn't be surprised that our grandchildren might have one-of-a-kind physical expressions that put our gag threshold to the test.

There are many things our grandchildren will either do or say that aren't inherently or biblically wrong. They are just different. One of the biggest mistakes parents make is when they pass moral judgments on things their children do that don't meet their tastes in either behavior or style. Grandparents can make the same foolish mistake. In actuality, there are many things our grandchildren may say or do that don't fit our personal tastes. It may annoy their parents or, because of their spiritual insecurity, perhaps embarrass them. But when you measure what the child is actually doing or saying against the grace-based standards of the Bible, God doesn't care.

When we moralize these innocuous expressions of our children and grandchildren or, even worse, pull a verse out of Scripture and misapply it against these expressions, we set children up to rebel against God and their parents. They know that what they're doing isn't bad. But because it is being framed as bad—when it's really just something that is different—they can't help but react.

There are two things we need to do as grandparents in this arena. First, make sure we don't fall into the legalistic trap. We need to allow our grandchildren the freedom to be who they are with all of their quirks and not make them feel like they are flawed just because they are different. Second, we need to be an example to their parents. We need to let grace rule the day. If we don't, legalism will.

The thing we must burn into our brains when it comes to legalism is: Legalism is *evil*! Anytime we superimpose our personal tastes on the Bible to get our grandchildren to look, act, or dress according to our wants, we are being a pawn of Darkness himself. Grace-based grandparents give their grandchildren the freedom to be different.

The Second Freedom: Being Vulnerable

Grace-based grandparents also give their grandchildren the freedom to *be vulnerable*. We create a safe haven for them where they can share their doubts and fears as well as work on their inadequacies. When they are around us, they need to know they can expose the fragile side of their hearts and be confident we will always treat them with care.

Someone has said that childhood is a 24-7, 365-day-a-year battle to keep from being embarrassed. The older we get, the more tender-hearted we should be toward other people's feelings of inadequacy. They need our patience and nonjudgmental attitude. They need to be confident that when they are exposing their doubts and fears to us, we won't trivialize them.

I (Tim) remember a time when I was having lunch with my grandmother Pearl. She was a wonderful lady who usually had huge tasks before her but always had time for whoever was with her. At the time, I was in the third grade. I had become painfully aware of the fact that I was a slow reader who struggled with grammar and was easily distracted. My report card screamed of my struggle. It had provoked my dad to scream at me a few times. I happened to mention the difficulty I was having with these basic skills to my grandmother. She let me talk. She asked questions about how this was making me feel. She listened to the fear I had about possibly being held back and being thought of as slow. She happened to know a couple of key people in history who also had similar struggles—people like Abraham Lincoln and Theodore Roosevelt. She told me their stories. She assured me I was going to master reading and grammar in due time. And she believed that, because it was more difficult for me, I'd ultimately be forced to master them more thoroughly than most people do. My struggle would probably serve me well.

It was one of many times I let my guard down around her. And it played a huge role in helping me get through the many frustrations that came with being a kid who wasn't academically gifted. Grace-based grandparents allow their grandkids the freedom to be vulnerable.

The Third Freedom: Being Candid

Grace-based grandparents give their grandchildren the freedom to *be candid*. Kids need to know they can tell us what they are thinking and be confident it will not come back to haunt them. Young people need the freedom to think out loud around us without fearing they are going to get a lecture if they say something that doesn't align with our personal worldview. We're not saying there isn't a time for us to weigh in on certain ideas they are entertaining. But many times young people are simply processing life. They need to be able to share the deeper feelings of their hearts and know there is someone who doesn't simply write them off as being idiots.

Sometimes they need to vent about things that are going on around them that don't add up. It might be about politics, spiritual issues, or the family. Grandchildren need to find grandparents who want to know what's bothering them, what they think about issues, and how they are doing with their spiritual pilgrimage. Our willingness to give them the freedom to be candid, even though they may expose how far off they really are, makes us natural candidates for them to turn to when they need advice or counsel.

Because their candor might involve frustrations they may be having with one of their parents or siblings, we need to make sure we listen in confidence. They may be angry with God. He can take it; so should we. And we shouldn't be surprised that every once in a while, the primary object of their frustration is *us*. We make mistakes. We sometimes let them down. They need to know they can voice their disappointments and not get a lecture or rejection in return.

There are many things happening around our grandchildren and so many people crossing their paths who frustrate them. Grace-based grandparents provide an exhaust system for those frustrations that preserves hope within their hearts. They give them the freedom to be candid.

The Fourth Freedom: Making Mistakes

Finally, grace-based grandparents give their grandchildren the freedom to *make mistakes*. Childhood is often a series of missteps and mishaps stacked up one against the other. One of the greatest ways to turn those mistakes into lessons in virtue is to respond graciously to the person who is making them. Grace recognizes our propensity toward sin. It understands the toxic nature of selfishness. But it never writes people off just because they fall short of the glory of God.

Our grandchildren may get into fights, cheat on tests, lie to us or their parents, get kicked out of school, go too far with their boyfriends or girlfriends, experiment with drugs, disrespect alcohol, or take advantage of people. When things like these happen, grace says we have every right to voice our disapproval and disappointment. If it falls to us to discipline, grace also says we have every right to mete out consequences for these mistakes. Correction and discipline are sophisticated forms of grace. They say to the person, "I love you too much to sit idly by and watch you grow up to be a bad person. I'm going to correct you in order to help you become an ally to yourself and everyone around you."

But since home is where "life is supposed to make up its mind," it must be a place where disappointments are processed, hurts are endured, and mistakes never mark the end of a relationship. Grandparents can play a huge role in making sure this happens.

Grace never writes people off just because they fall short of the glory of God.

We have some friends who have had a series of problems with their teenage daughter. She's a great girl who occasionally has serious flurries of stupidity. Unfortunately, because so much of her unacceptable behavior is directed toward her mother, it's been very hard for her mom to serve as an ointment in her life. Fortunately, there's Grandpa. He's a godly man who wears several layers of wrinkles around his chubby face. He's also a man who has maintained a sober, street-level view of life. He knows full well how easy it is to let your foolishness get the best of you. Yet he also deeply understands what the grace of God looks, tastes, and feels like to a person who has lost her way. It has given him a grace-filled understanding for his granddaughter.

The grace she finds when she turns to him in her shame has helped her get through some extremely difficult setbacks she created for herself. He's the grandpa without guile. Sure, she sometimes hears him voice disappointment, but she never hears him voice condemnation. He treats her the way God has always treated him when he's done something stupid. In the process, we've seen this girl become more responsive to correction and more desirous to move beyond many of her selfish habits. The bonus in all of this is that Grandpa has been a stabilizing agent in this girl's relationship with her mother. He loves his granddaughter's mother as much as he loves her.

A Ditto of Jesus

You might wonder where we came up with these four freedoms of grace-based grandparenting. We got them from the way Jesus deals with us. He gives us the freedom to be different, be vulnerable, be candid, and make mistakes. His grace is that sufficient bridge over the tougher challenges of our lives. When we give the same freedoms to our grandchildren that God gives to us, we place ourselves in a far better position to carry out our strategic roles.

Incidentally, these are the same freedoms parents should give their kids. If you want to take a far more in-depth look at them, you might want to breeze through the book I (Tim) wrote on this subject titled *Grace-Based Parenting.*[1] Your children may not have the understanding or tools needed to create that wonderful room temperature of grace. That book will show them how. In the meantime, you can either be used by God to introduce a grace-based environment to them or enjoy the privilege of reinforcing the grace-based home they have already established.

In the next five chapters we are going to develop four biblical roles that God has handed to grandparents. You're going to love them. But the thing that is going to help you best implement them is your choice to format your relationship with your grandchildren around this wonderful gift we have been talking about the past few pages—God's amazing grace.

For Further Thought and Discussion

"Truly I say to you, unless you are converted and become like children, you will not enter the kingdom of heaven. Whoever then humbles himself as this child, he is the greatest in the kingdom of heaven. And whoever receives one such child in My name receives Me." (Matthew 18:3-5, NASB)

1. What have you seen in the lives of your children or grandchildren that illustrates the faith of a child Christ was talking about in Matthew 18?
2. What unique emotions and connections do you feel for your own grandchildren that you don't automatically have for your friend's grandchild?
3. Which one of the four freedoms (the freedom to be different, be vulnerable, be candid, and make mistakes) do you have the hardest time extending to your children or grandchildren? Why do you think this is?

Heavenly Father,
Thank You for the grandchildren You have brought into my life. Thank You that I get another chance to experience Your love through the eyes of a child. Please plant the seeds of faith in my grandchildren, and help me to be part of growing their childlike faith. Lord, please help me to treat my children and grandchildren the way You treat me—with amazing grace. Amen.

5 Role #1: Giving a Blessing

One of the features that sets a great actor apart from those who just *think* they're great is the ability to embody the person being portrayed. He or she takes on the persona of the character so thoroughly that you actually believe the actor is that person. This is especially impressive when the actor plays many different roles. You can see him in a couple of movies in the same year, and yet he makes a seamless transfer to the new character.

Robert Duvall is one of those actors who seems to consistently become the person he's playing. On one occasion we found ourselves waiting in the same line for an airplane. He said hello first. I came back with, "It's good to meet you, Gus." I said it without thinking. I knew his name was Robert Duvall, but he had so filled out the character of Gus McCrae in the movie *Lonesome Dove* that he had become that person to me. I corrected my mistake and introduced myself. He smiled and told me Gus McCrae was one of his favorite parts. We had a nice visit about playing roles.

Lights, Camera, Action

We all have various roles we must play. Some of you are employers. As such, you expect certain things from the people who work for you, and they from you. When you are functioning in a particular role, it is your responsibility to become the essence of what that role calls for.

And we all must play multiple roles. Darcy is a daughter, sister, wife, mother, and friend. I've seen her playing all five of those roles at the same time and doing a superb job with each. It's not hard to play multiple roles. The trick is to play them well.

Many years ago we were vacationing in the Black Hills of South Dakota, in an area where a passion play had been performed annually. Each summer a cast of hundreds played out the drama of the life, death, and resurrection of Jesus. We had rendezvoused with some friends and were planning on going with them to the play one evening. They were very familiar with some of the main characters in the play. As a result, they arranged for us to have lunch with "Jesus."

We had a great visit over a meal and got a real feel for the heart of this man. We were interested to hear how much his playing the Son of God every evening had affected his life. He said he was so taken by the significance of the character he played that he felt compelled to act like him in his day-to-day life. Obviously, he wasn't in the same galaxy as the King of kings and the Lord of lords—and he would be the first to admit that. But because of the importance of the role he played, he didn't want to do anything in his personal or private life that undermined his ability to portray the Savior of the world.

Taking On the Essence of True Grandparenthood

There are four roles we must play as grandparents. If we merely mouth the words to these roles or have to be consistently prompted in order to hit our marks and deliver our lines, most likely the people watching our performance won't be convinced. The best way to play these roles is to become the people the roles require.

Over the next few chapters we want to unpack these roles for you. They are all doable. All you have to do is make yourself available to God to play these key parts in your grandchildren's lives. But there's something we need to establish from the outset. If we choose not to fulfill these roles, we will by default become an antagonistic influence on our grandchildren. An unwillingness to take on these roles turns us into unwitting "heavies" in the minds of our grandchildren. Once you see what these roles are, you'll probably realize you're already playing them. But if you aren't, we think you will not only want to rise to the occasion, but also make sure you do nothing to undermine their essence in your private and personal life.

The Power of a Blessing

The first role we are called on to play is the role of *giving a blessing* to our grandchildren. This role is powerful, crucial, and urgent.

The concept of passing on a blessing was beautifully developed by Gary Smalley and John Trent in their book *The Blessing* in which they showed how instilling into a person a high sense of significance and a hopeful future is best done when a person is young.

Giving a blessing goes all the way back to some of the most famous names in the Bible. Before the great patriarch Jacob went on to glory, he called his sons to his deathbed and gave a unique blessing to each one of them. These were full-grown men who were married and had their own children. Yet he wanted to instill in them a unique sense of blessing before he died. Right before he blessed his sons, he had two of his grandsons brought in, because he wanted to make sure they received his blessing too. These were the two sons of Joseph.

Joseph was the son who had been pulled from Jacob's heart by the jealousy and subterfuge of Jacob's sons. Assuming that Joseph had been killed by a wild animal, Jacob spent many years of his life mourning the death of this special boy. In reality, Joseph had been sold into slavery in Egypt. God not only saw fit to protect Joseph but to move him into a position of authority over all of Egypt. When Jacob was once again united with this son he had given up for dead, he was amazed to find that he was the equivalent of the prime minister of Egypt.

There were two sons born to Joseph while he was in Egypt, isolated from his family. Their names were Ephraim and Manasseh. As Jacob prepared to take his last breath, he called these two grandsons to his bedside and laying his hands on them said these words:

> May the God before whom my fathers
> Abraham and Isaac walked,
> the God who has been my shepherd
> all my life to this day,
> the Angel who has delivered me from all harm
> —may he bless these boys.
> May they be called by my name
> and the names of my fathers Abraham and Isaac,
> and may they increase greatly
> upon the earth. (Genesis 48:15-16)

Just like the patriarchs of old, we have a chance to pass on a blessing to our grandchildren. It's one of the most strategic roles we will play in their lives. It's a combination of attitude and action. The blessing we bestow on our grandchildren will play a key role in establishing a sure foundation upon which they can build their lives. That foundation will sustain them through the storms they'll face in the future.

There's no denying the sheer power that our blessings can be to our grandchildren. Experience has proven that kids brought up with a clear sense of blessing can move into a hostile future and do just fine. But the flip side is equally true: Kids brought up *without* being blessed may move into an adult world that applauds and embraces them and still end up struggling with their concept of personal value.

All this said, it's obvious there is too much at stake for us to take our role as blessing givers lightly. If we want to effectively give a blessing to our grandchildren, it's crucial that we understand what their true needs are in order to bless them wisely.

Three Driving Inner Needs

The number one rule of public speaking is "Know your audience!" If you were trying to develop a product for a consumer, you'd work overtime to figure out what the consumer is looking for and what she really *needs*. In the same way, we'd all be much more effective blessing givers as grandparents if we could first clearly delineate our grandchildren's genuine needs.

But that's exactly where the problem lies with most people. Few adults—parents or grandparents—are confident they can articulate what their kids truly need deep down inside. In fact, if the average adult were given a quiz in this regard, he'd probably be surprised (and discouraged) to realize how hard it is to spell out the basic, driving inner needs of children. We know. We've quizzed people all over the country regarding this very issue.

Make yourself available to God to play these key parts in your grandchildren's lives.

The Bible outlines that children are born with three fundamental, driving inner needs. They are the result of being made in God's image. No other part of God's creation has these inner needs. Yet as vital as these are, most adults couldn't list them for you. There is one person, however, who, if he were standing here and I gave him a piece of paper, a pen, and posed this question to him, would be able to go 1 . . . 2 . . . 3 and list them out perfectly. His name . . . is Satan. Satan not only knows exactly what inner needs dominate our children's hearts, but he consistently offers them counterfeit ways to meet them.

By now, you're probably a bit curious as to what these needs are, so let us list them for you. If you keep these needs in the forefront of your mind as you work to be a blessing giver to your grandchildren, you will do wonders for their relationship with their parents, their view of themselves, their relationships to the people around them, and their attitude toward God. The three needs every child is born with are:

- a secure love
- a significant purpose
- a sufficient hope

Satan appealed to these three needs when he tempted Eve in the Garden of Eden (see Genesis 3). It's worth the personal study to see how effectively he framed his questions and statements to play right into Eve's overwhelming need for security, significance, and a sense of sufficiency.

If you want to see Satan appealing to all three of these needs in another person's life, all you have to do is open your Bible to Matthew 4 and read about Jesus' testing in the desert. He went without food or water for 40 days. When He was just about dead, Satan appeared and tried to tempt Him by appealing to these same three needs. He offered Jesus counterfeits, but Jesus didn't take the bait. He was so *blessed* through His relationship with His heavenly Father that He wanted nothing to do with Satan's knockoffs. Grandchildren who know they are truly blessed can have the same resolve when Satan moves in on them in their weaker moments to try to pull their hearts away from God.

Obviously, our grandchildren's parents have the greatest responsibility to meet these needs. They are usually in the best position to do so because of their relationship and the amount of time they spend together. We grandparents can reinforce what the parents are doing to meet these three inner needs. And we can also help fill in the gaps that exist when a parent is young and inexperienced, is absent, or drops the ball.

Let's look at these three needs individually and see how we can help meet them in such a way that we give our grandchildren an incredible sense of blessing.

A Secure Love

When it comes to transferring the assurance of a secure love to our grandchildren, there are three things we can do: First, grandchildren feel securely loved when they know their grandparents accept them as they are. We talked about this some in the last chapter when we developed the atmosphere of grace that should surround our relationship with them. It is crucial that our grandchildren know we accept them as they are.

We don't mean by this that we tolerate or condone sinful behavior. Most of the things over which kids feel rejected by adults or peers are not necessarily the things they do wrong. It's the things about them that the people around them simply don't like. It might be their music, their fads, their clothing, their way of communicating, their hair, their personality quirks, their body style, or the pace at which they work. Grandchildren need someone who doesn't make issues out of these nonissues and loves them for who they are.

A second thing we can do that gives them a sense of secure love is assure them that they enjoy a close affiliation within a loving and honoring family. Hopefully, they get to experience this with their immediate families. But some don't. Either way, it does wonders for their sense of security and love when they know that every time they cross your path, they are connected to a person who honors and loves them. Proverbs 10:7 says, "The memory of the righteous will be a blessing." The assurance that your grandchildren enjoy a close affiliation with you will give them a sense of secure love that can carry them through much of the rejection that their immediate context or their culture often brings their way.

A third way our grandchildren can gain a sense of secure love from us is when they receive regular and generous helpings of affection. God has hardwired children to respond to meaningful touch. They need to know there is always a safe and loving set of arms waiting for them when they come to see us.

A Significant Purpose

If a secure love was all you were able to offer your grandchildren, you'd be way ahead of the curve. But God also wants us to use our position as grandparents to help develop a sense of significant purpose in our grandchildren's hearts. Let's look at three ways this sense of significance and purpose can be transferred to your grandchildren.

For starters, grandchildren feel a significant purpose in their hearts when they are regularly affirmed. God did not design children to be irrelevant. He built great value, gifts, and skills into every person He created. We need to go out of our way to applaud the things they do well and whisper encouragement to them when they are working hard to conquer a challenge in their lives that isn't coming easy.

King David acknowledged the significance of an individual in his beautiful Psalm 139. Among other things, he remarks, "I will give thanks to You, for I am fearfully and wonderfully made; wonderful are Your works, and my soul knows it very well" (verse 14, NASB). We need to be reminding our grandchildren of their innate value as God's special creation. When we not only affirm them for what they do, but for who they are, we communicate to their inner beings that they have a significant purpose that makes them very valuable to the world around them.

A second thing we can do that helps build a sense of significant purpose into their lives is give them our attention. Not only were they not designed to be irrelevant, they weren't designed to be invisible either. Grandsons and granddaughters find it far easier to feel as if their lives matter when they know there is an older, smarter, and wiser person out there who has them on his or her mind. And when we get those chances to be involved up close in their lives and view them as assets to others, we can boost their confidence in who they are and why they matter.

We recall a tender conversation we overheard on an airplane. A grandfather had flown out west to pick up his grandson and take him back to his farm in the Midwest. The boy was about six years old. He carried on an animated conversation with the young woman sitting next to him about the trip he was taking with his grandfather. He was going to be with his grandfather for "a whole two weeks!" And though his grandfather was sitting right next to him, he talked about him as though he were some bigger-than-life entity. We were so tickled listening to him tell this woman about the animals he was going to touch, the tractor he was going to ride, and the hay barn he was going to sleep in on the last night he was there. "It has real bats in it," he said, "but my grandfather said he won't let any of them get me." Here was a grandchild who had a grandfather willing to cross the country to pick him up and give him his undivided attention for two weeks of a busy summer.

Too much is at stake for us to take our role as blessing givers lightly.

It is especially important for grandparents to notice their grandchildren during those times when the kids think they have been forgotten. Their parents may be struggling in their marriage or going through a divorce. These times can be devastating to a child's sense of significance. A grandparent who is paying close attention to their needs during this time can play a tremendous role in helping them process their pain.

A third way grandchildren develop a sense of significant purpose is when we gracefully admonish them. Children who lack accountability flounder to know who they are and how they can make a difference with their lives. We need to draw clear moral boundaries for them, applaud them as they honor those boundaries, and lovingly correct them when they stray from them. Our grandchildren's parents carry the primary responsibility for their training and correction, but we pass on a great sense of value to them when we love them enough to use our platform and example to challenge them to a higher standard.

A Sufficient Hope

The third priority we have is to help meet a child's inner need for a sufficient hope. The best way to instill the greatest hope is by helping each grandchild see the eternal hope found in a relationship with Jesus Christ. We'll discuss this key part of our role later on in this book.

We prepare the way for them to put their ultimate hope in the sufficiency of Jesus Christ by instilling a sense of hope in their daily lives. We'd like to suggest three ways to help meet your grandchildren's need for a sufficient hope that will dramatically enhance your role as a blessing giver.

For one thing, grandchildren feel a sense of hope when we help them recognize their God-given abilities and develop them. Helping them become the best they can be at what God has gifted them to be gives them hope that they'll have a viable contribution to make in the future. When they understand that these are gifts they have received from God, they are more equipped to use them in an eternal context.

One of the famous verses on this subject is found in the book of Proverbs: "Train up a child in the way he should go, even when he is old he will not depart from it" (Proverbs 22:6, NASB). If we were to give a literal rendering of this verse, straight from the Hebrew language, it would read something like, "Train up a child according to his unique inner bents, and when he is old, he will not depart from them." God has given our grandchildren divinely ordained bents toward things that make each of them a one-of-a-kind person and someone who can turn those bents into valuable contributions to society.

They might have a bent toward organization, or humor, or math, or entertainment, or sports. Maybe it shows up as stubbornness, or cleverness, or fearlessness. When we're paying attention and trying to help them isolate their God-given abilities, they gain a bigger-than-life hope. But we can't stop at just recognizing these gifts. We need to be willing to help them develop them too. Often grandparents are the catalyst and encourager for a young musician, golfer, scientist, or volunteer.

A second way we can help instill a sufficient hope into our grandchildren is by encouraging them to live a life of adventure. We need to challenge them to be willing to try new things, think on their own, and stretch themselves to their limits. It's the difference between raising a safe grandchild and raising a strong one. Too often, the priority of safety, born out of fear, denies a child the chance to blossom. The priority of safety might unwittingly doom your grandchild to a life of mediocrity. Strong kids, on the other hand, end up far safer in the end. That's why adventure is such an important quality to instill into their hearts and why it plays such a key role in giving a sufficient hope.

When our granddaughter Riley was first learning to swim, we had to encourage her to step up to each new challenge. On the one hand, we worked to instill a healthy respect for the swimming pool. But as she started taking lessons, it was evident that her healthy respect for the water in the swimming pool had a paralyzing effect when it came to taking new risks. We both got to play a key role in helping Riley make her first solo lap across the narrow end of the pool. Then we branched out to the length of the pool. Later it was our consistent encouragement as well as our presence in the pool directly below her that convinced her to take that first jump off the diving board. Before she was done, she was jumping off the diving board and swimming the length of the pool "all by myself!"

Riley has learned to not only trust our encouragement but to wrestle with her own fears when we aren't nearby. Her parents are committed to helping her live a very adventurous childhood, and we're more than happy to help them along the way.

We can boost their confidence in who they are and why they matter.

One time, when the grandchildren were very young, we vacationed as a family at Lake Tahoe. The ski area on the north side of Lake Tahoe once served as host to the Olympics. For our final day, we took the gondola to the mountaintop in order to take in the sights. Among the many options, we found there was an ice skating rink. Riley's parents gave me (Tim) permission to take her out for her first adventure on ice skates. Her excitement turned to sheer fright when she realized how quickly she could find herself on her bottom. But I kept working with her and encouraging her to be brave and keep trying. All along, I served as a source of balance and a check that kept her from hitting the ice every time she attempted to glide. She had a reasonable share of spills. They helped motivate her to perfect her skills. The last thing she did was skate the entire width of the rink (with me right behind her in case she fell) into the arms of her applauding parents.

Being a blessing to our grandchildren might cost us some blisters on our ankles, but they are a small price to pay for the long-term effect those blessings have on our grandchildren.

An adventurous life forces children to process their fears. Everyone has fears, but most people, because they are never forced to confront them, end up letting their fears define them. Children who are encouraged to regularly venture outside their comfort zones are more likely to be willing to depend on God in their lives. That's because adventures force them to trust God. God loves to come alongside them when they're frightened or lonely or overwhelmed or ready to give up. In these situations He teaches our grandchildren hope through His sufficiency. One of the best ways we can instill this kind of spirit into our grandchildren is for them to see it as a part of the way we live our own lives. The more adventurous a life each of us is willing to live—especially in the area of faith—the more inclined our grandchildren will be to step outside the ranks of those who know neither victory nor defeat and find out what they're truly made of.

As far as helping them live a great adventure, remember to get permission from their parents. We're not talking about taking your grandchildren skydiving!

A third way we can help instill a sense of sufficient hope into our grandchildren is by helping them turn their childhood into a series of positive accomplishments.

Children need to know they have what it takes to succeed. Too often they feel as if they are living in a world that only reminds them of how much of a failure they are. Sometimes there are extenuating circumstances, such as a disability or a disadvantage, which adds to this feeling. It's great when grandchildren know that when they are within our sphere of influence, they have adults who are committed to doing all they can to help them be all they can be.

Showers of Blessings

Our first role as grandparents is to give a blessing to our grandchildren. The best way to do this is by consistently meeting their needs for a secure love, a significant purpose, and a strong hope. In our next chapter, we'll list some specific ways you can make this happen in their lives.

For Further Thought and Discussion

May God himself, the God of peace, sanctify you through and through. May your whole spirit, soul and body be kept blameless at the coming of our Lord Jesus Christ. The one who calls you is faithful and he will do it. (1 Thessalonians 5:23-24)

1. How has receiving or not receiving a blessing in your childhood affected your life? How well did your parents or grandparents do at giving you a secure love, a significant purpose, and a sufficient hope?
2. What are some individual attributes you can affirm in each of your grandchildren? Do you see any of your child (their parent) in these attributes?
3. What are some of the ways you can celebrate the accomplishments of your grandchildren?

Heavenly Father,
Please help me to know my grandchildren's hearts well enough to see their true needs. Give me Your view of them as I accept who You made them to be. Thank You that You formed them in their mother's womb and that You have made them in Your image. I pray You will show me how to help them develop a secure love in their hearts, a significant purpose for their lives, and a sufficient hope in You. Amen.

6 Being a Blessing by Giving a Blessing

You might remember the movie *On Golden Pond.* It's now considered a classic, in part because two legends of Hollywood played the main characters. Henry Fonda and Katharine Hepburn were a set of grandparents who volunteered to take care of their teenage grandson while his mother went through some transitions in her life. This boy showed up at their place feeling angry, frustrated, and worthless.

He needed to be blessed.

What he found were two people who genuinely loved him, who believed he was significant, and who were able to instill in him some hope for the future. Their willingness to bless him helped him climb out of the hole of insignificance he had fallen into. Even though this story had some serious flaws and Henry Fonda's character was crusty, edgy, and profane, these flawed people were able to bring about a significant change in their grandson. How much more capable are grandparents who bless their grandchildren's lives with the power of God's Holy Spirit fueling them?

The Art of Giving a Blessing

In our last chapter we introduced our first grand role: giving a blessing. Before we introduce our second grand role as grandparents, we'd like to give you some practical things you can do to bless your grandchildren spiritually, emotionally, and physically.

Blessing Them Spiritually

One of the greatest things you can do for your grandchildren is to pray for them. Both Darcy and I had a surrogate grandmother named Vivian who prayed for us every day for over 20 years. She has since gone on to heaven. As much as we loved knowing she was praying for us, we loved even more the fact that she was consistently praying for our children . . . by name . . . every day . . . without fail.

Just like Vivian, you can pray. When it comes to children and grandchildren, there might be circumstances in their lives or yours that don't allow for the closeness you'd like. And there might be some stress between you and them, but you can still pray. Whether you live across the street or across the country, you can be a blessing giver through prayer.

Recently I (Tim) met a young mom raising three children. Her stick-on badge said she went by the name Katia. As soon as she said hello, I knew she was a transplant from the former Soviet Union. As it turned out, she hailed from the region of Kazakhstan.

She had immigrated in her early twenties to the United States. Her husband met her while she was finishing a degree program at a state college. They had been married about 10 years.

Katia spoke with great enthusiasm about her children and her desire to raise them in a safe environment. She mentioned the word *safe* so many times that I decided to find out what made her so frightened about the world that surrounded her in the United States. I figured I knew the answer before she responded, but I needed to make certain.

Sure enough, she talked about the incredible struggles she faced growing up in Kazakhstan. She was taught atheism from the time she started kindergarten. Once she reached her teenage years, the lack of any absolute moral standard hit her age group in its full fury. Teenage girls were encouraged by their parents to be sexually active, alcoholism was pandemic, and money was so scarce that a life of crime often started at this time in a person's life.

It is not uncommon that people who have endured extremely difficult circumstances in their childhoods often try to create safe enclaves in which to raise their children. In trying to learn why she was so preoccupied with the safety of her kids, I asked a question that got an answer I wasn't expecting. "So you came out of your teenage years in Kazakhstan with a lot of scar tissue on your heart?"

This is where she threw me a curve. "That's what's interesting. I didn't. I didn't surrender my virginity, I didn't drink, and I was able to get through the entire time there without ever having to experience any violence firsthand."

In explaining how she managed to live a life so counter to her depressing culture, she said two wonderful words: "My grandmother!" It turns out her grandmother had rejected the atheism of communism and maintained a vigilant commitment to her belief in Christ. Katia's parents were atheists, but her grandmother's faith carried her through. She said, "Every time I would visit my grandmother, she would tell me how much she loved me and how she was praying I would grow up to be a person who loved God. She would always remind me that she was praying for me every day and trusting that Jesus would protect me from the awful pressures that surrounded me."

> ***You can be a blessing giver through prayer.***

"So your grandmother introduced you to a relationship with Jesus?" I asked.

"Oh no. I was an atheist until I came here to the United States. But I loved my grandmother like crazy. She believed in a better me than I did," she said. "I just felt this enormous power to resist all the temptations I faced. It was after I got here that I figured out how much I wanted God's presence in my life."

A grandmother in the former Soviet Union defied the government and decided to live her life to give a spiritual blessing to a girl who didn't otherwise have much of a chance. Now that girl is working to replace her fears for her own children with a confidence in God's ability to watch over them in the midst of our culture.

We bless our grandchildren's spiritual lives not only by praying for them but also by showing them how to grow in their faith and use their spiritual gifts. It's not just a case of us urging them to do this. The apostle Paul recognized the power of example when he wrote to Timothy, "I have been reminded of your sincere faith, which first lived in your grandmother Lois and in your mother Eunice and, I am persuaded, now lives in you also" (2 Timothy 1:5). Our grandchildren must see what faith looks like by watching us grow in our love for Christ and for the people around us. They've got to see us using our spiritual gifts in substantive ways that force us to trust God. Too often grandparents want to leave the "heavy lifting" of the Christian life to younger people. We need to be exceptions to that tendency. As hard as life may be, we need to keep *keeping on* so our grandchildren understand what it means to finish strong. Our prayers and our godly example will help build that heart of blessing that each grandchild longs for.

Blessing Them Emotionally

When it comes to this key part of their makeup, there are a couple of strategic things we can do that will make a powerful impact on their sense of blessing.

We can celebrate their accomplishments. For the grandchildren who live close by, that might mean showing up for Grandparents Day in the elementary school or on the sidelines of some of their athletic endeavors. For those who live far away, it might mean keeping up with their achievements through their parents and then encouraging them directly through emails, phone calls, and text messages. We'll strengthen their confidence if they know they can count on us to provide that nonjudgmental voice in their lives that can't always be provided by their parents.

For the past 14 years, I (Darcy) have gathered every Monday school-day morning to pray with a group of moms for our students and their schools. All of my kids have been blessed by the love and prayers of the other moms in this Moms in Touch group. As we were praying our thanksgiving last week, one of the mothers thanked God for her daughter and son's grandparents. She gave thanks for the safe haven they provide for her kids as they are processing the challenges of high school. She was so grateful that these teenagers, who were giving her a run for her money, still loved going to Grandma and Grandpa's house and loved being with them and felt safe opening their hearts to them. Obviously, this grandmother and grandfather had been cheering them on and encouraging them in a nonjudgmental way all of their lives. Now, as teenagers, these grandchildren were still comfortable coming to their grandparents for some emotional blessings.

Keep keeping on so grandchildren understand what it means to finish strong.

And while we're talking about blessing them emotionally, we have to at least brush on the issue of *showing favoritism.* It's an easy trap to fall into, and it can have a devastating effect on the grandchild who doesn't get invited into the inner recesses of our hearts. Whether it is intentional or accidental, favoritism can be counter-productive and cause jealousy between grandchildren and between the parents and the grandchildren. On this subject, physician Arthur Kornhaber says, "In most instances a grandparent favors a certain grandchild because the two of them share a common quality—for example, being the same gender, being a youngest or eldest child, and having similar personality traits, temperaments, physical characteristics or talents . . . intelligence, musicality, athletic ability."[1] There are also some practical issues that make it difficult to show equal attention to all our grandchildren. Some might see you more because they live nearby or live with you or share some interest that naturally allows them to get more of your attention. Perhaps they need more help due to a family crisis, and you have been playing an active role in their lives.

We had one grandmother share with us that, while treating every grandchild the same may be the true desire, it can be difficult when the parenting style of your children is so radically different from your own. "The less well-behaved grandchildren are often that way through no fault of their own, and it is very tricky not to blurt out correction. This does not go over well with the parents and totally befuddles the kids." The pleasantness of our other grandchildren could even subconsciously cause us to favor one over the other. But whether proximity, interests, ease, or age determines your contact with them, you should love all of your grandchildren with the same *intensity.* Each one needs to know you are delighted to be his grandparent, regardless of how easy he makes it for you to love him.

Avoiding Favoritism

- Be careful not to set an unrealistic precedent with your first grandchild.
- When a crisis or ongoing challenge in one family or grandchild's life requires more of your time and energy, go out of your way to make sure your other children and grandchildren know you would do the same for them.

- Avoid comparing your grandchildren to each other or to their parents.
- Though you may have a natural connection with one of your children, don't fall into the trap of showing preference to that child or his or her children.
- Make sure your grandchild doesn't overhear his parent using you as a sounding board regarding problems with him or a sibling.

Blessing Them Physically

We can give a blessing to our grandchildren when it comes to their physical lives by providing a safe and comfortable home where they are always welcome. And we'll do wonders for them if they know we are proud, on their behalf, for the body and the looks they were given. The world most kids live in has a way of picking them apart when it comes to their physical appearance. The media, their community, and sometimes their educational environment are quick to point out where they are substandard in their looks, weight, and athletic abilities. We have been around long enough to understand the fickle nature of public opinion and the shallowness of the people who thrive on superficial beauty. We can bless them by assuring them they are beautiful or handsome in our sight . . . and always will be. It's simply seeing them the way God sees them.

Count Your Blessings

Spiritually, emotionally, and physically—on each level we are afforded ample opportunities to give a blessing to our grandchildren. When we do, we'll also be giving a blessing to their parents. It might be a reinforcement of the way we raised them, or it might be a dramatic contrast.

When we approach every contact with our grandchildren as an opportunity to bless them, we are truly carrying out the essence of this first critical role of grandparenthood. If it has been your custom to view certain events like birthdays and Christmas as times when you bless them, and all the other contacts are just time spent with them, we hope you'll be willing to rethink that custom. Being a blessing to our grandchildren isn't supposed to be something we do in parentheses, but rather something we *are* every time we are around them.

If it hasn't been your practice to voice words of assurance and hope to your grandchildren, now is as good a time as any to make this your new habit, because when it comes to giving a blessing to the generations after us, it's never too late, and it's never too much.

For Further Thought and Discussion

Blessed are all who fear the LORD,
    who walk in his ways.
You will eat the fruit of your labor;
    blessings and prosperity will be yours. . . .
Thus is the man blessed
    who fears the LORD.

May the LORD bless you from Zion
    all the days of your life;
may you see the prosperity of Jerusalem,
    and may you live to see your children's children.
        (Psalm 128:1-2, 4-6)

1. List each of your grandchildren by name and then put two prayer requests by each name. Pray regularly for these needs. (In our DVD study *Extreme Grandparenting: The Ride of Your Life!* we have an example of a simple-to-use *Grandparent's Prayer Journal.*)

2. How have you already seen God answer prayers for your grandchildren?
3. What are some specific ways you could bless your grandchildren spiritually, emotionally, and physically?
4. Why is it easy to fall into the trap of favoritism with our grandchildren? How can showing favoritism undermine our relationship with our children?

Heavenly Father,
Please help me to be a blessing giver to my grandchildren by praying daily for them, by celebrating their accomplishments, by modeling a genuine faith in You, and by always communicating my delight in being their grandparent. Help me be deliberate in using my time with them to touch their lives in ways that serve them for the rest of their lives. Please reveal to me how I can bless them spiritually, emotionally, and physically. Thank You that as much as I love them, You love them more. Amen.

7 Role #2: Leaving a Legacy

Family is one of God's greatest ideas for securing a culture and for sustaining His grace from one generation to the next. Every once in a while, an event happens that reminds us just how powerful these bonds are between the generations.

I (Darcy) have a picture album that captures one of those great moments in time. It is also near and dear to me because it depicts one of the best road trips we ever made with our children. The pictures capture the day we celebrated the 100th birthday of my grandmother.

It was an unforgettable event. Five generations converged on a small town in California to toast the life of a wonderful lady. My grandmother had crossed the United States in a covered wagon as a young girl and crossed the Atlantic Ocean in the Concorde as an adult. When she was born, society was moving at a snail's pace compared to what it was on the day all her grandchildren and great-grandchildren gathered around her to help her blow out the one hundred candles on her birthday cake.

By that time, life was moving at several times the speed of sound. In the decades she had lived, she saw the influence of family encounter stiff competition from forces that didn't necessarily have the family's best interests at heart. But she was a great example of how one person, paying attention, and operating from a clear set of values, can stand strong against all the cultural challenges around her.

Besides being a tender and moving time for me as a granddaughter, the whole event was a fabulous time for our children. My entire extended family stayed at one of the few hotels in town. It was a low-budget place right next to a convenience store. The kids loved it. They could move back and forth between their cousins' rooms, and they got more than their share of slushies, Doritos, and beef jerky. The dads loved that part too, with a little coffee thrown into the menu.

It was a powerful event because it was a great reminder of our second role as grandparents. In the last two chapters we explained that one of our roles as grandparents is to give a generous blessing to our grandchildren. The second role we have been given by God is to *leave a good legacy* for our grandchildren.

As you know, when it comes to the issue of leaving a legacy, none of us has a choice of whether or not we're going to leave one. It's a foregone conclusion. The only choice we have is what kind of legacy it will be. We are writing our legacy every day by the choices we make about how to invest our time and by what we decide to do with our God-given talents. Our legacy is written in how we use the personal resources we've been given and what we do with the various opportunities each day brings.

These choices make up the script of our lives, written over a lifetime and left for all to read. Young sets of eyes will study that script and take careful notes. And because of who we are in relation to them, they will take what they've found and draw serious conclusions about their own lives. It is essential that we leave them a legacy that points them to God and inspires them to follow a noble path.

Older and, Hopefully, Better

Psalm 102:28 says, "The children of your servants will live in your presence; their descendants will be established before you." As grandparents, we get to see what kind of legacy we are establishing through our descendants. We get to see our grandchildren filter life and begin the process of leaving their own legacies. Because of that, some of us would like to skip to the next lesson and act as if this one never happened. We look back on choices we made and the negative impact they've had on people close to us, and we feel discouraged about our legacies.

Maybe we didn't have good role models when we were young. Maybe we didn't come to know God until we were much older. Or maybe we knew Him when we were younger but neglected to make our daily choices according to the mandates of His Word. It's easy to list the "maybes" that helped mold our legacies along the way, but none of them are legitimate excuses for not trying to *improve* our legacies. Nor do they represent valid reasons to just give up trying to make a positive imprint on our grandchildren. We're leaving an imprint whether we like it or not. And refusing to try to repair a bad legacy is to resign our grandchildren to being negatively affected by it. Since leaving a legacy is unavoidable, we ought to do everything within our power to leave one that helps rather than harms.

How's That Working for You?

Most people have some dark chapters in their past. And it's equally true that some of those chapters were written at the expense of our children. In the process, we may have left a bad taste in their mouths about us. As a result, we may not have the kind of relationship with them that we wish we had. And because of that, they may not want us to have much of a relationship with their kids.

We received an email from a heartbroken grandmother. She and her husband had raised a daughter in the midst of their rocky marriage. Now that their daughter was married with two children, she was denying access to her children as a way of punishing her parents for the mistakes they made in her life. This grandmother was longing to lavish her love on her grandchildren, but their mother was telling them that Grandma was mean and wasn't allowed to see them.

In this chapter we are going to discuss what we shared with this grandmother and many like her who are trying to restore a broken legacy with their children in order to have the opportunity to leave a legacy of love for their grandchildren.

New Beginnings

What's great about grandparenting is that it gives us a chance to reinvent ourselves as pacesetters for our families. We can actually use these final decades of our lives to become full-time ambassadors of God's grace to some of the very people we have disappointed in the past.

My (Darcy's) father is a good example of this. When I think of the kind of legacy he was leaving as I was growing up, the words *anger, isolation,* and *regret* come to mind. There were six kids in my family, and my father seemed to grow more distant from us as we grew older. When the bulk of my siblings were teenagers, we found ourselves under the roof of a man who was preoccupied with *his* life, but uninvolved in ours. He seldom said words of encouragement and was quick to remind us of our faults. As we all grew up, got married, and started to go our separate ways, there was a clear sense of disappointment as we looked back over our years under his influence.

But then something amazing happened. Within months of each other, my brother and his wife and Tim and I gave birth to my father's first two grandchildren. These two little girls melted my dad's heart. He loved being around them. He was patient, tender, and interested in the fine points of their lives. Some of my fondest memories of my dad are of him holding our daughter on his lap and singing songs to her. It made me wonder, *Where was this man when I was growing up?*

But it didn't make me bitter. I realize it does for some children, but it didn't for me. I longed to have a great relationship with my dad, and through my own children, I was able to get to know a man who either didn't exist for me or hid himself very well when I was a young girl. My father learned that one of the ways to make up for mistakes in his past was to love my children in ways he wasn't able to love me.

What we're talking about is so obvious that it almost seems absurd to bring up, but the fact is, life changes us. We aren't the people we were when we got out of high school or when we were going through the early years of raising our children. Fathers who would have nothing to do with the daily care of their young children are known to turn into Mr. Grandma once the grandchildren show up. Baby-boomer grandpas are being reborn to relational domesticity. Men who wouldn't be caught dead changing a diaper or pushing a stroller when they were young fathers now are ready to put up a fight for the opportunity to do those exact things with their grandchildren.

My (Tim's) father sure illustrated this point. He would come out to visit our kids and would stuff cash in their piggy banks or whisk them away to the mall to get them ice cream. For a while I felt that this man, who looked similar to the man I grew up with, was really an imposter in our midst. I recall how when I was a boy and would ask him for 10 dollars, he'd give me sad stories about the Great Depression. And then he'd finally respond to my request with something that sounded like, "Get a job." He changed as he got older, and one of the ways had to do with how he viewed his money and his grandkids. He felt that one of money's roles was to put ice cream and candy into their tummies.

When it comes to the issue of leaving a legacy, none of us has a choice.

Listen, most of us aren't even similar to what we were five years ago. We live in a *constant* state of change. But here's the important point: Growing older is *supposed* to make us *better* and *wiser* people. It's supposed to give us that experience and perspective that helps us temper our lives into ones that are more valuable to the people around us.

Obviously, not everybody comes to their position of grandparent with a long list of regrets. Many of you were conscientious parents who were guided by the love of Christ as you raised your children. You steered your family with an accurate moral compass, and you are enjoying the fruits of your labor. You have a rich relationship with your children and an even richer one with your grandchildren. If you just keep on doing what you are doing, you'll no doubt get to leave a wonderful legacy of love. But there are many others who are feeling the effect of some bad choices when it comes to their grandchildren.

Gatekeepers

Our relationship with our own children is the single most influential factor in the access we have to our grandchildren. Our children are the gatekeepers to our grandchildren. It's their job. While their children are under their care, we must go through them to reach out to our grandchildren. With that in mind, we would like to talk in depth about restoring a fractured relationship with a child.

In the book of Joel, the children of Israel had made the choice to ignore God and go against His wishes for their lives. One of the consequences of their sins was a plague of locusts that swarmed through their land and destroyed their crops. They were an agrarian culture almost completely dependent on a good harvest. This plague of locusts devastated their economy. The consequences had their desired effect. They repented of their sins and asked God for forgiveness and mercy. God said something profound to these punished people that rings true to people today, men and women who are realizing the consequences their wrong choices have had on their role as grandparents. Listen to what God says in Joel 2:25: "I will repay you for the years the locusts have eaten."

One of the ways God often chooses to restore lost years for us is through our role as grandparents. By loving our grandchildren, we get to be something for our children that—for whatever reason—we could not be when they were young.

It shouldn't surprise us that our sudden willingness to play a large and positive role in our grandchildren's lives causes some of our children to experience feelings of resentment. We have heard many laments like this one from a friend we encountered at a soccer game: "He never showed up for one of my games when I was little, but he hasn't missed one of his grandsons' games. Go figure." Our gracious and kind involvement in our grandchildren's lives may open old wounds for their parents. If we just trudge ahead like nothing ever happened, we might never get to leave the kind of legacy God meant us to leave.

A Legacy of Regret, Times Two

We know of two boys, identical twins, whose parents were not careful as they passed an early inheritance on to them. It was obvious to one brother that they had shown clear favoritism to his twin. He thought the other brother was given a much bigger piece of the family pie. The actions of the parents caused such a deep divide between the twin brothers and their wives (who were sisters) that each couple decided to have nothing to do with the other. They decided not to speak to each other and refused to have contact with each other's families—this in spite of the fact that both families lived in a tiny rural town where everybody knew everybody.

It's been over 50 years. Three generations have come from these two original couples. There was a point when the original parents realized they'd hurt their one son deeply. They were in the best position to rectify the problem, but their enormous pride and fragile egos played them like puppets. They didn't want to have to admit, out loud, that they were wrong. As a result, they became estranged from the family of the son who felt he'd been shortchanged. Two families of cousins, second cousins, and third cousins have had to avoid one another in a small rural village for over half a century.

One grandmother told us that the birth of her grandchildren was the motivation she needed to try to make things right with her daughter. However, her son-in-law was very resistant to this idea. He had lived with the bitterness between the mother and daughter for years and was opposed to the idea of having more of his mother-in-law in his life. As far as he was concerned, "murder-in-law" described her more precisely.

Rather than accepting defeat and falling back into the despair of the past, the grandmother decided to carefully rebuild her relationship with her daughter and establish one with her son-in-law. As she told me about this, she said it was the hardest thing she has ever done. It wasn't without pain and disappointment, but it was worth it. She and her daughter and son-in-law have established a workable relationship that involves ever-expanding boundaries of trust. She is now able to see her grandchildren and have them visit her at her own house. Had she not made the effort to take the first step, as well as persevered through the tough years, she would have missed out on all the joy she is presently experiencing as a grandmother. It may take years to tear down the walls one has spent so much time building, but it is well worth it.

Let's just stop for a minute and take an inventory. Maybe you were the kind of parent who was present but unaccounted for. Or maybe you were absent, because either work or divorce caused you to play a minimal role in your child's life. Maybe you carried a chip on your shoulder for some reason, and you seemed to take your frustration out on them. Maybe you made some major mistakes that cost them or embarrassed them or caused them to resent you. Here's the good news! In spite of what happened, we serve a God who wants to help restore those years you lost. And in the process, He wants to give you a chance to do something in your grandchildren's lives that will live on long after you are gone.

I Repent

It starts with repentance. Repentance is not just admitting you are wrong; it's recognizing that what you did hurt people. And it's asking for forgiveness. The last half of Ephesians 4 outlines the rules for how to fight fair and resolve conflict. The capstone of Paul's advice hits directly on the issue we're dealing with. He writes, "Be kind to one another, tender-hearted, forgiving each other, just as God in Christ also has forgiven you" (verse 32, NASB). When it comes to intergenerational conflict, forgiveness is best when it takes place at three levels.

First, we need to ask God to forgive us. We need to go to Him with humble hearts and acknowledge we did things that hurt our children. We need to let Him know how sorry we are for our actions and for the negative impact they have had on our children. In the process, thank Him for His mercy.

Second, we need to forgive ourselves. Some people think they have to beat themselves up for past mistakes and wallow in misery as a way of doing penance. That doesn't help anyone, and it insults the finished work Christ did for us when He took our sins on Himself on the cross.

Third, we need to ask our children for forgiveness. We need to specifically acknowledge the big and small things we did to them that have made it hard for us to play a good role in their lives. We may also need to go to our son-in-law or daughter-in-law and ask forgiveness for things we have done to alienate them from us. This is not something that is going to change the relationship over night. It didn't happen that quickly and it won't heal that quickly either, but repentance is the first step to opening the door that leads to restoration.

Helping Things Heal

While you are waiting for love and repentance to redeem the relationship, you can take some action to remain connected to your grandchildren. Prayer is by far the most effective and the least intrusive action you can take. No matter what restrictions are put on your contact with your grandchildren, God can work in their lives and bless them on your behalf through prayer. You may also be able to write your grandchildren notes or emails, call them on the phone, and send them gifts for special occasions. Make sure none of these in any way undermine the greater goal of restoring your relationship with your grandchildren's parents.

As we write this, we know what some people are thinking. They think that whatever mistakes they might have made are no big deal. For decades we have heard young people say that when they confront their parents about the pain they received from them, the parents start to chuckle or shake their heads and tell them that perhaps they've lost their minds.

Here's reality: Everyone edits his or her history. You either put on filters that block out the negative, or you put on filters that block out all the good times. When children have experienced a lot of disappointment, they may see things as worse than they really were. Conversely, when parents have made it a lifestyle to trivialize the severity of their problems, they have a bad tendency to remember the past as being much better than it actually was.

We have some dear friends who had to bury their eighteen-year-old son. He was killed trying to save a dog that was caught in traffic. Few things could devastate a couple more than what they had to go through, but one set of grandparents actually gave their grief a run for its money. They tried to top it with insult.

This particular set of grandparents were people you'd never suspect of being off-the-chart high controllers. They were leaders and key benefactors to their church. They sat on prestigious boards and had a Who's Who set of Christian friends. But when it came to their children, they trafficked in guilt, manipulation, and gossip. It was because of this that our friends had made the hard decision to distance themselves from these people shortly after their last child was born.

This only caused these grandparents to ramp up their highly

controlling words. One of the things they told our friends when they moved away was that God was going to punish them for taking their grandchildren from them. At the funeral of their grandson, these grandparents approached the grieving parents and said, "This happened because you moved away from us."

It has been many years since they heard these chilling words. Yet, as people of faith, they have been torn with the responsibility of forgiving these grandparents for their jaded insensitivity and crass high control. At the same time they want to protect their remaining children from their grandparents' manipulative ways.

The years have had a tempering effect on these grandparents. Recently, they actually started to talk about some of the mean things they said and wrong things they did. But they have yet to come right out and take full responsibility for the pain they caused in the past. When confronted point-blank with the harsh words they said over the years, they trivialize them by responding, "I think you're reading more into those words than what we meant at the time."

That's a form of self-protection we might employ when we are young, naive, and a bit self-absorbed, but as we get older, life should season us in such a way that we are more honest with ourselves. Part of that honesty is willingness to be forthright with people we've hurt and take responsibility for our actions.

When I hear this issue being discussed, I think of that old expression about "eating crow." It refers to a process of swallowing pride, admitting guilt, and asking for forgiveness. By this point in our lives we should all be able to write a cookbook for eating crow.

The Upside of Eating Crow

The benefits of seeking forgiveness are many. One benefit is that we take steps to relieve the tension between our children and us, tension that may be blocking us from having the involvement in our grandchildren's lives that they need and we desire.

A second benefit is that it frees our children to be better parents to our grandchildren. Often our mistakes leave open wounds that undermine our children's ability to function properly as parents. We can play a significant role in helping those wounds heal.

A third benefit to seeking forgiveness is that it strengthens the kind of influence we get to have on our grandchildren. They see grandparents who are actively involved in loving and encouraging their parents. And keep in mind the obvious: If we don't initiate the healing process through forgiveness, we may never get to have a relationship with our grandchildren that is even remotely close to what God intended it to be.

Maybe it's time for some of you to raise the white flag and do everything you can to call a truce over some longstanding conflict with your children. Don't expect it to happen overnight. Healing takes time, but it has to start with you.

And we've got to be diligent to make sure we *keep* our relationships reconciled. The normal back and forth between families can create hurt. We need to make sure we're dealing with issues as they come up—like disagreements, opinions expressed that may have hurt, or statements that were made inappropriately. It's important in these situations to focus on the problem and not the person with whom you're having the problem. This is especially true when we're dealing with our daughters-in-law and sons-in-law. They don't have the lifelong relationship with us—whether good or bad—and we may not have gotten off to the kind of start with them that we would have preferred. A practical way to develop this kind of love is to always acknowledge and greet both parents when you see them, give hugs, kisses, or handshakes to both, and include both of them in your admiration and affirmation.

One grandmother observed that the more your son-in-law or daughter-in-law sees you as a partner on their team, the more trust and freedom they will extend to you. You can become their ally by carrying out their wishes when you are with their children, by always speaking positively about them in the presence of their spouses and children, and by letting them know you appreciate all they do for your child and your grandchildren.

10 Ways to Be an Ally to Your Son-in-Law (or Daughter-in-Law)

1. Truly see him as an answer to your prayers for a spouse for your daughter.
2. If the circumstances of his marriage to your daughter were less than ideal, ask God to help you forgive those mistakes and the ones who made the mistakes.
3. Extend to him a clean slate, and give him the benefit of the doubt.
4. View him and your daughter as a team—one in God's eyes—and don't do anything to undermine their oneness.
5. Accept his parents, and do your best to establish a good relationship with them.
6. Respect his and your daughter's standards and rules regarding their children, even though you may disagree.
7. If he is open to it, make sure you show him the same type of affection you show your daughter.
8. Keep short accounts. If you have a conflict, don't let it fester. Make sure to take responsibility for your shortcomings and forgive his.
9. Show a genuine interest in who he is and what he does.
10. Pray for him daily because he has incredible influence over those you love the most.

Leaving a Great Legacy

Because our pasts can undermine what we're trying to do in the present, we've dedicated much of this lesson to redeeming our legacies. As we work through those past disappointments or continue on the productive path we're on, we ask the question, "What should we be doing *now* to make sure we are leaving a legacy that will impact our grandchildren in a positive way?"

This question brings to mind another one of our road trips. Many years ago, before we had any children, we were driving across Wyoming on a two-lane road. For a half hour we were stuck behind a long line of cars poking down the highway. We could see half a mile ahead what was holding us up. It was one of those state-of-the-art RVs that had more whistles and bells on it than the space station. It took awhile for everybody to pass it. When we finally got our turn to poke along behind the RV, we had plenty of time to read all of the bumper stickers they had collected in their travels.

One of the stickers explained how they could afford to drive such a sophisticated home on wheels. It said "We're Spending Our Children's Inheritance."

We laughed. Here were two senior citizens enjoying their twilight years in a high-tech Winnebago. The bumper sticker's message seemed appropriate on the back of an RV, but as we reflect on it now, we can't help but feel how easily it could be reworded and stuck on the back of some grandparents: We're Squandering Our Legacy.

Some are under the impression that you can leave a legacy without making sacrifices—a sort of "this is who we are, and this is what you get." Our grandchildren need more from us. They need us to use what time we have left to write the script to a legacy that will last forever.

So how about we go through a quick laundry list of some things that help us leave these kinds of legacies. If we take these suggestions to heart, it will put us light years ahead of most grandparents.

1. Bring honor to our families' reputations by living lives of integrity publicly and privately. What our grandchildren hear about us from others and what they learn about us firsthand needs to be consistent with a lifestyle of integrity. They need to see our "yes" be "yes" and our "no" be "no" and our character having no ambiguity. Proverbs

20:7 says, "The righteous man leads a blameless life; blessed are his children after him."

We also bring honor to our families' reputations by reinforcing, rather than undermining, the rules and guidelines our grandchildren's parents have established. If a rule is unclear, we sincerely ask for clarification, especially if a rule differs from those we set for our own children. We can't assume we will always agree with the rules our children and their spouses have established, but unless we're being asked to do something that endangers a grandchild, we need to honor the parents' rules. At times it may be appropriate to give input if the parents are seeking advice; otherwise we praise their positive efforts and applaud their desire to run a tight ship.

Our children are the gatekeepers to our grandchildren.

2. Make decisions with an eternal perspective. Life here on earth isn't all there is. It's just a forerunner to eternity. Our grandchildren need to see our consistent confidence in the salvation we have in Jesus Christ, demonstrated in how little we fear and how much we hope. Our eternal perspective leads us to finish well and finish strong. It reminds us to always keep our end goal in mind. We need to take opportunities to remind them of how God has been faithful to us, how He continues to show us His goodness, and how He empowers us to endure through suffering and hardship.

The attitude we have toward people as compared to things also demonstrates our eternal perspective. Kids need to see grandparents who love people and use things, not the other way around. Our grandchildren need us to keep wealth and material possessions in perspective. It's not that status and money have no place; often they are the reward of hard, deliberate work. But they are not most important. Our attitude will be a powerful contrast to the world that surrounds our grandchildren and wants to define them. Our diligence to maintain an eternal perspective will help our grandchildren view themselves in the light of eternity.

3. Leave clear tracks for them to follow. I (Tim) remember when I was about eight years old, spending a few days at my grandparents' house. It had snowed pretty heavily overnight. In the morning my grandfather decided to walk down to my uncle's house through the drifts. He invited me to go along, but the snow was too deep for me to make it on my own. Fortunately, I found that if I stayed behind him and walked in his bootprints, I could keep up.

We have grandchildren following us. It behooves us to cut a straight trail through life for them. They need to see us choosing grace, backing up our words with actions, avoiding cynicism, and demonstrating faithful living. We have a powerful opportunity to show them how people avoid a self-indulgent life and how they invest their time in serving God and others. They will be proud to receive and carry on your legacy here on earth and in heaven.

When You Finally Run Out of Time

Several years ago, two unrelated grandparents lay in an intensive-care unit in a small-town hospital in Pennsylvania. One was a woman named Winnie. The other was a man who was a financial pillar of the community. Winnie was a high-school graduate. The man across the room had an Ivy League education. Winnie had worked for slightly more than minimum wage all her life. The man was a titan of local industry. Winnie was dying with a few hundred dollars in the bank. The man was dying with more money in the bank than most people make in five lifetimes. But the difference was that Winnie was truly rich, and the man had little to show for his life.

They both had children, and they both had grandchildren. For the entire time they lay across the room from each other, Winnie had a constant stream of children and grandchildren coming to be by her side. The numerous people she had lived her life for were now traveling from all points of the compass just to hold her hand and stand by her side to the end.

The man had no visitors. He had lived for himself when he was young and had indulged himself as he got older. He had purchased recognition, accolades, and applause. But because he had not left his mark on the hearts of the people in his life, no one came to hold his hand and to weep over him when he died. Now, with time running out, he suddenly realized it was too late to do anything about it.

Late one evening, as the nurse was preparing him for a night of sleep, he inquired about the woman across the room with all the children and the grandchildren. The nurse told him her name and a little about her family. He asked, "What are her chances of surviving?"

The nurse said, "None. She will be fortunate to live another few days."

After a long pause, he said, "I wish I could change places with Winnie. I'd give everything I have to be what she is to her family."

A few days later Winnie died. And very soon so did the man. People came from all over the country and stood outside in the rain for three nights for a chance to pay their last respects to Winnie. Her children and grandchildren stood proudly by—two generations eternally touched by this humble lady. The titan of business, the Ivy Leaguer who had followed her to the grave, well, he had more family members show up for the reading of his will than he had at his funeral.

Winifred Olive Dean Kimmel, my (Tim's) mom, passed on a legacy that we now will pass on to our own children and grandchildren.

We grandparents have roles to play. One of them is to give a blessing to our grandchildren. Another is to leave a legacy that never dies. We are all making choices. Time will prove, and eternity will tell, whether or not our choices added up.

For Further Thought and Discussion

I will utter hidden things, things from of old—
what we have heard and known,

what our fathers have told us.
We will not hide them from their children;
we will tell the next generation
the praiseworthy deeds of the LORD,
his power, and the wonders he has done. . . .
Teach [the] children,
so the next generation would know them,
even the children yet to be born,
and they in turn would tell their children.
Then they would put their trust in God
and would not forget his deeds
but would keep his commands. (Psalm 78:2-7)

1. How would your children say you have changed as a grandparent from when you were their parent?
2. Assuming we could all have been better parents, what part of your legacy to your children do you need to repair and do differently with your grandchildren?
3. What are you doing in your life now or have you done in the past to bring honor to the family reputation and to live your life with an eternal perspective? How are your grandchildren benefiting from this legacy?

Heavenly Father,
Forgive me for the things I have done that have damaged the legacy I want to leave for my children and grandchildren. Give me the courage to ask for their forgiveness and change my ways to be honoring to You and them. Please restore the years the locusts have taken and allow me to live a life of faith, integrity, and eternal significance to my children and grandchildren. Thank You that You are the God of the second chance. Amen.

8 Role #3: Bearing a Torch

One of the requirements of my (Tim's) professional work is that I travel a lot. In my travels I've been surprised how often I've passed by one of the famous Olympic stadiums that have served as stages for the International Games in the past. Darcy and I even stood in the stadium in Athens that played host to the first Olympic Games of the modern era, in 1896. I enjoy visiting a piece of real estate that once was a venue for the finest athletes in the world.

On the occasions when I had the benefit of a local guide or a talkative cab driver, my first question was always the same: "Where did they position the Olympic flame?" It's easier for me to picture the hundreds of thousands of people in the stands and the world-class athletes on the field once I've oriented myself to the flame. In fact, it's impossible to envision the Olympics apart from that flame. It's a symbol. It's like a torchlight shining out to a longing world inviting them to put aside their conflicts, at least for a brief few weeks, and pull up a seat.

Why am I heading this direction? It's my way of introducing this chapter on one of the key roles of grandparenting—*being a torchbearer* for our grandchildren, a steady light that illuminates their paths.

We can draw a wonderful parallel to grandparenthood from how the Olympic flame gets to the stadium. You see, this eternal flame burns on Mount Olympus in Greece (with the aid of some huge propane tanks), and months before the Games begin, the Olympic torch is lit from that flame. Then it makes its way over continents and oceans to the site of the competitions. How the torch is carried, at least across the thousands of miles of land, is poignant: The flame is carried by people—thousands of them who relay it through villages, towns, and cities—across the outbacks and off-ramps of many nations until it is finally used to ignite the cauldron that will burn over the Games. And the folks carrying the torch are not world-class runners. They're a cross section of humanity: old, young, tall, short, fast, and slow.

The analogy? We grandparents are all participants in a long line of people who have been called on to hold up a light and pass it down through the ages. We aren't chosen for our skills or our intellects. In fact, neither of those are requirements. God can effectively use any grandparent, regardless of résumé, to light the way for grandchildren.

Neither of us has ever had the privilege of participating in the relay that delivers the Olympic flame. But there's a good chance one of you readers actually has. If we could put ourselves in your running shoes and go back to when you carried that torch, we know exactly what thought would be uppermost in our minds. It's probably the same one you had: *Don't fall. Don't trip or stumble or do anything that risks this torch going out.* And that is exactly what we need to keep in mind as we pick up the challenge of bearing a torch for the benefit of our grandchildren.

Glowing in the Dark

Jesus told us some important things about ourselves in the Sermon on the Mount, among them, "You are the light of the world" (Matthew 5:14). Notice He didn't say, "If you'd like to be, you can be the light of the world." He simply stated it as a foregone conclusion based on our being His followers.

The Bible uses the images of darkness and light to contrast good and evil. Jesus is saying that we are the beacons of righteousness to a world overshadowed by the negative effects of evil. And we don't have to think hard to come up with illustrations of just how evil our world can be. The early years of the twenty-first century brought us several incidents that reminded us just how far evil people will go to harm people they don't care for.

In the same sermon, Jesus said, "Let your light shine before men in such a way that they may see your good works, and glorify your Father who is in heaven" (Matthew 5:16, NASB). Our integrity and good character are supposed to stand out in a culture gone astray. And the goal of the light we carry is to enable people to see God at work in us, light the path to Him, and ultimately give glory to Him.

What are the first recorded words of God's when He decided to create the universe? He was going to set the universe in motion and place the human race on its fifty-yard line. And as though He was trying to establish a standard for all that was to follow, He said, "Let there be light" (Genesis 1:3). Later, after mankind chose to rebel against God—thus defining the relationship between the Creator and the created—God decided the human race desperately needed to be redeemed. So He sent His Son.

See how God's Son described Himself and defined His mission: "I am the light of the world. Whoever follows me will never walk in darkness, but will have the light of life" (John 8:12). And further, "I have come into the world as a light, so that no one who believes in me should stay in darkness" (John 12:46). As His followers, you and I are called by God to be that light for the people around us. This obviously, but especially, includes our grandchildren, because, as we discussed in some of the earlier chapters, we have a natural connection to them that gives what we say and do extra clout. Paul says in Ephesians 5:8, "For you were formerly darkness, but now you are Light in the Lord; walk as children of Light (for the fruit of the Light consists in all goodness and righteousness and truth)" (NASB). Our grandchildren are born in that dark condition. God wants to use our lives and our influence to show them the way out of it.

This Little Light of Mine

God has called us to be torchbearers for our grandchildren, so let's consider two ways we can carry this light for them. The first way is *by being a torchbearer of the gospel* to them. Our grandchildren need to see a grandmother or grandfather whose thinking and choices are formatted by the assurance that they have been forgiven by Christ. Obviously, this gets a little difficult if you've never put your hope in Jesus. If you're reading this book and have suddenly hit a snag because you've never decided where you stand with Jesus, then let us suggest a little homework assignment. You might want to read either the Gospel of John or the Gospel of Luke, two powerful books that outline the life and claims of Jesus. They can give you a clear understanding of who He is and help you answer the question of where you stand with Him.

This gets a little difficult if you've never put your hope in Jesus.

But assuming you are a follower of Christ, and you want to be used as a torchbearer of the gospel to your grandchildren, let's look at some dos and don'ts regarding letting your light shine brightly.

One thing we need to do is make sure our grandchildren hear the gospel, but we have to go about this carefully. (We'll address the issue of parental permission to share spiritual lessons later in chapter 14.) Some children feel spiritually ambushed or browbeaten into believing when they visit their grandparents. The primary way we can expose them to the gospel is by treating them as Christ would. He was gracious, gentle, long-suffering, and patient. Let them experience what it's like to be in the presence of a joyful heart when they are around you. Possibly let them see the power of the gospel at work as you share the love of Jesus with your friends and neighbors. They may be fascinated to hear someone you know share his testimony of God's redemption in his life. Of course, they also will be exposed to the gospel through books you read to them when they are young and church events you might take them to as they grow older. But far more of the gospel is going to be impressed upon them by how you live and how you treat them than by what you say. The key here is to let them have a comfortable and natural exposure to the gospel by watching the Good News as it is lived out in your life, "when you sit at home and when you walk along the road, when you lie down and when you get up" (Deuteronomy 6:7).

High-Beam Christianity

When being a torchbearer of the gospel to our grandchildren, it's important to trust the Holy Spirit to draw them to Himself on His timetable. We could tell you stories of well-intended but misguided grandparents who did serious harm to their grandchildren's relationship with God by trying to help the Holy Spirit speed up the process of drawing them to Himself. We've got to remember that salvation is a work of God, not something orchestrated by us. God may well choose to use us in introducing one of our grandchildren to Him. But we've got to let *the Holy Spirit* draw them in when He is ready.

It's one thing to make the gospel real to them, but we step on thin ice when we continue to ask them if they'd like to make that decision to follow Christ. Some grandparents have been known to go from coaxing to badgering their grandchildren into saying some words and praying a prayer with them. From our decades of working with young people, we have seen that in the majority of cases, this has the potential to do more harm than good. Often, the grandchildren are merely going through the motions because they either don't want to hurt their grandparents' feelings or they just want them to back off. In the process, they may resent the pressure and those who are exerting the pressure. They may get just enough of an inoculation to keep them from truly seeking a personal relationship with Christ.

These might come across as tough words, but we mean them graciously. We all want to be spiritually effective grandparents. That means we hold up a torch. It doesn't mean we chase them around with it. You know, some Christians' idea of being the light of the world resembles the high beams of a car on a deer at night. First we blind them and then we run them down. This is not necessary if we're willing to leave the Holy Spirit in charge.

We also need to show compassion for those grandchildren who have chosen at this point not to give their lives to Christ. They might be feeling pressure from their parents, their church, or their friends—especially if they are making lifestyle choices that clearly communicate a rejection of God. They need to find in us someone whose love never dims, whose arms are always available, whose ears are always open, and whose time is always theirs.

In, but Not Of

A second way we can carry the light for our grandchildren is by *being a torchbearer of moral living in an immoral world.* Our grandchildren are being raised in a world that is turning more secular as we get older, a world antagonistic to the things of God.

Some parents and grandparents try to compensate by doing their best to raise their children in a hermetically sealed-off spiritual environment. This is a mistake. We know parents who have chosen this route, somehow thinking it is their only option to keep their children safe. It's not, and in the long run, it usually turns out to be a poor option. Besides, there's a far more effective choice.

Grandchildren need to see us function in the midst of a secular society and come through it remaining faithful to God. They need to see us engage the people around us and move among the icons of darkness but not be the least bit intimidated by them. In fact, they need to see us flourishing within a culture hostile to Christianity.

Our grandchildren need to see compassionate grandparents who aren't afraid to venture out into the lost world and turn the lights on for those who need a Savior. The only way we can do that is by maintaining a daily dependence on Christ. No doubt all of us have had enough experience at trying to live life on our own power. We've seen the folly that comes with bending the rules to fit our desires. By now, we should be ready to let our days belong to Christ. And that's exactly the kind of torchbearer living that can help our grandchildren work their way through the darkness around them.

Lights That Talk

Another way we can bear the torch of moral living in an immoral world is by taking bold yet gracious stands on moral issues, especially ones we see our grandchildren violating.

Grace-based grandparenting doesn't mean we condone the immoral choices our grandchildren make. Immorality ultimately destroys people. Condoning their wrong choices either verbally or through our silence makes us accessories to their demise. But when we do take stands against an immoral world and the influence it is having on our grandchildren, we must do it with a spirit of gentleness and compassion.

Paul reminded the Galatians how to treat someone who is struggling with wrong choices: "Brothers, if someone is caught in a sin, you who are spiritual should restore him gently" (6:1).

A real-life example is a woman who struggled through her late teens and twenties with agonizing gender confusion. She acted out her confusion in choices that brought condemnation and rejection from her parents and isolation from her siblings. During this time, she was brash, argumentative, and profane. She was tough to be with and tough to look at. She finally straightened out her life thanks to the patient and consistent understanding she received from her grandfather. Her grandfather was the only one in her family willing to be out with her in public and introduce her to his friends. He never condoned her choices, but nonetheless he loved her with a love without strings attached. When our grandchildren find a grandparent holding to an unflinching standard steeped in mercy, they will be much more likely to view that grandparent as a resource when they are trying to figure out the mysteries of life.

They need to see us flourishing within a culture hostile to Christianity.

As we remain compassionate and loving toward our grandchildren, we can teach them to develop discernment and make right choices. But in order to earn the right to be heard, we may need to walk with them through some of their movies, music, video games, fashions, and fads. We need to replace the stigma of "old-fashioned grandpa" with "up-to-date, well-informed, savvy, wise, and discerning grandpa."

Those last two sentences might have given some of you the sudden urge to step up your meds. The thought of having to actually listen to some of their music or be interested in some of their video games might seem way over the line. You might be saying, "There's got to be a way to carry a torch on behalf of our grandchildren without having to log time in their world."

The answer is: Yes, you can bear a torch for the gospel and for moral living without having to step over the threshold into their world, but the torch won't be very bright. Our torches will illuminate our grandchildren's paths more brightly when we are, in their eyes, both timeless and timely grandparents. Things that are timeless have a constant appeal. Things that are timely have an urgent relevance. If we want to be used by God to help our grandchildren develop discernment and make right choices, we need to be willing to both welcome them into our world and hang out in theirs.

Because this is such an important part of our calling as grandparents, we devote an entire chapter (16) to grandparenting our teenagers.

Passing the Torch

Someday, just as at the Olympics, we will come to that point in our lives where God will say, *It's time for your closing ceremony.* Our chance to be a living, breathing torchbearer for our families will come to an end. What do you want your life to say on that day? How much of what you stood for do you want to have imprinted into the hearts of your grandchildren?

> ***The torch passed twice to the next generation.***

I know one family where these questions were answered in a vivid way. In college, I (Tim) had a great buddy named Terry Hill. I never met his grandmother, but I could tell a lot about her just by the way her children turned out. She had three sons and one daughter. All three sons became pastors, and her daughter married a man who was a spiritual pillar of their church. I had gotten to know Terry's dad during my college years. He was a gracious man who always had a lot of patience for us quirky college kids.

A couple of years ago, Terry's grandmother died at the age of 90.

She died rich in love, purpose, and hope. Four generations of her offspring gathered at the church to celebrate her life as a torchbearer of God's grace. Her son, Terry's father, stood behind the pulpit and quoted a verse that this sweet saint could claim at the moment she took her last breath. It was 3 John 4: "I have no greater joy than to hear that my children are walking in the truth." She lit the way for all of them—and there they were, four generations, walking in the truth she had illuminated with the torch of her life.

Terry's dad—a wonderful pastor, husband, father, grandfather, and great-grandfather—was now standing before his extended family bearing the torch his mother had so clearly shown him how to carry. The next words out of his mouth were to be the closing remarks of his eulogy to his mother, and then Terry—my old college buddy—now a grandfather himself, was going to lead the gathering in the hymn "When We All Get to Heaven."

But something went wrong. Terry's father's words started to run together and become incoherent. He'd obviously been under intense stress since his mother's death and had been up late the night before finalizing funeral details. Terry's mother whispered that Terry needed to go up and stand next to his dad until he regained his composure. Just as Terry stood next to him, his father turned to him and said very clearly, "And now, Terry is going to take over." With that, he collapsed into Terry's arms.

He was dead by the time Terry laid him down on the floor. On that day, the torch passed twice to the next generation. A new grandfather was called on to pick it up and hold it high. He did, and he is carrying the torch with the same courage and kindness demonstrated by his father and grandmother.

We're all given the same responsibility. The question is, "What will we do with it?" We hope, for the sake of those who follow after us, that we'll choose to humbly and happily bear the torch and hold it high for them to see, all the way to the end.

For Further Thought and Discussion

"You are the light of the world. A city on a hill cannot be hidden. Neither do people light a lamp and put it under a bowl. Instead they put it on its stand, and it gives light to everyone in the house. In the same way, let your light shine before men, that they may see your good deeds and praise your Father in heaven." (Matthew 5:14-16)

1. Without being overbearing, what are some ways we can let our light shine to our family?
2. Why is it so tempting to try to strong-arm our children and grandchildren into putting their faith in Christ? Why doesn't this work? What is a better alternative?
3. What are you doing right now that could show your grandchildren how to turn on the spiritual light in their community or neighborhood?

Heavenly Father,

Thank You for taking me from darkness into light. I want more than anything for my children and grandchildren to know You and to live for You. Use my life as a light that illuminates the path to You. Help me be a consistent example of good deeds that bring glory to You. Please keep my loved ones in Your care as You work in their lives and draw them to Yourself. Amen.

9 Role #4: Setting a Standard

We learned in previous chapters about our roles as blessing givers, legacy leavers, and torchbearers. *Being standard setters* by modeling good and clear benchmarks for our grandchildren, caps off the four roles we play as grandparents.

Several years ago, we were invited to speak at a marriage retreat in California. It was at a beautiful getaway about 40 miles north of Santa Barbara. We thought it would be fun to fly into Burbank airport, rent a car, and enjoy the drive to the retreat location. We figured we could head up the coast, slip into the interior of the state, and follow some of the beautiful California back roads to our destination.

The car we rented came equipped with a global positioning system (GPS)—a new device at that time. Darcy got out the address of our destination, programmed the GPS into the computer, then told it what kind of course we wanted it to map out for us. Within a few seconds, a nice lady's voice came out of our speakers. She said hello, welcomed us to Burbank, and then started giving us directions that would get us out of town and heading up Highway 1. The pleasant voice gave us a great sense of assurance as we were screaming down the highway. It was nice to know that someone or something knew where we were, where we were going, and how to get there.

What I (Tim) liked about this audible system was the Australian accent and the lead time it gave. As we'd come up on a transition from one freeway to the next, the voice would give me a heads-up:

"You need to make sure you are merged into the right lane because you will be exiting in one mile." We'd get about half a mile away from that exit, and the voice would say, "Please take the next exit off to your right and bear to the left when the road splits about a quarter of a mile after you exit." We were in the midst of a vast sea of cars, and a satellite 25,000 miles out in space was tracking our progress and giving us careful directions.

The problem came a little south of Santa Barbara. Both of us got our minds fixated on a cappuccino—because there's nothing like a *four-dollar cup of coffee.* We decided to take a side trip into the heart of town. The signs to the older part of town were obvious, and we figured we had the time, so we exited the highway in search of a coffee shop.

That's when the voice went nuts. It almost sounded hurt that we had taken off on our own little side trip. It warned that we were heading in the wrong direction. It then sounded frustrated as it explained how it would have to recalculate our destination for us. The deeper into town we went, the more the voice tried to get us to turn back to the prearranged path.

We got such a kick out of ticking off the GPS. We started thinking how much more fun these things would be with famous voices as tour guides. Imagine Woody Allen getting all paranoid when you slipped off the beaten path. Or how about Bill Cosby? He'd tease and harangue you until you got back on course. Jerry Seinfeld would be a hoot, doing his best to insult you into turning around.

The Long and Winding Road

All of this leads to a discussion about the fourth role we have as grandparents. That role is to *set a clear standard for our grandchildren to emulate.* Like a GPS for our grandchildren, we need to use our lifetime of wisdom and knowledge to help them set a clear course for their lives.

We all understand the expression, "They can't see the forest for the trees." That's what grandchildren often feel as they are processing the various aspects of their lives, with limited vision because they're standing so close to the dilemmas they face. Using our road trip as an example, it's easy to take a wrong turn, get confused, and even be frightened at street level when cars are whizzing by at 20 MPH over the speed limit and you're not certain where you're heading. As long as we're following the GPS's route, it communicates, "Relax, don't panic. I know right where we're going. Follow me." That satellite—way out in space—can see both the forest *and* the trees. It sets an exact path, not just because it can see our destination on the globe, but because it can see all the bends in the road we'll encounter along the way.

Similarly, our years of living on earth, our good decisions and our mistakes, and all the experiences we've turned into principles for living give us an advantage in setting a clear standard for our grandchildren. This is the big payoff for being a wisdom hunter for so long. But what if you weren't a wisdom hunter in the past? What if only recently you made a decision to start thinking like a senior statesperson for your family? The good news is that it's never too late. When a person makes a clear decision to grow up and act his or her age, it's amazing how quickly God can retrofit that person's thinking.

Moving Violations

Let's limit this GPS analogy to our legitimate role as grandparents. It's not our role to tell our grandchildren where they *have to go* and what they *have to do* with their lives. Our role does not require us to chart their personal course. Our role is to set such clear standards for living that by simply studying our example, our grandchildren can get all the inspiration they need to chart their own courses wisely.

Obviously, some grandchildren might lean on us for specific advice and leadership as they make certain decisions. Sometimes, because of who we are or what we've accomplished in life, our grandchildren might ask for our help with decisions regarding college education, career, marriage, how to raise kids, finances, and spiritual leadership. The key is to offer advice when asked, then let them take it or leave it. We must avoid framing our advice so that they feel they can't go against it without being punished with guilt, shame, or a lifetime of "I told you so." And we shouldn't be surprised if grandchildren take off on a few side trips that cause us concern. Just try not to overreact when they do.

And remember, nothing we do should undermine the leadership they get from their parents. Rather, we should reinforce their parents' guidance. Sure, their parents are young—as we once were. They may offer a good path, but it might suffer from some inconsistencies because of their lack of maturity. What is great for our grandchildren—and their parents—is when they know they have in us grandparents who present such a clear and unwavering standard that both generations can feel comfortable using that example as a guide.

Surefire Weight-Loss Plan

So we set the standard. But obviously a standard is only as good as its accuracy. Throughout history, people who have relied on inaccurate maps have come to tragic ends. Our government has a department of weights and measures to insure accurate standards.

I (Tim) once lost seven pounds in one day simply by replacing our bathroom scale. But then I wondered which scale was right—the new scale, which I hoped was accurate, or the old one . . . or maybe neither. Because I couldn't be certain, I ended up taking my new scale with me on my next visit to the doctor. He has one of these expensive scales that are checked for accuracy about every three months. With so many inaccurate measuring tools around us, it's nice to know there's someone we can turn to who has the truth.

It's much the same for our grandchildren. They are surrounded by many people and things serving as benchmarks in their lives. But not all of them are accurate. Some are downright wrong.

That's why our role as standard setters is so crucial. Our grandchildren need to have confidence in us as reliable means of gauging their life's direction. We get some great insight on this from Psalm 92 where it says, "The righteous . . . will still bear fruit in old age, they will stay fresh and green, proclaiming, 'The LORD is upright; he is my Rock, and there is no wickedness in him' " (verses 12, 14-15). As our confidence in the Lord increases with age, our grandchildren should be able to count on us all the more.

Being a standard setter is even more crucial today since our grandchildren are being raised in a culture that has jettisoned clear moral absolutes. The worldview that surrounds them embraces relativism, pluralism, spiritual curiosity, and a general ignorance of Christian beliefs. Unfortunately, some of our grandchildren are being raised in homes that reflect bankrupt worldviews. Others are being brought up in homes with parents who fear God, trust His standards, and want to use them to format their families. Here's what's tough: Whether or not your grandchildren are being raised in an environment that teaches a biblical worldview, they will ultimately have to learn how to flourish in a culture that has clearly abandoned the perspective of the Bible. They are growing up in a world that elevates the importance of personal feelings over decency. And when it comes to ethical standards, today's culture assumes we all have the freedom to create whatever morality is convenient for us.

> ***A standard is only as good as its accuracy.***

Wishy-Washy Grandparents

Even though we hate to admit it, we have all been affected by the relativism of our culture—a culture that rejects moral absolutes. Sadly, some grandparents give up the good fight and cave in on the convictions of their youth. This sets us up to be poor finishers and gives our grandchildren misleading directions for life.

We've seen grandparents mislead their grandchildren by overprioritizing the role that money and success should have in their lives. We've seen them encourage their grandchildren to make looks and beauty a higher priority than character when picking a mate. We've seen them be quick to encourage divorce and condone sex outside of marriage. These are horrible recommendations to give the young and vulnerable. It's the equivalent of telling them to speed down a road knowing full well that a bridge is out along the way. Failure to model a moral standard for our grandchildren can sabotage their futures and guarantee they will reap what they sow.

Facing Life's Storms

John Steinbeck's novel *The Grapes of Wrath* offers a powerful lesson about how children find confidence in the face of danger. The setting is a farming community in Oklahoma during a time of severe drought, crop failures, and the poverty that resulted from these setbacks. Often families were at the mercy of wind and dust storms. On the plains, these dust storms could be seen coming from a long way off. The families would gather out in the yard, and the fathers—sometimes two and three generations side by side—would stare off into the distance and try to evaluate how severe the impact would be and what needed to be done to prepare for it. But the wives and the children didn't stare at the storm; they stared at the faces of the men. They could gauge whether to be calm or to panic by what they saw in the eyes of their leaders.

Today, nothing has changed. With a world in crisis, jets smashing into skyscrapers, a global war on terror, and a fickle economy, kids look to us to figure out whether they should be worried. Our grandchildren need to see grandparents who look past the storms on the horizon and see a mighty, sovereign God who's got everything under control. Grandparents need to represent to grandchildren a patriarchal and matriarchal standard of character, much like the influence the great patriarchs of the Bible carried into their old age.

Through our travels, we have come to know a wonderful family from Shiner, Texas. Doug and Laura Kaspar are part of a fourth generation of Kaspars who oversee the great Kaspar Wire Works. Started by Doug's great-grandfather, this family business has been passed down through the years from a man who had very specific standards regarding his product, his employees, and his customers. These high and clear standards not only guide Doug and his brothers, but also serve as a call to accountability as they carry on the family business. They have a standard to live up to in the eyes of their employees and their customers, a standard forged through the character of strong ancestors. Because that standard is so clear and uncompromising, Doug's extended family, and the company that bears their name, has enjoyed a cherished place in the history of southeast Texas.

That's the power of a good standard. That's also the power of a good grandfather and grandmother. It's the kind of influence God offers to every one of us as we hold closely to a core set of convictions. And when you do, you cover your grandchildren with grace. You're saying to them, "I realize life is confusing and you could easily find yourself bewildered along the way. That's why I want to use my life as a clear standard for moral living. I'm far from perfect, and I walk on feet of clay, but to the best of my ability I want to create an example to help you around the next bend in the road of your life."

Living Lives of Great Character

Setting a high standard is the logical outcome of a well-developed and balanced character. There are six character traits that form a complete standard for grandchildren to follow. As they observe and benefit from your life of character, they will be more likely to embrace these character traits themselves. These six character traits are developed in detail in Tim's book *Raising Kids Who Turn Out Right.*

Character Trait #1: Contagious Faith

Faith is essential because without it, it is impossible to please God: "He who comes to God must believe that He is and that He is a rewarder of those who seek Him" (Hebrews 11:6, NASB). People aren't born with a propensity to seek after God. In fact, we're born with just the opposite attitude. We rebel against Him and want to live by our own rules.

Now you might be thinking about one of your grandchildren, wrapped up in selfishness and testing the limits of God's standards. Don't panic. God hasn't stopped loving your grandchild. He wants to draw your grandchild to Himself, and one of the best tools He has is you and your uncompromising confidence in Him. Your unshakeable faith in the face of whatever life may bring is a powerful example when your grandchild finally realizes he or she needs God too.

If the Dow Jones Industrial Average plummets and our grandchildren see us handle it calmly, they'll notice a huge contrast with the world in general. We may have lost a great deal of money with that plunge, but it's just something that occasionally happens with the stock market. Our security shouldn't be found in *what* we have but in *whose* we are. When our grandchildren watch us get bad news from the doctor or be pink-slipped by an employer, yet continue to trust God, they'll, observe the clear confidence that comes when God is the director of life. Our faith will be contagious.

A wonderful senior lady named Mildred is a great example of this contagious faith. She buried her husband over a decade ago and was known for her faith then, though she's known for it even more now. Every one of her children and grandchildren reflects her powerful faith because they've seen this little lady take the worst that life can dish out and not be defeated.

When Mildred's grandson was spending a few days at her home in Tennessee, one or more phone solicitors would call each evening around dinnertime. The grandson answered the first call, gave the caller a polite "Thanks, but no thanks," and hung up. Grandma Mildred answered the next call, but instead of dismissing the solicitor as an intruder, she said, "You know, I'm an elderly woman with limited finances, and most likely I will have to turn down your request. But I would be glad to listen to your presentation if you'll promise to let me ask you a few questions and visit briefly with you when you're through." The person on the other end agreed, figuring it was better than an abrupt dial tone in his ear. After she heard him out and politely told him why she wouldn't be able to accept his offer, she asked questions about his life, his family, his hopes, and his fears. She said, "Honey I'm getting older, and I've got lots of time on my hands. I'd be glad to pray for you. Is there anything you'd like me to bring to God?"

Her grandson was stunned. She prayed with the young man on the phone and wrote down his needs with a promise to pray for him every day for the next month. It turned out she'd been doing this for years. Her prayer notebook was full of the names of phone solicitors for whom she had been praying. Because they had her number anyway, she'd encourage them to call her back in a month or so to let her know how things were going in their lives. What her grandson saw most of all in Grandmother Mildred was how much her faith had given her an intense love for people—even total strangers trying to get her to switch over her phone service or credit cards.

A contagious faith is a powerful cornerstone for our character.

Character Trait #2: Consistent Integrity

As a standard setter, a contagious faith is a powerful cornerstone for our character. It makes it easier to model the second character trait: a consistent integrity. Our grandchildren need to have grandparents known for unwavering honesty—who don't bend the rules for their own self-interests. We need to represent to them a place of moral rest.

When our kids were teenagers, they liked to shop at thrift stores. It's still considered cool. We loved it because their back-to-school clothing budget didn't put much wear and tear on our debit card. On one particular trip to the thrift store I (Darcy) saw a well-heeled lady who was probably in her sixties shopping with her granddaughter. The granddaughter found three T-shirts she liked. But I was shocked to see the grandmother encourage the girl to pull off her sweatshirt, slip two of the T-shirts on, and then put the sweatshirt back over them. Here was a grandma teaching her granddaughter how to shoplift—and in a thrift store at that!

Once, while standing in a long ticket line, I (Tim) heard a man behind me telling the two teenagers with him that he was going to say they were both 12 years old in order to get the child's ticket price. One of the boys said, "Okay, Grandpa."

> ***These adults were willing to sell their integrity.***

This grandfather at the movies and this grandmother at the thrift store were giving their grandchildren self-destructive standards for their lives that were guaranteed to sabotage their futures if they were embraced. I couldn't get over how quickly and how cheaply these adults were willing to sell their integrity—and to undermine their grandchildren's integrity along with it. We shouldn't be surprised if, somewhere in the future, these same grandchildren practice their lack of integrity on the very people who taught them how to lie and steal.

> O Lord, who may abide in Your tent? Who may dwell on Your holy hill? He who walks with integrity, and works righteousness, and speaks truth in his heart. He does not slander with his tongue, nor does evil to his neighbor, nor takes up a reproach against his friend; in whose eyes a reprobate is despised, but who honors those who fear the Lord; he swears to his own hurt and does not change; . . . He who does these things will never be shaken. (Psalm 15, NASB)

Character Trait #3: Practical Poise

Poise is a well-developed sense of what is appropriate. Because of their inherent immaturity, young people are known for their excesses, awkwardness, and lack of tact. We grandparents need to show them how a person lives a balanced and poised life. Ecclesiastes 7:18 says, "The man who fears God will avoid all extremes." We need to model for our grandchildren how to celebrate, how to mourn, how to win, how to lose, how to avoid being manipulated by friends or intimidated by enemies, and how to dine with kings but never lose the common touch. They need to see emotional poise, intellectual poise, social poise, spiritual and biblical poise, and even political poise.

One evening we had dinner at the home of a man who had been a highly decorated World War II hero. He had gone on to a life of politics and was now an articulate senior statesman with conservative political convictions. Many people were at the gathering, and during our dinner conversation one of his teenage grandchildren was leveling some criticism against the then-current president of the United States. For effect, she even gave him a disparaging nickname.

After dinner I (Tim) took the trash outside and while returning to the house, I overhead this grandfather speaking to his granddaughter on the patio. He was correcting her about using a demeaning expression to refer to the president of the United States. Ironically, this lesson in poise was coming from a man whose positions had been personally and publicly attacked by that president. He said "Even though we may disagree with this man, he is still the president of our country. He lives in one of the most influential homes in the world. Always refer to him and any other occupant of that house as 'the president.' " This grandfather could have upbraided his granddaughter at the dinner table, but instead he displayed practical poise through his gentle and private correction.

Character Trait #4: Personal Discipline

Personal discipline requires the willpower to do what is necessary to accomplish what is important. Grandchildren need to see grandparents who exercise discipline in many ways: spending time with God through prayer and reading His Word, restraining our tongue and our tempers, and pursuing new knowledge and experience. Observing our insatiable appetite for new knowledge will provide powerful inspiration to exercise personal discipline when they are in the dog days of college and become tempted to quit.

Character Trait #5: Steadfast Endurance

The world is overrun with quitters. People back out of commitments, get dream teams to get them out of contracts, and make excuses to walk away from covenants. Our grandchildren need to see how people run the race of life regardless of what obstacles are thrown in their way . . . and finish well. As we get closer to heaven, many challenges present themselves that allow us to demonstrate steadfast endurance. A great way to demonstrate this character trait to our grandchildren is by never giving up on *them.*

Character Trait #6: Inspirational Courage

The sixth character trait we need to model for our grandchildren is inspirational courage, the subject of Tim's book *Home Grown Heroes.* It is a trait best taught with silent resolve, because when it comes to inspiring courage, actions speak louder than words.

My (Tim's) father fought in the Battle of the Bulge. You'd never hear about his war record from him, but you could see the evidence of the courage he brought to the battlefield in the way he stood for righteousness as an older gentleman. My father's ethics had muscle. He wasn't afraid to stand alone if he had to, and he always stood up for people who couldn't stand up for themselves.

When I think of inspirational courage, I also think of a man named Charles Rush. When I first met him, he had recently retired as a captain from a navy career. Charlie was a senior at the United States Naval Academy when the Japanese attacked Pearl Harbor. His orders came the next day to ship out to the South Pacific, where he served as a lieutenant on three submarines.

But that was the past—ancient history—and he figured that's where whatever he did was supposed to stay. But that's not what the Navy felt. You see, it turns out that Charles Rush was an unusually courageous young lieutenant. About midway through World War II, Lieutenant Rush was on the USS *Billfish*, patrolling the Makassar Strait, when three Japanese destroyers discovered their submarine. Submarines are fairly easy to sink once you've located them. Technically they are already "sunk." You just have to fill them with water. The destroyers immediately set up a grid to crisscross the sea and drop depth charges over the submarine's location. The first three they dropped blasted against the hull of the sub, knocking over drums of acid, cracking pipes, breaking seals, and creasing the external fuel ballast tanks.

With the streak of diesel fuel to follow, the Japanese destroyers just kept pounding away on them—relentlessly and without mercy for the next nine hours. The executive officer was incapacitated in the orginal depth charging and put under sedation in his bunk. Lieutenant Rush checked in with the engine room and found the crew already resigned to impending death. He immediately took charge of the situation. The men found his courage inspiring and quickly responded to his calm and confident resolve. Together they fought the leaks and worked to keep the batteries dry and the engines going. Meanwhile, the depth charges kept dropping.

After several hours of desperately working to keep the submarine from sinking, Lieutenant Rush went to the conning tower to see if he was needed. That's when he saw the real problem: The captain of the submarine was almost comatose with fear. He gave no orders, no one was at the helm, and the submarine had been simply tripping along, an easy target for the destroyers above.

He asked for permission to take over the con. The captain refused. Realizing how desperate the situation was, Lieutenant Rush pleaded with his cowardly captain for permission to take control of their plight. Finally the captain relinquished the control, and Lieutenant Rush immediately found a helmsman, ordered the submarine below crush depth, and then—using an instrument that had been marking their path, reversed their course, charted a mirror image of where they had been, and escaped by slipping out under the trail of fuel they had been leaving. Nine hours after the attack began, Lieutenant Rush and the men of the *Billfish* escaped from the destroyers into the night. They immediately surfaced, got clean air back into the submarine, and were able to recharge their batteries. Eventually they finished their patrol and returned to their port in Australia.

The men of the *Billfish* always wondered why Lieutenant Rush was never decorated for his bravery. They all believed he had single-handedly saved their lives. A half-century passed before the mystery was solved. That's when the Freedom of Information Act required that the records of the war be opened, available to be viewed by all. And that's when his fellow submariners found out that their former captain, the man who had caved under the stress of battle and had served them up to the enemy, had falsified his ship's log by minimizing the extent of the engagement and trivializing the seriousness of the damage.

They quietly petitioned the Department of the Navy to investigate. It took them 10 years to uncover the truth and right a wrong.

And just after the turn of the century they called Charles Rush back to the Naval Academy, where he had been a student so long ago, and before a gathering of his remaining former shipmates, dignitaries, and friends, they awarded him the Navy Cross, one of the highest honors the navy can bestow on one of its own.

None of his friends or family knew any of this until the Navy finally brought it to light. But it explained the quiet courage we have observed in Charlie over the years we've known him. You see, this Lieutenant Charles Rush, now Captain Rush, who saved the men of the *Billfish* so long ago, is Darcy's stepfather. But there's more. It turns out that his former captain, the man overcome with fear, ended up living his last days in a community not far from ours.

Many years before he received the Navy Cross, Charlie and Darcy's mother visited his old captain. The two former seamen laughed together, exchanged old war stories, and remembered the dead. But the discredited captain never mentioned the incident, nor did Charlie Rush ever bring it up—to him, to us, to anyone. Charlie was glad his captain wasn't alive when the Navy recognized him for his courage. Charlie never wanted to see his former captain embarrassed.

This is the kind of standard setter we're talking about—someone who sets a standard for all his kids and grandkids to follow—a grandparent who shows inspirational courage, consistent integrity, personal discipline, steadfast endurance, contagious faith, and a practical poise to the generations to come. Our grandchildren are watching, folks. Let's set a standard they can bet their lives on.

Consider how you can help build character in the next generation:

- Contagious Faith—Show them how to take God out of a box and make Him their life.
- Consistent Integrity—Show them how to do the right thing even when no one is looking.
- Practical Poise—Show them how to maintain balance.
- Personal Discipline—Show them the power of self-denial and self-control to achieve what they have always wanted.

- Steadfast Endurance—Show them how to keep going when everyone is telling them to give up.
- Inspirational Courage—Show them how to do the right thing even when they are scared to death.

For Further Thought and Discussion

Whatever is true, whatever is noble, whatever is right, whatever is pure, whatever is lovely, whatever is admirable—if anything is excellent or praiseworthy—think about such things. Whatever you have learned or received or heard from me, or seen in me—put it into practice. (Philippians 4:8-9)

1. How have you seen grandparents set a poor standard for their children and grandchildren? What do they communicate to their grandchildren when they say one thing and do another?
2. Why is it so hard to not push our advice on our children and grandchildren? What might you do to "win" the right to be heard?
3. What is going on in your life that you can use to model a contagious faith or inspirational courage to your children or grandchildren?

Heavenly Father,
Forgive me for times my life has failed to set a good example for my children and grandchildren. I pray they would see me as a wise ally and I would be available to come alongside them when they ask for my help. Please guide me as I demonstrate true character to them. Thank you for the power of the Holy Spirit in my life and theirs. Amen.

part three

A GRAND OPPORTUNITY

10 Dealing with Divorce

I (Tim) love new technology. I get a kick out of the way someone comes up with a fresh idea then moves it into the mainstream of everyday life. We've seen new inventions go from toys for the rich and elite to staple products for the rank and file. Most of you readers have technological tools you use each day, tools that weren't even invented a decade or so ago. And the speed at which these new innovations move from changing our lives to defining our lives can leave your head spinning. None of this bothers me, because I'm one of those people who welcomes change. In fact I thrive on it. I love it when my days are filled with a string of unknowns, whereas Darcy prefers predictability in her life—which is why we had some conflict when I had a phone installed in her car many years ago. This was way before cell phones.

I (Darcy) didn't feel I needed a phone in my car. I had been fine without one, and I didn't like the idea that people could invade my privacy while I was driving around town. But you can probably guess what I think of cell phones now. I don't leave home without one and neither do most of you. What was first considered a luxury has now moved to being a necessity.

We think that's what has happened with grandparents. They were once an added bonus to the nuclear family—like an extra luxury item. But because of the sophisticated pressures families face today, grandparents are now far more necessary to their family's success. The modern-day family is in a battle, and the cultural enemies are formidable. Much like the giants and overwhelming armies that the Israelites faced as they entered the Promised Land, today our families sometimes feel outnumbered and outmatched when facing the stresses that work to devastate them. As Moses needed Aaron and Hur to keep his arms lifted up to ensure victory, parents and grandchildren need grandparents to provide the extra support and encouragement necessary to win the battle for the family. Grandparents are indispensable as today's families contend with life.

We are a link to the past, an anchor for the present, and a bridge to the future.

Grandparents intensely identify with the pleasure of seeing their children enjoy their own child. But the opposite is true as well. We hurt deeply when our children and our grandchildren go through pain and heartache. As we lift the weary arms of our loved ones in the midst of the dark corridors of their lives, God wants us to be blessing givers, legacy leavers, torchbearers, and standard setters. And He calls on us to carry out these roles in a spirit of grace.

Grandparenting is a sacred trust. Our position offers a link to the past, an anchor for the present, and a bridge to the future. As such, we sometimes become involved in sticky situations. That's what we want to address in these next chapters. But before we get into these issues, we acknowledge that the very nature of these situations makes some extremely sensitive subjects. And because we're trying to deal with them in a succinct manner, the forthrightness of some of our statements might cause some pain or discomfort. Please know that is not our intention. As we clarify and correct in some of these sticky areas of life, we hope your grandchildren will be the beneficiaries.

Sometimes things happen within our children's families that can really make life difficult for everyone involved. And sometimes we find ourselves stuck in the middle. In this chapter, we want to deal with the stickiest of all sticky situations: What should you do if your children divorce? We tackle this first because it's what usually creates the other two situations we'll address in the following chapters: when your grandchildren come to live with you and how to deal with blended families.

With the divorce rate where it is, well over half the grandparents reading this book either have dealt with, are presently facing, or will face this problem of a child's divorce. And the more married children you have, the more likely it is that somewhere along the way you will *have* to deal with divorce. Some of you have been divorced yourselves. You know what the pain is like, and you've seen firsthand the negative impact it can have on the children involved. You know that the way parents handle the dissolution of a marriage plays a huge role in their children's health and well-being. That's why it is crucial that grandparents handle themselves properly before, during, and after a child's divorce.

When the Cradle Is Rocked

When you first realize that your children are having serious problems in their marriage, it's normal to want to move in quickly and closely to help avert a divorce. But as you do, you need to make sure that you do not undermine your ability to provide the love and support your children, your in-laws, and your grandchildren will need now and in the future.

Let's step back for a second and take in the big picture regarding divorce. First, we need to keep in mind that divorces are seldom the result of a sudden blowout in a relationship. In most cases, they result from an emotional and spiritual "slow leak" over a long time. It may take you or the involved spouse by surprise, but in most cases, the love and resolve were slowly slipping out of the relationship.

Second, since the breakup of the marriage has likely been coming for some time, the deteriorating situation has been doing damage to your grandchildren's emotional systems well before you hear the *D*-word mentioned.

Third, because no one is perfect and everyone has blind spots, each spouse is capable of contributing to the deterioration of the relationship. One may be far more responsible for it than the other, but both bring a humanness that can cause love to erode.

Fourth, one of the great myths about divorce is that it removes two spouses from each other's lives. That is only a possibility if there are no children involved. Otherwise, they are still part of each other's lives and will continue to be for the rest of their lives. They are going to have to see each other at celebrations, graduations, weddings, and when their kids start having kids. They may be drawn together because of a child's injury, illness, or negative actions. Because of all these points, how we respond to the divorce is going to determine if, and to what degree, we will be used as an agent of grace and healing for everyone involved. We want to be part of the adjustment and solution rather than the problem.

One grandfather told us how hurtful it was when his former son-in-law tried to turn the grandchildren against him and his wife. The father filled his children's heads with false accusations against the grandparents, and for a while it seemed the children believed everything. This grandfather said the only thing they could do was follow Jesus' advice in Luke 6:27-28, "Love your enemies, do good to those who hate you, bless those who curse you, pray for those who mistreat you." This set of grandparents is still trusting God to fully restore their relationship with their grandchildren, and for now they are using their energy to pray for and love everyone in the picture, including their former son-in-law. They chose to respond to the unfounded accusations with grace, so when their grandchildren reach adulthood, the grandparents will have no regrets about how they responded. In the meantime, their attitude toward the former son-in-law who is clearly disparaging them to their grandchildren is serving to neutralize his words in the hearts of his children.

What a great example this will be to these grandchildren of what the Golden Rule looks like when lived out under stress.

How We Can Help: Getting Perspective

The first thing you need to do when your children split up is get perspective. This may sound too mellow, and please don't assume we're saying we don't consider divorce a serious problem. We think it's the primary problem attacking the family. We have dedicated our entire professional lives to trying to help families stay intact. But perspective helps you realize that as bad as divorce is, it's not the end of the world for you, for your children, or for your grandchildren. It's a storm you may pass through, but there is hope on the other side. We're offering you some ways to gain perspective.

God did not mean for us to go through these times by ourselves.

Make a commitment to not beat up on yourselves. It's easy to turn on yourselves; you wonder what you either did or didn't do that might have contributed to it. This serves no positive purpose. The sad fact is that people get divorced. Torturing yourself can do nothing to change the situation.

Find a personal outlet for your pain so you don't add to everybody else's. Your child and your child's spouse are hemorrhaging emotionally. They aren't in any position to help you process your own pain.

In fact, it's just the opposite; they need you to help them process theirs. That's why you need to immediately secure a strong source of support for yourselves outside of your children. You need to lean on the prayers, encouragement, and advice of friends, pastors, and counselors so you can prove yourselves a worthy support to your children and grandchildren.

We belong to a fellowship group with friends who have been through thick and thin together. We shed many tears together as we bare our hearts and hurts when our children or grandchildren are going through rough waters. One of the things that has broken our hearts the most as a group is when we have to walk with one of our friends through the pain of dealing with their child's divorce or the ongoing residue of that divorce. Our friends have been able to openly share their sorrow and confusion and be comforted by the gracious love and fervent prayers of those in this group.

God did not mean us to go through these times by ourselves. We do ourselves and those we are grieving for a lot of good when we have a safe place to vent our feelings and receive encouragement and sympathy. It does no good to try to wear a mask and pretend we have the ideal family when in reality we all go through difficult times. Trying to do image control makes matters far worse. We need our friends to surround us with love and understanding.

Ask God for objectivity. We all have natural parental reflexes that cause us to want to side with our children and protect them when they have a conflict with their spouses or ex-spouses. Indeed, our son or daughter may be the lesser contributor to the downfall of the marriage and a victim of some serious betrayal. The tendency to want to lash out and vent our anger toward the spouse may be understandable, but it is the very thing that could prevent us from being a source of healing for that person either now or in the future. What's worse, it could sabotage our access to our grandchildren. The other reason we need objectivity is we might find it is not our in-law who is the major problem in the collapse of the marriage but our own son or daughter. If this is the case, our disappointment and frustration is compounded. Obviously we have a right and responsibility to voice our opinions, but we've got to pray all the way through that we always function in a spirit of grace. Grace doesn't mean there isn't a time or a place to sternly voice disapproval, and it doesn't mean there won't be a serious injury to the ongoing relationships, but it does mean we leave the door open for reconciliation. And both parties need to know this.

Keep in mind that the grandkids need us the most. They are the ones who are bearing the brunt of the pain. They have the least amount of maturity for processing the divorce, and they have the most to lose. They need a mother and a father working as a team to help them build their lives. The divorce of their parents attacks their three inner needs for a secure love, a significant purpose, and a sufficient hope. We can help fill that void.

A couple of years ago, during a New Year's holiday in the Arizona mountains, we got to watch firsthand how a set of grandparents can play a stabilizing role in a grandchild. In this case their daughter, who was going through a divorce, was the leading cause of the marital meltdown. These two grandparents made it their primary focus to provide a safe haven and sense of normalcy for the young man caught in the turbulence. On that getaway weekend the grandfather helped his grandson get the hang of shooting clay birds with a shotgun. The grandmother helped him get into the party mood on New Year's Eve and dance with everyone. The grandfather told me he was committed to spending the next ten years of his life helping this boy move into adulthood prepared and confident.

We grandparents represent a stability that our grandchildren desperately need when their parents' marriage implodes. We are in a position to play an even larger role in stabilizing their emotions during a time when their parents are emotionally spent. Too often, their parents are so wounded that it takes years before they are able to provide the emotional and spiritual help their children need during or after a divorce. A lot of damage can happen in that time. Fortunately, God gave the family grandparents.

How We Can Help: Preserving and Protecting Our Relationship

The second thing we need to do when our children divorce is to help preserve and protect a supportive relationship with our grandchildren, thus playing a pivotal role in how much or how little damage they will take away from the divorce.

Maintain neutrality around them regarding their parents. We must not take sides when we're with our grandchildren or pit ourselves against one of their parents. This attitude must draw on the power of the Holy Spirit, because most grandparents in a divorce situation find it to be one of the hardest times to show self-control and unselfish love. Criticizing either of his parents compounds a sense of insecurity and instability the grandchild is already feeling about his parents. He needs to find in us an unwavering love for him and for the two people he loves so much—his parents. When grandchildren confidently view us as a neutral party, they may ask us to explain a situation they cannot understand. Questions like:

- "Why don't my parents love each other anymore?"
- "My parents are saying some really mean things to each other, and I don't know what to believe."
- "If my father leaves, does it mean he is going to forget about us?"

This is our opportunity to let God's love shine through us as we honestly but kindly explain that adults make poor choices at times, and unfortunately, those choices can really hurt others. It does not mean they have stopped loving the child, but they are choosing to change their lives and perhaps where they live. This is a great time to remind your grandchild that you're still here and will always love him or her.

Maintaining neutrality when it comes to inflammatory words of judgment and accusation will not only play a huge role in the speed at which these grandchildren heal, but will play a large role in preserving and protecting our access to them. If we criticize either of their parents, we might alienate ourselves from that parent who could in turn prevent us from seeing our grandchildren and block our ability to give them the ongoing support they so desperately need.

Be a safe place for them to process their emotions. Often they just need someone who will listen as they express all the confusing feelings brought on by their parents' divorce. It is less about giving advice and more about understanding and reassurance.

When parents divorce, grandchildren feel grief. It's not that they feel as if one of their parents died; it's more like their whole family died. Their family was far more important in their lives than any individual member of it. It represented a security system and an identity. They need to know we will listen to them as they walk through and talk through their grief.

They are also filled with fear. Their parents' divorce presents them with many unknowns. They wonder: *Am I going to have to move out of my house? Will I have to go to another school? Will I be forced to live away from my sister or my brother? What happens if my parents start to date someone else? Will I get an extra set of parents, maybe some more siblings? What if I don't like them? What if they don't like me?* You can see how frightening a divorce can be for a young heart. They need steady and sure grandparents in their lives letting them know that no matter what happens, their love will never change or go away.

Often they're very angry. They are mad at their parents and might want to make trouble just to punish them. They may even strike out at us as they process their pain, hurt, and confusion. We all seem to vent most at the people whose love we're sure of. They need a patient grandparent in their lives who is not overreacting to their behavior and understands their anger. We can also help by showing them how to process their anger. It is not a good idea to try to talk or shame them out of their anger. We need to let them get these feeling out in a safe place. Responses like, "I can see you are having a bad day," instead of, "You need to control your anger!" or "It sounds like someone really important to you has hurt you badly," instead of, "Don't talk that way about your mom or dad," will let them know we support them.

Furthermore, we can demonstrate how to process anger by appropriately processing our own. They need to see that anger doesn't give us the right to strike out and hurt others. We can encourage them to reach for a higher standard rather than a lower one. Taking this higher road brings balm and salve to the tender hearts of everyone in the equation.

Children of divorce often feel a great deal of guilt. They might feel an irrational sense of responsibility, as though they are the reason their parents divorced. They may have heard their parents arguing about them. They need a patient and wise grandparent assuring them that they were not the reason their parents broke up. This is a good time to explain that all married couples argue and fight and even the healthiest of married couples have conflict. Parents fight about money, the house, their jobs, and how they spend their time. That doesn't mean their money or house or job or time is responsible for the conflict they are having. They need grandparents who can discern this false sense of guilt and give them hope. They need to hear a grandparent say, "This is bad, and I know you are hurting because of it. But this is not the end of the world for you. These things happen. This is a storm you are going through, but you will get through it, and there are bright days and lots of wonderful things waiting for you on the other side. And I am here with you. We'll get through this together."

Projecting hope into the future and assuring them you will always love them and that your love for them will never change can give them the security they need to keep going in their new way of life.

Kids can show various levels of anxiety. You might observe a new nervousness about them, feelings of panic and impending doom. They might have difficulty breathing, develop intense panic attacks, or get depressed. Signs of depression might be a lack of attention; lethargy; negativism; irritability; or a sense of helplessness, hopelessness, and worthlessness. They might act up, become a consistent behavior problem at school, develop chaotic sleep and eating patterns, and even become suicidal. The key in these situations is to work with their parents to get them serious and qualified help. And remember to not only pray for them but also enlist your friends to join you in taking their needs to God.

> ***Though their immediate world may look like it's falling apart, their bigger world isn't.***

Protect your legal rights of access to them. There are many factors created by the divorce that can complicate grandparents' continued involvement with their grandchildren. Often a custodial parent moves after a divorce, making contact for a noncustodial grandparent even harder. Though joint custody is what most courts prefer, it isn't always the way they rule. Your child may be the parent with the least access to the children.

If the custodial parent remarries, another set of grandparents is added, making the noncustodial grandparents' position even more tenuous. In the event the noncustodial parent drops out of his or her children's life (having rejected or abandoned them), noncustodial grandparents my even feel "unworthy or embarrassed" to pursue a relationship with their grandchildren. These difficulties are not generally the types that require any legal action. They are solved best by prayer, perseverance, and patience. Make sure the custodial parent knows you desire to be an ally and that the well-being of the children (your grandchildren) is your utmost desire. Offer your assistance in tangible ways such as babysitting, carpooling, or giving the parent a weekend off. Ask permission to continue your traditions of gift giving, travel, or special activities with your grandchildren. Welcome the new grandparents into the fold, and position yourself as a partner in this new family configuration.

There are situations where a parent may deny you contact with your grandchildren as a way to punish you for the sins of your child or to inflict pain on you because he is in so much pain himself. This is when grandparents may have to look into their legal rights to have contact with their own grandchildren. Each state is different when it comes to this issue. All 50 states currently have some type of "grandparent visitation" statute through which grandparents and sometimes others (foster parents and stepparents, for example) can ask a court to grant them the legal right to maintain their relationships with beloved grandchildren.

But state laws vary greatly when it comes to crucial details, such as who can visit and under what circumstances. Some offer a lot more protection of grandparents' rights than others. If you feel your right to see your grandchild could be in jeopardy, ask your son or daughter to make provision for your visitation rights in the divorce agreement. This is even more important when your child is the noncustodial parent. If your right to continue a relationship with your grandchild has not been provided in a legal agreement, then it might be necessary to petition the courts for visitation rights. Though this may require determination and resolve, all of this must be done in a gracious and godly manner, in a way that does not add more stress to an already tense situation and in a way that does not alienate anyone in the loop. If you are unsuccessful in gaining access when your grandchildren are young, remember that, with God's help, your grandchildren may want to establish a relationship with you independent of their parents when they are older.

How We Can Help: Help Them Heal

Divorce is a time that requires us as grandparents to rise above the ordinary. None of us feel qualified or up for this kind of role, but God will empower us to serve as His hands, His voice, His tears, His shoulder, and His heart on behalf of our grandchildren. When people ask Darcy or me what line of work we are in, we often reply, "We are in the *hope* business." There is no time in our grandchildren's lives when we need to be more preoccupied with the dispensing of hope than when their parents are going through a divorce. God can use our commitment to hope to help them heal. With this in mind, we want to share some specific things we can do to help them heal.

We need to focus on the best interests of our grandchildren. This might be a good time to review the definition of love from chapter 2. If you recall, we defined love as the commitment of my will to your needs and best interests regardless of the cost. Helping grandchildren process their parents' divorce will probably cost us a lot of our time, perhaps some of our personal goals, a large investment of energy, and in some cases, a chunk of our money. But for most grandchildren, we may be their best allies for getting them through this painful time as a whole person. For some, we may be their only one.

While teaching at a parenting conference in Colorado, we met two salt-of-the-earth people. They were a set of grandparents attending with their son—a single dad. He was a long-haul trucker. His wife had abandoned both him and their son. His parents stepped in to provide stability for their son and grandson. Because of some learning disabilities the young boy had, both grandparents were helping homeschool him until he could get up to speed. By their own admission, they were not highly educated people. But they were quite competent at helping this boy get a good foundation in the fundamentals of academics.

They confided in me (Darcy) that this was not how they envisioned their golden years, but they were quick to say they wouldn't have it any other way. The joys of seeing their grandson grow up in a stable, loving home far outweighed the inconvenience and sacrifice. Perhaps we're stretching a biblical meaning here, but we think there may be a special commendation for these types of grandparents who for the joy set before them endure the hardships of standing in the gap for the sake of their children and grandchildren.

Because we may be their best ally during this painful time, our grandchildren need to consistently hear and see evidence that although their immediate world may look like it's falling apart, their bigger world isn't. We are part of their bigger world. As bad as divorce is, the aftermath of it offers grandparents an opportunity to show their grandchildren how we get on with the good things of life. Having this attitude will make it a lot easier for them to deal with the drastic changes in their lives. If they still see us on the sidelines at their sporting events, still have us sending them emails of encouragement, still see us celebrating their victories, know we are consistently hurting with them through their defeats, they'll be in a much better position to see beyond the trouble that surrounds them.

In chapter 5 we discussed our role as blessing givers and outlined the three fundamental inner needs of each child. Those needs are for a secure love, a significant purpose, and a sufficient hope; divorce works against development of all three. But we can minimize the damage. When our grandchildren find in us the secure love they so desperately need, when they find in us a confidence in their significant giftedness and the contribution they will make to the world around them, when they see in us a steady and supernatural hope, they'll know they can make it. Meeting these three inner needs should be our goal and our focus as we help walk them through this confusing time in their lives.

As you commit to being an agent of healing, you need to be available to those grandchildren who need you more at that time. A dad or a mother might have abandoned the family. You may have to step in and fill their place on almost a daily basis. This means you need to be willing to be called out of retirement or to take a sabbatical if that's what it requires. You might have to move closer to them. Emails and phone calls might have to become a daily part of your life.

We read a great article about a grandfather who helps his grandson with his math homework online at night. A passing comment in the article mentioned that the boy's parents are divorced and he lives with his mother. We thought, "You go, Granddad!"

This will definitely be a time to show these grandkids who are having a bigger struggle a lot of extra love and attention. It may help to have a particular grandchild come for a visit or spend the night once a week. You might need to single him or her out for special events like a ball game, concert, a trip to a museum, or going out for a burger on a regular basis.

One of the most effective ways you can serve as an agent of healing is to be positive. Don't be grim. Be upbeat. Keep your demeanor as joyful as possible and continue to show them how to celebrate life. And as a further gift to them, take care of yourself emotionally, physically, and spiritually.

How We Can Help: Come Alongside the Parents

So far, we've named three things grandparents should do when a child divorces: get perspective, preserve and protect the relationship with the grandchildren, and help them heal.

We also need to come alongside our children and their spouses. This is hard to do if we allow our anger and disappointment to become so great that we burn the bridges that connect us. No matter what they have done to *us*, we must avoid severing our relationship with *them*. One parent may have done something evil, and though we do not condone what was done, we must act in the best interests of our grandchild's future. The parent in question is in a position to undermine our connection to our grandchild. And, who knows, someday that parent just might want to cross that bridge you've left intact and seek your forgiveness and get help. As mentioned earlier, Galatians 6:1 cautions us, "Brothers, if someone is caught in a sin, you who are spiritual should restore him gently. But watch yourself, or you also may be tempted."

When people go through a divorce, it doesn't have to mean the end of the world for those involved. As the grandparent you could play a major role in just how devastating the divorce turns out to be, especially for the children. God could use you to provide the stability and hope that helps your grandchildren not only get through this difficult life chapter, but have much to smile about once they finally turn the page on it.

10 things to do or remember if your children go through a divorce:

1. Make sure you have a support system and outlet for your hurt and anger so that you can be strong for your grandchildren.
2. Don't torture yourself with guilt and regrets. These are adult children, and they are ultimately responsible for their decision to divorce.
3. Let your adult child and her spouse know you are available in any way to help them through this difficult time.
4. Though the two main adults in your grandchild's life may be in turmoil, you be that stable, calm, reassuring adult your grandchild needs.
5. Make sure the grandchildren know that the divorce is not their fault and that they will not be abandoned by you.
6. Be available to answer their questions, and be a safe harbor for them to express their emotions of fear, anger, and pain.
7. Remember they love both of their parents and do not want to hear you speak negatively about either one of them.
8. Devote extra time to praying for them and their parents.

9. Whether you live near or far, be in contact often with your grandchildren as a part of their lives that is not changing during this divorce.
10. Frequently reassure your grandchildren of your love, their parents' love, and God's love for them.

For Further Thought and Discussion

He has sent me to bind up the brokenhearted, . . .
to comfort all who mourn,
    and provide for those who grieve in Zion—
to bestow on them a crown of beauty
    instead of ashes,
the oil of gladness
    instead of mourning,
and a garment of praise
    instead of a spirit of despair. (Isaiah 61:1-3)

1. How is a grandchild's life changed when his or her parents divorce?
2. What should a grandparent avoid doing to add to the pain of the divorcing parents and their children?
3. What can a grandparent do to comfort and help a grandchild going through the separation or divorce of the parents?

Heavenly Father,
O Lord, I need Your help to deal with my pain and bitterness during this difficult time. Use me to help bind up my brokenhearted grandchildren, to comfort them and project a hopeful future. Please wrap Your arms around them and assure them of Your constant love. Open my eyes to ways that I can be there for them and their parents. Amen.

11 When Your Grandkids Move In

It clearly wasn't part of your original plan.

In the back of your mind you imagined the last third of your life playing out more like a television sitcom. At best it was to look like an episode of *The Cosby Show* where you knew your grandchildren were in extremely capable hands and all you had to do was live close enough to drop in at your convenience and enjoy a comfortable involvement with everyone in the picture. At worst it was to look like an episode of *Everybody Loves Raymond* where you lived across the street from your kid's house, got to come over to "smell" the grandchildren anytime you wanted to, and otherwise spent your days driving your grown children crazy.

Instead, your grandchildren are living in your home. Some of you are also shouldering the majority of their care. If your grandchildren are living with you, it may not be much of a comfort, but you join millions of grandparents in North America who also have their grandchildren living with them. In 75 percent of these cases, the grandparents are considered the head of these households.

If you don't fall into this category, you may be inclined to skip this chapter and head to something that applies directly. However, most grandparents who are raising their grandchildren didn't think they would be in this situation either. There are unforeseeable circumstances that could cause you to join those millions of grandparents raising their grandchildren. Because of this, you might just want to keep reading.

Having your grandchildren live with you may be a labor of love on your part, but it can also come with serious frustrations and disappointments. As well as being outside your original plan, having to provide much of their primary care is often complicated by circumstances that make the job harder.

Sometimes you find yourself in this position for incidental but positive reasons:

- Your children are moving into another house but have to get out of the one they are in until their new one is ready.
- The father has accepted a job in another state, but the rest of the family is staying with you until the school year is over.
- It might be during a military deployment.
- It's part of a summer routine.

These scenarios are more like camping—occasions when you slide over and make room for everybody and work overtime to make sure all feel welcome.

But there are some unfortunate reasons that your grandchildren may have to live with you, and when these occur, the grandchildren are usually going to have to stay longer. "In the past, grandparents reared their grandchildren mainly because the parents had died or divorced. But the reasons in recent years have more to do with substance abuse, mental health disorders, incarceration and teenage pregnancies."[1]

These problems have caused the percentage of the grandparents providing primary care to rise substantially over the last decade. It's not uncommon in these situations that both the mother and the father of the grandchildren struggle with serious spiritual, intellectual, or emotional problems. They can't be much help and often complicate an already difficult configuration. If one of the parents is in prison or caught up in the world of drugs, the situation is more than a little parenthesis in your schedule. These scenarios require complete retrofitting of your life.

Déjà Vu All Over Again

It's a huge adjustment to move from thinking you'd put the sweat labor and heavy lifting of raising young children behind you for good, then suddenly finding yourself in the middle of the parenting business. There's no question this configuration is often emotionally wrenching for both grandparents and grandchildren. But for a lot of the grandchildren involved, you may be their only hope.

Having your grandchildren live with you might be your calling.

The apostle Paul teaches us that we are to "carry each other's burdens, and in this way you will fulfill the law of Christ" (Galatians 6:2). Jesus said, "A new command I give you: Love one another" (John 13:34). Coming to the aid of your children and grandchildren is one way you may be called on to take Paul's admonition and to meet Jesus' expectations. What's more, having your grandchildren live with you may be far more than a solution to a crisis; it might be your calling.

And there's some good news coming from the efforts of these millions of grandparents who are accepting this calling: These grandparents are doing some of the best parenting being done today. And that makes sense. You're a veteran, seasoned by decades of raising your own kids. You have a better idea of what matters most and what doesn't. It's nice to know there are a few things besides cheese that improve with age.

But this good news doesn't relieve the stress that comes with the decision to take in your grandchildren. Becoming a surrogate parent to your grandchildren creates a whole series of challenges for you emotionally, financially, legally, and spiritually.

Adding Up the Human Toll

Having grandchildren live with you comes with some serious sticker shock: loss of privacy, the delay or complete cancellation of your retirement plans, and the added daily responsibilities in your schedule. These usually aren't welcome surprises, no matter how much a grandparent loves her child. And often, grandparents lack the energy or health to keep up with the time and physical demands of parenting children. At best they feel inadequate and overwhelmed.

Taking grandchildren into the home can raise health risks for grandparents. A study conducted by researchers from Harvard School of Public Health and Harvard Medical School showed a direct correlation between women providing more than nine hours of care for their grandchildren per week and an increase in heart problems. The grandmothers in this kind of caregiving relationship have a 55 percent greater chance of developing coronary heart disease than those women who don't provide such care.[2] These grandmothers often lack social outlets that can relieve stress. "The demands on caregiving grandmothers probably also results in less time caring for themselves. For example, they may have less time to sleep, rest, exercise, and get regular checkups."[3]

But declining health isn't a foregone conclusion, just a greater risk. Even if the grandparents have the stamina to do the job, many feel like they lack the up-to-date know-how to handle today's children. Their grandchildren's culture, the schools, the neighborhoods, and even necessities such as cell phones and computers have changed since they were raising their own children. Just when they thought they were at the top of their learning curve, they are now faced with a cliff to scale in order to be relevant and adequate with the raising of their grandchildren.

Who's on First

Among the most significant obstacles to feeling adequate and empowered is grandparents' lack of authority to make important daily decisions regarding their grandchildren's education and medical care. Without the documents that grant them legal status, these grandparents can be blocked from enrolling their grandchildren in the local school, picking up their grandchildren from school, or even filling out the paperwork for a sports team.

When a grandchild needs medical attention, a grandparent may not have the legal right to sign insurance reimbursement forms or even authorize medical treatment. Fortunately, because of the number of grandparents raising their grandchildren and the magnitude of this problem of caregiver rights, state and federal regulations are being passed to rectify this situation. There are Web sites that offer guidance in getting the legal status you need. Because these are constantly changing, we aren't going to list them here. But tapping "grandparents and caregivers' legal rights" into your search engine should give you plenty of sites. There are also social and government agencies that can help you sort through this legal tangle. These government programs include, but are not limited to, Temporary Assistance to Needy Families (TANF), Medicaid, and State Children's Health Insurance Programs (SCHIP). The AARP Web site provides a comprehensive array of the latest government agencies and policies that provide assistance to grandparents raising their grandchildren.

As you research the options available for outside assistance and legal rights, keep in mind that the law tends to give deference to the parents. Though they may have a negative influence on the situation, the system is slanted in their favor. You may not be able to get all the rights and privileges you prefer or need.

Besides the health risks and legal frustrations, there are also financial demands when it comes to raising your grandchildren. Many grandparents who are called upon to provide care for their grandchildren (and sometimes the parents of those children) struggle with limited financial resources. There are many reasons why money may be scarce including having children of their own in college or new and increasing medical costs because of advancing age.

Grandparents also may be financially strapped because they are part of the "sandwich generation." That expression describes members of the baby-boom group who have the responsibility to care for aging parents at the same time their own children are dropping their grandchildren off at their home. If their aged parents require financial assistance or need to live with them, these boomers can find themselves sandwiched between the demands of their own parents and their children's children. It's not out of the question for them to have an 80-year-old mother in one bedroom and an eight-year-old grandson in another.

This is when a realistic assessment of the needs and resources to meet those needs should be taken. There's a limit to how much time, energy, and money a grandparent has to spread around. And the worst thing that could happen is if this grandparent, who has so many people depending on her, ends up being sucked dry and needing to be rescued herself.

Level Heads and Carefully Laid Plans

Often, the grandchildren in these situations are struggling with confusing emotions. Besides those we mentioned in our chapter on divorce (grief, fear, anger, guilt, and anxiety), they may also feel adrift, lacking any sense of permanence in their lives. They often feel abandoned. Separation anxiety can cause disruption in their sleep, serious mood swings, and discipline problems. Therefore, when we find ourselves having to take our grandchildren in to live with us, there are some basic things we need to do.

First, do the exact same things in this scenario that we listed in the previous chapter where we dealt with the issue of divorce:

- Get perspective.
- Protect and preserve a supportive relationship with your grandchildren.
- Help them heal.
- Come alongside their parents.

Second, ramp up your commitment to meet the three inner needs we outlined in chapter 5:

- a secure love
- a significant purpose
- a sufficient hope

By focusing on meeting these needs, we minimize many of the problems children face when their parents cannot provide a home for them.

Third, carry out the four grandparenting roles explained in chapters 5–9. Use this opportunity to be a blessing giver, legacy makers, torchbearer of the gospel and moral living, and standard setter. The good thing about having your grandchildren live with you is the opportunity you have to do all this in a more intense way.

There are some additional practical guidelines that we need to embrace if our grandchildren come to live with us. These minimize the negatives and maximize the chances of turning this situation into one that can be enjoyed by everyone in the equation.

Deal with your disappointment. You raise the chances of turning your grandchildren's presence in your home into a positive experience if you commit to dealing with any resentment you may be harboring toward their parents for putting you in this situation. You may feel robbed of a time in your life when you were looking forward to more leisure and less stress. Go to a counselor or get involved in a grandparents' support group. These are ideal places to share your frustrations and disappointments and exchange practical tips. These places also offer resources, such as speakers with professional advice on finances, legal issues, and other parenting matters.

Whatever you do, don't take it out on your grandkids. They had nothing to do with creating this problem. They are the unfortunate victims of these unforeseen circumstances. Even though you have to make some adjustments, your grandchildren need to know you are ready to do what you can to make their lives better.

Whatever you do, don't take it out on your grandkids.

Make your grandchildren feel as if they are in their permanent home, not just visiting. It may sound crazy, but life will vastly improve for everyone in this new family picture if you do that. What does this look like? It could mean letting them decorate their rooms. It definitely means giving them the freedom to access and enjoy the various amenities of your home without needing to ask permission every time. If they are teenagers in a growth spurt, they need to feel like they can open your refrigerator or cupboards without a reprimand. You have to be willing to listen to their music and welcome their friends. Friends are such an important part of childhood, no matter what the age. By allowing your grandchildren to bring their friends to their new home, you are empowering them to keep that one part of their lives intact. These friendships can help reestablish a sense of permanence in life.

Everything we just mentioned in the previous paragraph assumes adhering to the moral boundaries and practical standards of your home. Listening to a grandchild's music doesn't mean he or she can have every kind of music in your home. Not all music is acceptable for young people. And satisfying hunger doesn't mean a grandchild gets to spoil a dinner about to be served.

But bringing grandchildren into your home is much easier on them when they know they can relax and settle down. The more comfortable they feel in your home, the more at ease they can become with you.

One of the challenges of raising a grandchild is that the youth culture is so different from when you raised your own children. It's easy for a grandparent to want things to remain as they were in the past. We need to remind ourselves that there has never been such a thing as "the good old days." That's a myth. The past has always had its share of challenges. Each generation feels like it's got a plateful of responsibilities that push patience to the limit. Trying to make things work like they did in the past could make you appear to be rigid and irrelevant. This doesn't mean you can't enforce some old-fashioned standards of moral behavior. They aren't really old-fashioned—they're timeless. But you do want to create an environment that takes into consideration some of the basic needs of a technologically sophisticated society.

You might want to talk with the youth pastor in your church or read some Christian books targeted at teens and their culture for a crash course on what is considered "normal" nowadays—even for Christian kids. Just like a parent, you will want to focus on the child's heart and not get too sidetracked on how they dress or the style of music they are listening to. You might really surprise them and offer to buy tickets to a concert you know they would enjoy. If you go with them, remember to show respect for their musical tastes. They need to see you doing whatever you can within your limitations to provide them an environment as close to a home with their own parents as possible.

Don't make them feel guilty. Don't remind them of the inconvenience or sacrifice you are making. They don't need to hear how difficult it is. Take those concerns to God. Your grandchildren need to sense your enthusiasm over their being a part of your daily life. They need to feel you look on this situation not as *having* to take them in, but rather that you *get* to. It may be that you are like Queen Esther who was called upon to take some courageous and sacrificial steps and was put in her situation for such a moment.[4]

Establish reasonable standards and discipline. When your grandchildren live in your home, it is important to *discuss with their mother or father (if they are still in the picture) what the standards of your home will be and who will carry out discipline.* In multigenerational households it is important to clarify things that might be taken for granted in other homes. Have as few rules as possible but enough boundaries so you don't experience burnout or feel like you are going to go crazy if you don't have some space.

If their parents are either living with you or still involved in their children's lives, you'll have to discuss discipline options. You should put the onus of discipline responsibilities on them. They are the parents. Don't be surprised if their discipline style is radically different from yours.

If the parents are out of the daily picture, they still may want to have some say in disciplining their children. This may impede or destroy your ability to correct and direct your grandchildren. You may need to get the courts involved; you may have to petition for custody rights in order to protect your ability to adequately raise your grandchildren.

For grandparents who are stepping in to help out, there is a fine line between feeling useful and feeling *used.* Establishing the standards of your home and making a plan for discipline minimizes the chances of feeling like you are being exploited. And don't apologize for the standards of your home. It's your home. Just make sure that what you expect of your grandchildren is tempered with grace that accounts for their ages, their belongings, and their idiosyncrasies.

Be their grandparent first. Even though you may be carrying most of the responsibilities of a parent, grandchildren prefer that you remain their grandparent. They have parents. Most likely, they are processing a lot of different feelings about them. If you try to supplant those parents, you'll create more trouble for yourself. As you establish a balance, you may have to surrender *some* of the grandparent/grandchild dynamics. For instance, you may not get to be known as much for playfulness as you'd prefer. And that loving conspiracy that grandparents are known to enjoy with their grandchildren may not be appropriate under the circumstances. Obviously, the joy of positive spoiling of the grandkids is diminished. Regardless, do your best to keep your role as much as possible in the grandparent camp.

Don't abandon all hope, but keep in mind that people grow and change.

There are two very practical reasons why you want to carry out your responsibilities of parenting them from your platform of a *grandparent.* First, grandchildren tend to respond more respectfully to their grandparents than they do to their own parents. Therefore, you are more likely to gain their cooperation if you maintain the mantle of grandparent. Second, you'll better preserve their parents' position in their hearts. Should circumstances change, their parents need to be able to assume their responsibilities with as little confusion as possible.

Don't write off their parents. Even though you may have lost some respect for your grandchildren's parents, don't abandon all hope, but keep in mind that people grow and change. Keep praying for them. Keep the door of your heart open to them. At the same time, do not accommodate any of the behaviors that keep them from being able to parent. Though you are extending financial help to your grandchildren, it only hurts to extend financial help to their parents if they use it to continue their destructive choices. Grace, of course, takes into account those with mental illnesses or serious debilitations, but it does not license us to accommodate sinful behavior simply because we feel sorry for our children. It's painful to accept, but the truth is that some people have to hit rock bottom before they'll reach up to God for help.

In the meantime, you might want to discuss with an attorney what the best legal configuration is for you as custodian of your grandchildren. Some of your options may include adoption, managing conservatorship, guardianship, or, if you have the parents' cooperation, a special power of attorney.

Love Is a Two-Way Street

As difficult as it is to make room for your grandchildren in your home, this special calling can be a source of immense joy if you view it as an extension of your love for God. God can use you to salvage and stabilize an unfortunate set of circumstances. He can use this opportunity in your life to energize your relationship with Him as well as give you a chance to stay on the cusp of significance during your twilight years.

He might even use your willingness to take your grandchildren into your home as a way . . . of saving your life.

Shortly after my (Tim's) mother gave birth to her fifth child, my brother Todd, she came down with rheumatic fever. My father did his best to keep food on the table and take care of us kids. During the day, my older brother was able to shoulder a lot of the supervision of me and our siblings. But poor Mom was confined to bed and had absolutely no energy to care for her newborn. So she asked her mother if she could help.

At the time, our family was living in Pennsylvania. Grandmother Dean lived in the little village of Eastbrook, just a few miles from our home. She gladly agreed to take care of baby Todd. Granddad wasn't as excited about the idea. He was a broken man who had fought in

World War I in the wicked trenches of France, where he had been gassed by the enemy. He came home from the war with the effects of that awful gas in his system. On top of that, the Great Depression took its toll on his view of himself as a provider and protector.

My grandparents' life had become that of two people living under the same roof with hearts that were miles apart. Grandma spent her days working hard and serving others. Granddad had withdrawn into his own private world. Because of this, Grandma had developed the habit of sleeping in the living room on the couch each night. Although there was a crib set up in the second bedroom upstairs, Grandma had been putting Todd down for bed in a baby buggy in the living room so she could continue her practice of sleeping downstairs.

Just after eleven o'clock on a quiet night, Todd awakened and started to cry in a way that held the entire house hostage. My grandfather woke up and yelled down to my grandmother to quiet him down. She tried all the tricks she knew, but his crying just got more intense. Todd's crying that way was an anomaly because he had never had a prolonged crying fit before that night. Grandma pulled out all the stops trying to figure out how to calm him down. In exasperation, my grandfather swore down the stairs for her to "bring that !# baby upstairs and put him in his crib." Grandma complied.

Just as she got to the top of the stairs, they heard the explosion. What neither of them knew was that two intoxicated teenage boys had decided to race their hotrods several miles down the inclined country road that ultimately passed through Eastbrook. There was a sharp bend in the road just as it came into the village. My grandparents' house was a few feet back from the road just around that bend. Neither driver could control his car through the turn. Both cars crashed through the wall of the living room. One flipped over and landed on the couch upon which my grandmother had been lying. The other car was right beside it. The baby buggy that Todd had been lying in was crushed like an accordion into the grill of that car. Both drivers managed to walk away from the wreckage.

The next day, people came from all over Lawrence County to view the devastation. It was obvious to everyone that anyone in that living room would not have survived. My grandmother was a follower of Jesus. The way she explained it was like this: "Both my husband and I are sound sleepers. I'd grown accustomed to sleeping on the living-room couch each night. God saw fit to have my grandson living with us so that He could send one of His angels down to tickle him into a crying frenzy enough to get me to take him upstairs. The reason I'm here today is because God sent our grandson to live with us."

No doubt grandparents who open their homes and their hearts to their grandchildren make a major sacrifice. It's a profound act of love, mercy, and grace. But they shouldn't be surprised to find that God uses their act of kindness to do some wonderful things in their own lives. Some of God's greatest gifts come with the word "grand" as a prefix. And His love is a two-way street.

If Your Grandchildren Come to Live with You

- Hold the parents accountable for whatever financial and time contribution they are capable of making.
- Don't allow things to get off to a poor start by not setting boundaries and expectations.
- As much as possible, whether the parent of your grandchild lives with you or not, make sure the parent realizes he or she is still the parent and is expected to get his or her life back together and take on the responsibility of the child. (In some cases of abandonment, incarceration, or addiction, this may not ever be possible.)
- Investigate all public-assistance programs and don't be too proud to access them.

- Ask other family members to pitch in (siblings, aunts, uncles, other grandparents). No need to play the martyr.
- Get in a grandparents' support group. If you can't find one, start one in your church or neighborhood. You may be surprised at how many other grandparents are going through the same things you are. (Our DVD study *Extreme Grandparenting: The Ride of Your Life* is a great tool and resource for gathering a group together in your church or neighborhood.)
- Take advantage of childcare or Sunday school classes at church to allow others to care for your grandchildren and give you a rest.
- Don't feel guilty if you can't provide the optimum care and environment for a grandchild. Do what you can with God's help and the help of others.
- Make sure your marriage and your relationships with your other children, grandchildren, and friends aren't completely neglected because of your added responsibilities. Consider these people you love and who love you to be resources and part of your support system.
- Get others praying for you. Consider joining a Moms In Touch group in your area, or you may even find or start a Grandmothers In Touch group. Go to www.momsintouch.org for more information.

For Further Thought and Discussion

Do you not know?
    Have you not heard?
The LORD is the everlasting God,
    the Creator of the ends of the earth.
He will not grow tired or weary,
    and his understanding no one can fathom.
He gives strength to the weary
    and increases the power of the weak.

Even youths grow tired and weary,
    and young men stumble and fall;
but those who hope in the LORD
    will renew their strength.
They will soar on wings like eagles;
    they will run and not grow weary,
    they will walk and not be faint. (Isaiah 40:28-31)

1. What are some things that have led or could lead to resentment if your grandchildren come to live with you? What have you given up or would you have to give up when your grandchildren live with you?
2. Why is it important to set boundaries and expectations with the parents when your grandchildren, with or without their parents, are living in your home?
3. How can you make your grandchildren feel welcome and at home if they come to live with you? What might be the most challenging adjustment you would have to make?

Heavenly Father,
I need Your help dealing with my feelings of disappointment and worry during this time when my grandchildren need to live with me. Please renew my strength and provide the resources I will need right now to have a safe and secure home for these precious children. Please give me patience, wisdom, and endurance so that I can show Your unconditional love to them and they can know they are loved no matter what. Work in the lives of their parents so they can give their children what they long for. Thank You that You never leave us or forsake us. Amen.

12 Stepgrandchildren and Adopted Grandchildren

When the two of us were growing up, we lived on opposite sides of the continental United States. Other than both having families with six kids, our homes had more things different about them than they had in common. Neither of our families started out with much, but only one would have been considered poor while the other was lower middle class. The family that started out poor climbed the ladder to the top of the middle class. The one that started out on the low side of the middle class held a fairly good grip on that rung until the kids were all grown and gone. One of us grew up in a Republican home. The other's family tree was full of Democrats.

In spite of these different backgrounds, one thing we shared in childhood was our exposure to Sunday school. One of us was taken to church by our parents; the other was sent on without them. But even in these different contexts, we both got an early taste of the truths about God. God has an amazing way of spreading His influence over very different types of people.

There was one Sunday school song we both learned the words to by the time we were about four years old. You probably know it too. It's the song that tells about Jesus' overarching love for children—in fact, all the children of the world: "Red and yellow, black and white, they are precious in His sight."

You'll probably have that song stuck in your head for the remainder of this chapter. That's okay. It's a nice song. It's too bad it doesn't reflect the true nature of God's actual family.

Splitting Some Theological Hairs

The issue here isn't whether or not Jesus loves the children of the world. He obviously does. It lies with the fact that the bulk of the children within the world who choose to love Him back are technically stepchildren and adopted members of His family.

We don't mean to belabor this technicality, but we do want to make a point here. God established a family relationship with the patriarch Abraham early in the history of humanity. He made a covenant with him and his descendants—the future nation of Israel. Throughout the Old Testament, the Jews of Israel are referred to as God's children. When God sent His Son, Jesus, to pay the price for our sins on the cross and then validated His finished work by raising Him from the dead, He established a new covenant with His people. But He extended it outside the boundaries of His original relationship with Israel. He offered redemption to the Gentiles as well. It's interesting how the Scriptures refer to the non-Jews who became members of God's family. In Ephesians 2:11-19, Paul puts it like this:

> Therefore, remember that formerly you who are Gentiles by birth and called "uncircumcised" by those who call themselves "the circumcision" [the Jews] . . . remember that at that time you were separate from Christ, excluded from citizenship in Israel and foreigners to the covenants of the promise, without hope and without God in the world. But now in Christ Jesus you who once were far away have been brought near through the blood of Christ.
>
> For he himself is our peace, who has made the two one and has destroyed the barrier, the dividing wall of hostility. . . . He

> came and preached peace to you who were far away and peace to those who were near. . . .
>
> Consequently, you are no longer foreigners and aliens, but fellow citizens with God's people and members of God's household.

Here's another reference to the non-Jews who have been brought into the family: "Praise be to the God and Father of our Lord Jesus Christ, who has blessed us in the heavenly realms with every spiritual blessing in Christ. For he chose us in him before the creation of the world to be holy and blameless in his sight. In love he predestined us to be adopted as his sons through Jesus Christ, in accordance with his pleasure and will" (Ephesians 1:3-5).

One more. In Romans 11:17, Paul refers to Israel as the olive tree and Gentiles who believe as, "though a wild olive shoot, have been grafted in among the others and now share in the nourishing sap from the olive root."

Jesus does indeed love all the children of the world. But of the millions who love Him back, the bulk of them are stepchildren, adopted children, and outsiders who were grafted to His holy family tree. Here's the bottom line: God loves His stepchildren, His adopted children, and the members of His blended family.

When it comes to dealing with stepgrandchildren and adopted grandchildren, we should take our cues from Him.

Spreading the Love

We cannot effectively prepare ourselves for our roles as grandparents without making sure we have the proper attitude toward those children who didn't enter our family through the delivery room. There are lots of ways that grandparents can find themselves looking at a family-reunion picture crowded with stepchildren. This can come about through divorce or death and the subsequent remarriage of either spouse. Up to half of all grandparents will have at least one stepgrandchild relationship. With that in mind, it's valid to ask, "How do you respond to these additional family members?"

Jesus made this easy. He said in Matthew 7:12, "Do to others what you would have them do to you." If you were a child in a new blended family, would you want a grandparent showing up and singling out your new brother or sister for love and praise and ignoring you? Would you want to be in a home where some older person brings gifts for your stepsiblings but never brings one for you? Would you want to be referred to as the nonbiological grandchild?

Jesus anticipated that we would all encounter scenarios where we ended up with more than we bargained for. His advice is simple: *Love them all.* It's similar to the attitude we talked about in our last chapter on having your grandchildren move in with you: It should never be a question of how many grandchildren you *have* to love, but how many you *get* to love. The great thing about stepgrandparenting is that it not only gives the stepgrandchildren someone else to love them, but it gives you someone else to love you in return.

Yours, Mine, and Ours

The standard way the family circle is widened is when our children go through a divorce and remarry, marry someone who already has children, or adopt children. Sometimes a grandparent's remarriage after the death of a spouse or divorce is the reason the family dynamic changes. We'll spend the next few pages learning how to make the most of these different opportunities to expand the sphere of our love.

Let's get the nasty stuff out of the way first. The absolute worst thing a grandparent can do is differentiate between "blood" grandchildren and those who were "added to the mix." We commit a horrific sin when we cater to and coddle our "natural" grandchildren and ignore the stepgrandchildren. This is the behavior of small-minded, mean-spirited grandparents who have clearly lost any semblance of God's heart. We have seen severe damage done to grandchildren's faith as a result of so-called Christian grandparents treating them like sub-family members simply because of the remarriage of their parents. If we claim to be followers of Jesus, this kind of behavior is inexcusable.

Jesus weighed in on this issue, and He didn't mince words. With a child sitting on His lap, He used the opportunity to tell what He thought of people who did anything that undermined a child's healthy relationship with Him. Here's how He put it: "Whoever welcomes a little child like this in my name welcomes me. But if anyone causes one of these little ones who believe in me to sin, it would be better for him to have a large millstone hung around his neck and to be drowned in the depths of the sea" (Matthew 18:5-6).

God expects us to treat our stepgrandchildren and adopted children the same way He treats His. He extends an unconditional, magnanimous love to each one of them. We should do the same. The circumstances that created the blended family might not be ideal. Choices made by some of the adults involved might definitely have been misguided. But the children had nothing to do with those decisions. If anything, they are often the collateral damage of the foolish choices of their parents. We need to play a redemptive role in these unfortunate scenarios and offer love, mercy, grace, and acceptance to every grandchild caught in the middle.

Making the Most of Tense Situations

When we find ourselves with new grandchildren in our lives, the number one rule is: *Go slowly.* We need to move carefully, building a deliberate and patient relationship with these new grandchildren. We need to let *them* determine the speed at which the relationship develops.

It takes awhile for stepgrandchildren to feel as if they know us well enough to be comfortable around us. Because most of them are not infants when we first get to know them, we don't have the advantage of bonding with them from the beginning. Depending on the circumstances that created this new relationship, we may be viewed as part of the repercussion of the divorce of their parents or grandparents. Perhaps we should stay in the background and allow things to settle in and develop at their own pace. Most children need some time to get used to a new family situation before they can start to forge extended relationships.

One principle vital to establishing this new family dynamic is *allowing the previous primary relationships to continue without any threat by us.* If it's your remarriage, the people on your spouse's side can see you as an interloper or competition to the memory or the presence of the person who used to be married to your spouse. On top of that, your own children might find it difficult to accept this new configuration for their parent.

How do you respond to these additional family members?

It's essential to your children that you don't use this new marriage as an excuse for abdicating your role as the matriarch or patriarch of your original family. At the same time, you must be careful not to undermine your new spouse's relationship with his or her own children and grandchildren. So often we hear offspring say that once their parent or grandparent remarried, they abandoned their original family and spent most of their time with their new one. Sometimes they abandoned them both.

We need to think of our family as a series of concentric circles, overlapping to represent the existing relationships. A new circle does not replace any existing relationships but instead adds new opportunities to love the people within each circle. These circles will overlap to differing degrees as our grandchildren, and in some cases their new parent, allow us into their lives.

When it comes to opening up hearts, it is often easier with younger children than with the older ones. We can more easily meet younger children's physical and emotional needs. They are more trusting and usually less aware of the circumstances that brought us into their lives. Many older children have established strong loyalties to a parent or grandparent. These loyalties are stressed when a new marriage takes place; they are tragically lost when a parent or grandparent dies. The older grandchildren may view us as unnecessary or even intruding upon their lives.

Once again, a savvy stepgrandparent will view the new relationship as a new opportunity rather than a substitute for an existing or previous relationship. It might even be possible to verbalize this with an older grandchild. Certainly you will never want to compare yourself to another grandparent or in any way disparage that person. We must also never compare the divorced or deceased parent to the new one. Our job as grandparents is to do what we can to enfold and love these new grandchildren.

Hedging Their Bets

Because of the circumstances that put them in a stepfamily, some kids feel they've been burned. As a result, they are reticent to give their hearts to their new grandparent. They're working through some huge emotional adjustments with the new marriage of a parent or grandparent. Once again, we need to take our time. In this situation, patience is our finest virtue. We need to ask their permission to take the relationship deeper. And we need to assume that with the older grandchildren, authority may be an issue. For them, we might serve more as mentors and friends. Prior to our coming onto the scene, our stepgrandchildren had a history that didn't include us. It might take them awhile to figure out where we fit in.

When it comes to family gatherings, the onus is on us to do what we can to make everyone feel welcome. We need to use our example to cast every family member as an honored part of the family circle. You might ask why the onus is on us. That's simple: We're the oldest. We're the ones who have walked the fairways and back roads of life the most. We've been given more time and experience. Jesus said, "From the one who has been entrusted with much, much more will be asked" (Luke 12:48).

We've seen this played out in several families close to us. A divorce and remarriage takes place. The new person on the parent's or grandparent's arm may have played a role in the demise of the first marriage. Family gatherings could either be carried out in twos: two birthday cakes for separate visits, two Christmas celebrations, and so forth, or the people involved in the divorce and remarriage could decide to put away the animosity and inclinations to compete for the grandchildren's hearts and enjoy all the family gatherings without hurting someone's feelings. Yes, this type of dynamic is very difficult to create when the wounds are fresh and the hurts still sting. And because of some of the reasons for the new family configurations, it may never be possible. But it's definitely the goal mature adults should try to achieve. It's a lot easier if forgiveness is asked for and granted by the various people involved. It takes appropriating enormous amounts of God's grace to see this become a reality, but the peace and the security of the grandchildren are all the reason people need for burying the hatchet and forgetting where they buried it.

One final caution about the dynamics within the grandparent/stepgrandchild relationship: Never pit children or grandchildren against an ex-spouse. Unless there is a real possibility of danger or abuse, we should see ourselves as agents of God to bring healing and hope to these relationships.

In the meantime, as you establish a relationship with your new stepgrandchildren, you can start including them in your daily prayer time. It's powerful when we see these relationships as sacred opportunities to extend our time with God to include the goals and hopes of these new children He has brought into our lives.

The Chosen Ones

And speaking of new children brought into our lives, adopted grandchildren are very special gifts. They are the chosen ones. There are few greater acts of love than giving a child your heart, your home, and your name. It is a loving illustration of how God accepts and adopts us into His family.

In our research for this book, we surveyed many grandparents. As a result, we received some follow-up correspondence and quite a few photographs from some very proud grandparents. One grandmother wrote that her son-in-law had gained full custody of his daughter from a previous marriage. This happened when the girl was just a few years old. Those early years were about as traumatic as they could get. Her daughter and son-in-law started going to counseling with this little girl as soon as they brought her into their home. The daughter was proud to legally adopt the little girl as quickly as the papers could be processed. She did this even though she knew her newly adopted daughter came with massive scar tissue on her heart.

> ***Young eyes are looking to us for a reason to believe.***

This grandmother was so excited to share that, after years of counseling and the unrelenting love of the parents and herself and her husband, her granddaughter had placed her faith in Jesus. "She's in high school now, and she is clearly at peace with herself and her family. She is as beautiful on the inside as she is on the outside." These grandparents had opened their lives to a child in need of all the love she could get, and God has honored their open arms and loving hearts.

Jesus summarized it well. He said in John 15:13, "Greater love has no one than this, that he lay down his life for his friends." The greatest friends each of us have in life are family members. Most likely, none of us will be asked to lay down our physical lives for them. But God calls us to communicate a love to them that resonates with the assurance that we would be willing to die for them. It's really not that difficult to make sure they sense this. All we have to be willing to do is *live* for them.

Young eyes are looking to us for a reason to believe. Some have watched their parents leave each other, some inherited us with their new mother or father, and others were grafted in through adoption. To some of you, they may look like sticky situations, challenges that are going to tap your love to its limits. But God sees them as an opportunity for you to expand your wonderful role as a blessing giver, a legacy maker, a torchbearer of the truth, and a standard setter for living an abundant life. Those stepgrandchildren and adopted grandchildren need to be able to say one of two words and know they are getting all that these gifts have to offer: Grandma and Granddad.

Five Ways to Be a Better Stepgrandparent

1. Keep God's perspective that this is an extension of your ministry to your family.
2. Always take the high road and refuse to traffic in disappointment or blaming when it comes to the circumstances and people that brought about the new family configuration.
3. Take it slowly and gently. Allow the new grandchildren to figure out where you fit in.
4. Always speak with respect about the other adults in the picture.
5. Count it an honor to pray for these precious children. "And whoever welcomes a little child like this in my name welcomes me" (Matthew 18:5).

For Further Thought and Discussion

> The wisdom that comes from heaven is first of all pure; then peace-loving, considerate, submissive, full of mercy and good fruit, impartial and sincere. Peacemakers who sow in peace raise a harvest of righteousness. (James 3:17-18)

1. What are some things that can make it hard to love and treat our stepgrandchildren the same as our other grandchildren?
2. How can we use our adoption into the family of God as an example of how we should welcome these new children into our own families?
3. What positive results can happen to us and them when we accept our blended grandchildren as special gifts from God?

Heavenly Father,
Please give me insight into the hearts of these new grandchildren. Give me a heart of compassion and understanding, and help me patiently wait for opportunities to love them and show them acceptance. Use me as an agent to sow peace into the lives of those who may be hurting in this expanded family. Please show me ways to help meet their need for a secure love, a significant purpose, and a strong hope. And ultimately, use me to help them learn how to find all of those in You. Amen.

13 Positive Spoiling

Some of you reading this have lived through some very frightening moments in your lives. Maybe you've been on a battlefield and faced a well-armed enemy. Or perhaps you've been stuck in the middle of a violent storm with no place to hide. The feeling people get in those situations is similar to that terror felt when you're sitting next to a grandmother with a big purse on a cross-country flight. The pilot has barely gotten the wheels tucked underneath the jet, and she pulls out her picture album of the grandkids. She starts in with her unsolicited history of each child, then brandishes photocopies of their report cards; meanwhile, her seatmate gets this glazed look in his eyes. The next thing you know, she's pulled out a DVD. She's showing him her granddaughter's swimming lessons and her grandson's band concert, sound and all. Just as the trapped fellow starts looking around for something he can make a noose out of, grandma grabs a little device, pushes some buttons, and her grandson appears in virtual reality floating above her purse.

Though we're exaggerating to make a point, there's one person on this writing team who can't wait to get her hands on one of those virtual-reality thingies. And though they haven't been invented yet, that's not stopping her from writing a note to herself to inquire about one the next time she's at Best Buy.

It's impossible to talk about grandparenting without acknowledging the natural pride grandparents have in their grandkids. It's different from the pride we have in our own children. It's almost irrational.

Sometimes it borders on obnoxious—at least in the opinion of the poor creature sitting next to the overzealous grandmother on a long flight. But it's no doubt a God thing. Our wonderful Creator knew that each boy and girl would need a couple of cheerleaders who could maintain pride and praise for them regardless of whether they're winning or losing.

Obviously, a child's parents play that role too. But because they are also the child's primary life coach, they don't have the luxury of being able to filter out their son's or daughter's shortcomings as easily as grandparents do. That's good. Parents play a very important role in disciplining and training their children. But grandchildren also need people who look at them through the filter of a generation of years—whose joy in them isn't as tied to their behavior at any particular moment, but rather to the mere fact that the child *exists* and is part of that grandparent's lineage. And while we're on the subject, it's probably smart to mention that grandmothers aren't the only ones who can get obnoxious about their grandchildren.

Grandfathers can be endowed with excessive pride too. It's a contagious side effect of being blessed with a new and tender limb on your family tree. But grandparental pride and excitement can have worse results than just boring others if not kept under control. In this chapter, we want to look at a related sticky situation that virtually all of us have to deal with: spoiling our grandchildren.

We Don't Want to Be Name-Droppers, but God Said . . .

The writer to the Hebrews gives us some good overriding advice when it comes to this issue: "Make every effort to live in peace with all men and to be holy; without holiness no one will see the Lord. See to it that no one misses the grace of God and that no bitter root grows up to cause trouble and defile many" (12:14-15). It falls to us as the senior members of the family tree to bring a strong commitment to peace and maturity within the dynamics of our families. God wants us to be set apart from the world's way of thinking. He says that if we aren't willing to let Him oversee the way we process our day-to-day dealings with the people around us, He leaves us to our own devices. Our unwillingness to deal in grace with the people we love can plant a seed of bitterness that can grow and completely overtake the entire extended family. We can do better than that—we've got to do better than that, and it starts by knowing where the boundaries are when it comes to spoiling our grandchildren.

Too Much of a Good Thing

Spoiling is the natural outgrowth of the relationship we have with our grandchildren. Because we don't usually have the daily responsibility of their care, we are one step removed from their discipline, development, desires, and demands. Whereas the average parent is in the position of having to say no to most things, we're in the position where it is easier to say yes.

When most of us were parenting our children, our bills were high and our income was limited. We didn't have the money to accommodate many of our children's wants. We were tired most of the time, which often caused us to be impatient with them. And because we were working all the time, we didn't have the discretionary hours to spend with them that we would have liked. Now that we're older and better off financially, we may want to compensate for those years of relational and financial deprivation. But we usually skip the adult children and instead indulge the grandchildren with our extra time and, if possible, resources.

And Darcy can vouch for the fact that spoiling also gives grandmothers another excuse to go shopping . . . as if she needed an excuse.

But lest we put all the blame for buying too much stuff for our grandchildren on the grandmothers, we need to be honest: Grandma may buy a new book or another cute outfit for the grandkid, but Grandpa brings home a swing set, a computer, and a motorcycle.

The Past Defines the Present

How our children respond to our spoiling their children depends on two factors: the relationship we had with them as they grew up and the kind of spoiling we're engaging in.

The Parent-Child Relationship

If you came out of your parenting years with a close, healthy relationship with your children, they are more open to your blessing their children with gifts of toys, food, and fun. This is true even if, when they were growing up, your resources were limited. The solid, loving relationship you had balanced the lack of stuff you could give them. Now they welcome your desire to share your extra time and money with their children. Because things are positive between you, they don't automatically question your motives or see what you are doing as an attempt to undermine their relationship with their kids. For them, it simply seems like a nice bonus.

But you might get a completely opposite reaction from children whose relationship with you from their childhood nets out to a negative. They may harbor negative feelings toward you because you worked too much and saw them too little or you lacked the grace you have now developed. If you divorced and remarried, they may still be processing that. The bad memories and the tension that remains between you make it hard for them to appreciate your desire to lavish time and resources on their children when, as far as they are concerned, you didn't do that for them.

The solution to this problem will probably look more like a process than an event. You've got to close the loop between your child's heart and yours. As we talked about in chapter 7 regarding leaving a legacy, you may have to ask forgiveness for things you did to them and for some of the things you left out of their childhood. It might be worth it to go back and reread that chapter to understand the process better. The good news is that God is in the restoration business. He'd love to help you build the relationship with your adult child that you wished you had when he or she was younger. In the process, you may be freed up to spoil your grandchild without fear of hurting your child—that is, assuming the second factor of spoiling isn't an issue.

Spoiling: Helpful or Toxic

Just to remind you, the first factor that determines how our children respond to us spoiling our grandchildren is the kind of relationship we had with them growing up. The second factor has to do with the kind of spoiling we're doing. Our desire to lavish love and material things on our grandchildren can enhance the goals and objectives of our children, or it can be viewed as something toxic to family harmony. When we clearly understand and affirm the values of our children's homes, we can complement their provision with extras they are not able to provide. We can take our grandchildren to the park or library. We can TiVo their favorite shows for them to view later. We can spring for that extra pair of shoes or piece of sports equipment that is just out of range of the child's family budget. We can buy tickets to the play-off game or provide a plane ticket for a visit from one of the grandchildren. Doing the extras to reinforce the plans of your children is a special privilege grandparents enjoy.

We're in the position where it is easier to say yes.

Spoiling, however, can become toxic when it clearly undermines the parents' authority. Perhaps we let our grandchildren do something at our house we know is forbidden at theirs. Or we conspire with them to go behind their parents' backs to indulge some eating delight. When we do these kinds of things, we are setting a poor example for our grandkids and clearly crossing the line between spoiling and harming. Blatantly disregarding the values and desires of our children, just so we can pamper our grandchildren, damages everyone in the family circle.

Sometimes spoiling can neutralize consequences parents are using to teach our grandchildren a lesson. For instance, a grandson may have left his fifty-dollar baseball glove at the park, and it got stolen. To teach him responsibility, his parents are making him do chores until he has earned enough money to buy another one. If Granddad walks in and slips the boy fifty dollars, not only does this nullify the parents' lessons in fiscal responsibility, but it also gives the grandson a warped sense of value. In addition, many parents feel we're working against them when we give our grandchildren things their parents don't think they deserve or feel they aren't prepared to deal with responsibly. Buying your grandchildren a puppy without clearing it with their parents could be setting them up with something they aren't ready to handle.

Or perhaps a child has been bugging his parents for a drum set. They don't think he deserves one, because his grades have been down. Then the grandchild mentions it to his granddad, and a drum set shows up for his birthday.

Speaking of drum sets, sometimes our spoiling is toxic because our children suspect we're doing it to get even with them. Perhaps we don't like the way they are running their family, or there is some bad blood between us. So we do something nice for their child that we know will annoy the parents. Some grandparents give their grandchildren extravagant gifts to gain their love and loyalty. When we lavish gifts on our grandchildren with strings attached, the whole family gets tangled up in the mess.

We knew one family in Texas that had fallen apart because a grandfather was portioning out his attention and assets based on his opinion of his grandsons' chosen professions. His one grandson was aiming at a professional marketing career. The other wanted to head to seminary after he graduated from college so he could pursue a career in the ministry. Grandfather clearly placed more value on a degree and career in business than he did on a life devoted to ministry. He made his preference known verbally and financially. Fortunately, the grandchild who was slighted was able to deal with the inequity. His parents were not. They were wounded to think that one of their parents would single out one of their children and place less value on his chosen career path—especially one as noble as giving his life to serve God and others. The grandfather refused to change his ways. As a result, the parents refused to let the grandfather see either grandson. This conflict could have been avoided if the grandfather hadn't been so determined to continue his toxic spoiling.

Doing It Right

We've got good news. Constructive spoiling can be part of the charming relationship between you and your grandchildren. To make sure it helps rather than hinders the family dynamic, you must be careful to obey two basic rules:

1. Make sure what you are doing is okay with their parents.
2. Make sure what you are doing is helping your grandchild grow into a better person.

I (Darcy) have found that it makes sense to ask permission of parents in almost any purchase for a grandchild—especially when it comes to special occasions. In the first place, it is difficult in this age when kids already have so much to try to figure out something to get them for events like birthdays. Running things by the parents makes sure you're working with them on the best interests of the grandchildren and not buying something they themselves wanted to get for the kids.

When one of our grandchildren was turning four, I thought it might be fun and an ideal time for her to have a pet fish. Realizing that this would also involve the supervision and commitment of the parents, I asked permission first. Our daughter Karis thought it was a great idea, and so I bought a starter aquarium and a bright blue betta fish for our granddaughter. It was like déjà vu, because I had done this for several of our own children—including Karis. One of those children, our son Colt, saw the fish before I took it over to my granddaughter's house. Speaking from personal experience, he commented, "This will be Riley's 'fall from innocence.' I do not want to be there when that fish dies!" One of the lessons we all must learn is that we have to risk hurt in order to enjoy many of the good things in life. But because of the risk involved of a grandchild attaching to a fish that is destined to die, it made much better sense to first make sure it was all right with her parents.

You might want to get a grandchild a car for his sixteenth birthday. Though it might be perfectly acceptable to his parents, it might not be in the grandchild's best interests. This is where you've got to spend a lot of time on your knees praying for discernment. The more you do that, the more likely your spoiling will enhance their hearts and their greater good.

Money, Money, Money, Money . . . Money!

Let's talk about money for a bit. Some grandparents don't have a lot of extra funds to spend on their grandchildren. These grandparents are in the best position to give their grandchildren the kind of gifts that have a much more lasting impact on them than things bought in stores. Their blessing can be rich in time, wisdom, prayer, patient relationships, and the passing on of life skills.

We know one particular grandmother who didn't have a lot of financial resources to share with her granddaughter. But she knew how to run a VCR. It just so happened there was a television show her granddaughter absolutely loved, but her school schedule prevented her from seeing it. Grandma recorded the five shows each week, then had her granddaughter over for lunch every Saturday. They'd eat together, watch one of the shows, and she'd send her home with the rest. Her granddaughter had a great heart connection with Grandma because she saw a grandmother who was going out of her way every day to do something that meant a lot to her personally.

Another example is a grandfather who traded drum lessons for his granddaughter with a band leader in exchange for his once-a-week performance on the trumpet with this man's group.

Though many older adults live on fixed incomes and have limited financial resources, there are some grandparents who not only have the opportunity to treat their grandchildren to extra time and gifts but are also capable of helping them get a head start financially. For a lot of these grandparents, there is a strong desire to use the money God has blessed them with to enhance their grandchildren's lives.

But this can be a double-edged sword. Obviously, the same rules apply when giving money to a grandchild as apply to spoiling: Make sure it meets with the parents' approval, and make sure it ultimately helps the grandchild to become a better person. When it comes to our money, grandchildren are better off with too little of it than with too much. The job of parents and grandparents is to teach children how to create their own wealth and then how to handle it properly. You could give them a lot of money, but you'd probably do them a greater favor if you gave them just enough to help them get started—coupled with modeling the six character traits we mentioned in chapter 9. They'll be a lot better off with enough money and a lot of character to help them get off to a decent start. Along with your money, use your time to instill contagious faith, consistent integrity, practical poise, personal discipline, steadfast endurance, and inspirational courage into their hearts. If you attach these character traits to your financial investments, then you can watch them turn themselves into their very own ATM. Hard work, personal self-control, and good habits of stewardship are a far better inheritance than cash. The

Bible says in Proverbs 13:22, "A good man leaves an inheritance for his children's children." This inheritance may include money, but the most valuable bequest we can leave our grandchildren is the knowledge that whatever they possess belongs to God and is to be used for His glory.

Often, the motivation for passing some of our money to our grandchildren is driven by sophisticated tax-planning techniques such as income shifting and generation skipping. Though your accountant might recommend this, and your net worth might benefit from this, it might add up to a huge negative to your kids and grandkids. When it comes to this issue, we must be driven by love, not by tax laws and personal financial benefits. How much money we save on our taxes is irrelevant if it ultimately damages our grandchildren.

Spoiling Your Grandchildren's Parents

The better plan in most cases is to use your money while you're alive in such a way that it helps your *children* in their efforts to raise your *grandchildren.* Your adult children can benefit far more from your money when their children are young. This is normally the time when the cost of raising children is so high and parents have the least amount of income. It's a far more strategic financial plan than waiting until you die, your kids are around 60 years old, and they need your money the least. But you never want to give them so much that they couldn't make it without you. Nor do you want to give so much that it diminishes the respect the head of that home enjoys as the primary breadwinner. Obviously, there are cases where a child can't be trusted with any money from you. Perhaps she's got a gambling problem, a drug problem, or a habit of losing money in high-risk investments. In these cases it's best to get financial and spiritual counsel, and perhaps look into a trust account controlled by a third party.

After making sure your grandchildren's parents are okay with your offer of assistance, you can assist the family budget. You might want to use some of your money to help pay for tuition to a school that the parents have trouble affording, upgrade the vehicle in which they haul around your grandchildren, or take the family on an annual vacation.

This has been one of the most enjoyable splurges we have had with our children and grandchildren. Once a year, we plan a week of vacation with the whole clan. Of course, the more kids and grandchildren you have and the older they are, the more complicated this can become. But with some strategic planning and juggling of everyone's schedules, we have been able to work this out every year. And it has been an invaluable way to enhance the bonding among our children, their spouses, and the grandchildren. We don't go anywhere fancy or expensive, but that week of concentrated interaction is so valuable to the cohesiveness of our family. It has consistently been one of the best uses of our resources.

When we lavish gifts on our grandchildren with strings attached, the whole family gets tangled up.

Another way we've spent money well has been by taking our grandchildren with us to a Christian conference center we speak at every year. We had done this every year with our children too, and it played a huge role in helping our children galvanize their faith. But there came a summer when we realized our kids were grown to the point that they were occupied with studies, summer outreach projects, and jobs. There were no Kimmels left to take with us to camp. That changed when we became grandparents. We've been taking our grandchildren for several years now. They talk about it throughout the year, have the time of their lives when they are there, and their parents enjoy a nice week to themselves. It's clearly a chance to invest our resources in ways that pay dividends both now and for eternity.

There are lots of smart ways to positively spoil your grandchildren by spoiling their parents. You might want to temporarily supplement the parents' income while the dad is back in school or working to launch a business. If it helps the grandchildren's mother carry out her greater responsibility as a nurturer of your grandchildren, it could be money that ends up blessing your grandchildren all their lives. You may want to pay for some housecleaning so your grandchildren's mother has more time to spend with them. The point is that some of the best ways to positively spoil your grandchildren are to invest wisely in their parents. The main principle you want to use when investing money into their lives is to make sure it is always a "hand up" rather than a "handout." Time spent in prayer can help you tell which is which.

If you don't live close to your grandchildren, another great way to invest is to use your resources to buy more plane tickets and even rent an apartment near them for a few months so you might see them more often and invest valuable time into their hearts.

Fond Memories of a Spoiled Childhood

Spoiling and passing on money can be sticky situations if they aren't handled properly. But when we're careful to use them as a means to come alongside our children and grandchildren in positive ways, they can really enhance the bigger picture. Both of us were born into families with six children. Our dads had to work extremely hard to keep the lights on and put enough food on the table. My (Darcy's) grandparents owned a hotel in Ritzville, Washington. Every summer my siblings and I got to spend a couple of fun-filled weeks with them without our parents. It was two weeks of getting to run the big laundry machines, going to the one movie theater in town over and over again, eating candy bars out of the candy case, staying in our own hotel room, and playing the pinball machines up in the attic. Just before we went home, my grandmother would take my sister and me across the street to the beauty parlor to get us our annual perm. Our grandparents spoiled us for two weeks straight and lightened our parents' load in the process.

To this day, just about every time my siblings get together and reminisce about our childhoods, the Hotel Davis comes up. We each have vivid and special memories of those times with our grandparents.

One More Thing

This might be a good place to talk about building an honoring, noncompetitive relationship with your grandchildren's other grandparents. Your spoiling can create negative comparisons in the hearts of your grandchildren if you aren't sensitive to this. Just as you wouldn't want them one-upping you, you shouldn't do it to them. You should be encouraging a healthy relationship between them and the grandchildren you share.

A magnanimous attitude toward them adds to the peace within your children's home as well as builds a stronger base of love upon which your grandchildren can stand. That's why it is important to make every effort to build a mutually respectful and honoring relationship with your grandparenting counterparts.

They may be clones of you. Most likely they aren't even close. They may have a different kind of marriage, a different parenting style, and consequently, they may approach grandparenting differently. They may even be the polar opposites of you spiritually. You'll do everyone a favor if you avoid comparisons such as your opinion versus theirs, good ideas versus mediocre ones, right versus wrong. You should never do anything to upstage them—especially if you are in a position to spend more money or time with your grandchildren than they can. They are just as much your grandchildren's grandparents as you are, and they and your shared grandchildren desire a relationship with each other. You should not do anything to discourage your counterparts from having a wonderful relationship with the kids you mutually love.

Divine Spoiling

This book is fueled by a single theme: God's grace. We have said that we need to be grace-based grandparents. All that requires is a commitment to treat our grandchildren the way God treats us. God loves to lavish His blessings on us. The prophet Jeremiah put it this way: "Because of the LORD's great love we are not consumed, for his compassions never fail. They are new every morning; great is your faithfulness" (Lamentations 3:22-23).

God spoils us with His grace, but it is positive spoiling by a God who deeply loves us. Because He loves to spoil us, He knows how we feel when it comes to wanting to spoil our grandchildren. But as He lavishes His love on us, He only does the things that make us better people, that reflect well on His character, and that align with the agenda of His kingdom.

If we keep these same priorities in mind when it comes to the love we want to lavish on our grandchildren, they are more likely to prove to be assets to their greater lives.

And we become assets to their greater good.

Grace-based Spoiling

1. Less is more when it comes to gifting our grandchildren. Give gifts of time, character building, and prayer, rather than just money or things.
2. Never undermine the wishes or primary provision of the parents.
3. Whatever you do for your children or grandchildren should be more of a "hand up" than a "handout."
4. Never give a gift with strings attached.

5. When it comes to giving financial assistance, it makes a lot of sense to help your children in their efforts to raise your grandchildren.
6. Remember there is not a competition between you and the other set of grandparents. When it comes to the grandchildren, you are both on the same team.

For Further Thought and Discussion

Love must be sincere. Hate what is evil; cling to what is good. Be devoted to one another in brotherly love. Honor one another above yourselves. Never be lacking in zeal, but keep your spiritual fervor, serving the Lord. Be joyful in hope, patient in affliction, faithful in prayer. Share with God's people who are in need. Practice hospitality. (Romans 12:9-13)

1. How can spoiling cross the line from good to bad? Do you see ways you might be tempted to overdo it?
2. How does checking with the parents before lavishing a gift preserve your relationship with them?
3. What are some ways you can use your resources to come alongside your children and grandchildren without undermining their own responsibility to work and handle their money well?

Heavenly Father,
Thank You for the love You lavish on me. I want to be a giver of good things like You are. Please give me self-control and wisdom to know when and how to bless my children and grandchildren. I pray that my grandchildren will always have a spirit of gratefulness and generosity. Thank You for all You have blessed me with so that I may bless others. Amen.

14 Intervening versus Interfering

If wanting to spoil grandchildren is an occupational hazard of grandparenthood, then wanting to have a say in how they are being raised is even more so. Of all the areas that cause tension between grandparents and the parents of their grandchildren, the most problematic is grandparents' tendency to want to use their position and influence to play a decisive role in the day-to-day choices of their grandchildren.

This issue creates massive conflicts within families. It is the biggest joy stealer in family dynamics, the biggest creator of tension between brothers and sisters, one of the great contributors to marital breakups, and one of the worst things we could allow to happen to our grandchildren. The sad reality is that it is almost always caused by grandparents who don't respect boundaries.

That would be bad enough, but there's something even more tragic: The grandparents who are guilty of stepping over these boundaries are usually the last ones to admit they are the cause of tension. They won't admit it because they are certain they are justified. In their eyes, they believe what they are doing is solely in the best interests of their grandchildren. Only in rare cases is that reasoning actually true. In most cases the primary motivation of the grandparent is self-love rather than love for their grandchildren.

Here's what fuels this problem: There is absolutely no such thing as objectivity when it comes to assessing how our children are raising our grandchildren. Nor is there any such thing as objectivity in how grandparents view the innocence or guilt of their intervening actions.

Facing the Nasty Truth First

We need to get something out of the way at the outset of this discussion. Brace yourself; it's nasty: Some parents are high controllers. They micromanaged and nitpicked their children's behavior the entire time those kids were under their roof. They believe they have some moral right to slip over the lines that separate individual lives and make decisions for a child's life that aren't theirs to make. They traffic in guilt, gossip, hearsay, anger, manipulation, fear, and shame. They use love, money, compliments, blessings, privileges, intimidation, criticism, comparison, rejection, power, and abuse to foist their wills on their children. And because they are the parents, they think they have some God-given right to run the fine points of their children's lives indefinitely. High-controlling behavior ranges from mild to severe, but its impact is the same.

High-controlling parents are nightmares to children. They are the reason many kids can't wait to move out on their own. They are the cause of layers upon layers of lifelong personal problems in their children. They are also the complete antithesis of grace.

Often only one of the parents is actually a high controller. But both are guilty. The one is guilty for being a high controller. The other is guilty for not loving the children enough to make the spouse knock it off. And both can represent a severe loathing in the ongoing parent-child relationship.

I (Tim) wrote a book on this type of person, titled *The High Cost of High Control*.[1] Let's define what we mean by "high controller." High control is leveraging the strength of my personality or my position against my children's weaknesses in order to get them to meet my selfish agenda. This is toxic, vile, and destructive. There are a lot of reasons why people do this, but none of them justify it.

Unfortunately, it is commonplace in many, many homes.

High controllers are the last ones to admit they are doing anything wrong. That's because high controllers can always morally justify their high-control tendencies. High controllers create an intensely dysfunctional bond between themselves and their children in order to wield control over their kids all through their lives. They can even control their children from their graves.

The reason high-controlling parents wield so much power over their children goes back to those three driving inner needs we developed earlier in this book. Children desperately need a sense of security, significance, and sufficiency in their lives. The people they depend on most to receive this from are their parents. When we're doing our job correctly, we build into them a secure love, a significant purpose, and a sufficient hope.

A high-controlling parent puts a sick twist on these needs. In these types of homes, children only feel secure, significant, and sufficient if they fulfill all the superficial requirements this parent places on them in order to meet that parent's ego needs. Only then does the child gain the parent's approval. The problem is, approval can never be gained. Whatever the children do is never enough. They stay connected, desperately longing to know that who they are and what they do is acceptable to their parents. Unfortunately, it's a dysfunctional connection that never satisfies.

High-control parents make horrible grandparents. They take their toxic control to a new level.

That wasn't the nasty part. This is: If you are a high-control grandparent, most likely you're the last one to know. But should your children, son-in-law, daughter-in-law, grandchildren, or friends happen to love you enough to inform you that you are, you need to do one of two things: Get some serious help or move a long way away from your children and grandchildren. The benefits of your involvement in their lives never outweigh the damage you will continue to do. For once, love your kids and grandkids more than yourself. Beg for forgiveness, submit yourself to some intense counseling, get accountability in your life, and once and for all, set yourself and all the people in your family free . . . or move.

After decades of working with toxic high controllers, we know that if you are one, most likely you won't take either of those pieces of advice. And because of that, unfortunately, the rest of this chapter won't make much sense to you.

Respecting the Boundaries

Thank you for your indulgence. We felt it was necessary to deal with the most dangerous purveyors of interference in a grandchild's life so we could carry on a balanced discussion about how to stay within graceful boundaries when it comes to concerns about how our grandchildren are being raised. To begin our discussion, let's get some perspective.

Different generations bring different priorities and different values to their roles. If we're honest with ourselves, we'll admit that many of the priorities that ruled us when we were young and raising our own kids have gone through several adjustments as we've grown older. That's supposed to happen. It's called maturing.

On top of that, most of the children raising our grandchildren are married. That means that a person (let's say, your daughter's spouse) raised by different parents is in the equation. Most likely he was raised in a very different context. The priorities his parents embraced could be radically different from those you embraced when you were raising your daughter. One of the parents might have been brought up in the city while the other was being raised in the country. One might have gone to a Christian or other private school while the other was educated in a public school. One might have been raised in church while the other wasn't. There may be a mixture of races, nationalities, and cultures. That means the parents raising your grandchildren are very likely drawing from a composite set of values that may look extremely different from the ones you would use if it were left to you.

A Crash Course in Different Values

There are two types of values: *morally absolute* values and *personal* values. The Ten Commandments are a great example of some morally absolute values. Whether we like them or not, or agree with them or not, is immaterial. They are nonnegotiable laws that rule relationships. If you go by them, relationships develop more smoothly. If you don't, relationships head south. When our kids are going against one of them (e.g., committing adultery, lying, or stealing), they are obviously doing things that can bring great harm to themselves as well as our grandchildren. Our desire and need to speak up is legitimate.

Most family tension, however, isn't a result of speaking up because our children are breaking an absolute moral law, but rather the grandparents are giving morally absolute weight to their personal values.

Let's list some examples of personal values:

- not allowing babies to use pacifiers past infancy
- not permitting kids to suck their thumbs or develop attachments to blankets or stuffed animals for years into their childhood
- eating dinner together as a family
- not turning on the television on school nights
- letting kids eat dinner in front of the television set
- letting little children watch television every morning when they rise
- giving kids sweets before bedtime
- having everyone attend the same church
- letting teenage boys experiment with their hair
- having family devotions

- sending kids to Christian schools
- taking kids hunting or allowing them to carry a gun on a supervised hunt when they are 13 years old
- providing a personal car for a 16-year-old

These may or may not be our personal values, but they definitely are not in the league of moral absolutes. They might have guided you when you were raising your children, but they don't represent the only options. They are just some among many. Nor do they determine the character of a child who comes out of a family that embraces them. Families can raise great kids even if their children were attached to a blanket until they were seven, went to a different church when they were teenagers, were educated in public schools, and never had family devotions. In the same way parents can do an awful job of raising their kids even if they did everything on the list.

When it comes to interfering, there is a tendency to compare the way our kids are raising our grandkids to the way we would do it if the job fell to us. Here's where we make our mistake. When our children do something different from the way we would do it, we tend to place a moral value on that difference. Instead of thinking that our way is one way to do it and theirs is another, we assume that our way is right and their way is wrong. Unless we're dealing with a clearly stated, morally absolute precept in the Bible, we really have no grounds for giving moral weight to our personal values.

With these two huge issues behind us—toxic high control and differentiating between morally absolute values and personal values—let's mark the boundaries for giving input into our children's lives and getting involved in how they are raising our grandchildren.

When to Pray and When to Act

To what degree do we intervene in our children's and grandchildren's lives? There's a thin line between intervening and interfering.

Intervention becomes interference when it pushes our advice on our children when they aren't asking for it, when we criticize them in front of their children, or when we undermine their authority. Intervening can be done with words or with actions. Our intervention can empower them to be more self-sufficient and godly or cause them to remain in mediocrity and play the victim. Knowing when and how to intervene will make the difference in the outcome.

Our children are far more inclined to respond to our intervention when they are absolutely confident we aren't trying to take over their role or tell them how to raise their kids. The more we invest our hearts in theirs, and the more we bathe our relationship in grace, the more disposed our children will be to either ask our advice or be open to our help.

There are three levels of intervention we can employ in our children's lives:

- Level 1: We want to get involved.
- Level 2: We need to get involved.
- Level 3: We have to get involved.

Level 1 happens when see our children making decisions in the way they raise our grandchildren that are different from how we would do it. Usually these decisions entail a difference in personal values.

Level 2 happens when the parents may have a gaping hole in their parenting plan. Examples: They don't let their kids get enough sleep, they are at an impasse with a rebellious child, they are baffled about some medical problem with one of the grandkids, or they do things with their kids that can be morally harmful (such as taking them to R-rated movies when they are little, not taking them to church, or having them spend the weekend with them at a casino).

Level 3 happens when there is a clear and present danger for the grandchildren. Examples: the family is out of food, the family is living on the street, a parent is arrested, or a parent is violent or abusive.

Meddling

Before we review some basic guidelines on boundaries, let's take a quick and general swipe at the Level 1 types of intervention—when we *want* to intervene. This one happens just about every time some grandparents are around their kids and grandkids. They aren't doing things the way they think they should, and they want to let them know it. Usually, this has to do with unfairly moralizing a personal value. They're better off to stay quiet.

The standard example is in the way grandparents tend to view the issue of discipline. Usually, a grandparent thinks the kids fall short in this area of parenting. Every once in a while you hear them say they think their kids are too severe with their grandkids (an issue that might fall under Levels 2 or 3). But that is the exception. Normally it's their children's *inadequate* discipline that troubles grandparents.

Our ages and lifestyles often betray us. We might live in quiet, peaceful homes where things move at a sensible pace. We stop by to see the grandkids and notice two televisions on with no one watching them, the stereo blasting rap music, Mom and a teenager talking on their cell phones, the six-year-old racing through the house naked, and the other two grandchildren fighting over the Xbox. We think to ourselves, *The patients have taken over the asylum.* Actually what we're really observing is *a family*. It's just very different from the home environment we've grown accustomed to.

Because of our age, we aren't always as patient as we should be. We are more sensitive to turmoil, quick movements, and volume. If a child is making noise or doing things that annoy us, we think they should be immediately corrected. If the parents do nothing, we think they are pushovers when it comes to discipline. The actual problem might be that we are impatient and easily annoyed by children. The children might just be acting like *children.* And we're acting, well . . . old.

Sometimes our observations raise legitimate concerns—the grandkids are calling each other names, playing fast and loose with the furniture, or playing roughly with each other. The level of concern or the response of their parents might be quite different from ours. If we weigh in on this, it's natural for parents to think we are questioning the sincerity of their love and concern for their children. Many times, that's *exactly* what we are questioning. We're better off staying quiet.

When we think we need to point out our children's inadequacies in these areas, we create layers of tension. We do it even more when we pit our child against the other parent. When a grandparent says something like, "Son, I think your wife doesn't have a clue what she's doing when it comes to keeping your kids under control. You ought to do something about this," we've drawn unnecessary battle lines. When your son mentions this to your daughter-in-law, her relationship with you can only go one way—down.

> ***There's a thin line between intervening and interfering.***

We grew up around some families with strong-willed kids who were pluperfect brats. Their parents often appeared clueless or lame when it came to corralling them. But these kids didn't wonder if their parents loved them. And the good news is that most of these kids grew up to be fabulous adults. The point here is that just because you don't like the way things are going as you observe from the outside, doesn't mean your kids are necessarily doing an inadequate job. And even if they could step up their game, it doesn't mean we need to voice our concerns. Because when we do, we often build walls that ultimately end up coming between our grandchildren and us.

We wouldn't like it if we were trying to raise our kids and our parents criticized a lot of the personal values we embraced. We can't assume our children would react any differently in the same situation. We'd all do better if we prayed like mad regarding our concerns and kept our mouths shut.

Issues of Faith

One area where it is hard to stay silent is the area of our grandchildren's faith. The number one prayer of Christian grandparents is to see their grandchildren walking with God. When they aren't, our natural desire is to step in and convince their parents of their errors. This may be a Level 2 area where something *needs* to be done, but how we go about it determines whether or not we'll have any success.

The best way to get results on this issue is to first *pray faithfully* and *live godly lives* ourselves. We must not preach at the parents or nag them about going to church with us. If the parents don't want to attend church, ask permission to take the grandchildren. If nothing else, it will give them a few hours without the kids.

Some children use this faith issue as an opportunity to get back at their parents. They might feel that Jesus was shoved down their throats when they were young. They heard a lot of spiritual talk but didn't see the actions that should have backed it up. Perhaps you raised them in a legalistic church or maintained a strident spiritual environment at home. The lack of grace in these scenarios often turns kids cold to church when they are adults. It might be that this is the condition of just one of the parents' hearts, but the other feels the need to go along with it.

Your child or your in-law might feel that the disconnect between the faith and practice of their parents or their church leaders has created a lot of spiritual struggles for them now that they are adults. They may forbid you from taking their children to church or even talking to them about God. The best way to keep this spiritual battle going is to defy their wishes.

Their spiritual frustrations are real issues. They need to be dealt with. If we get defensive, trivialize their severity, or act like there's no truth to them, we're only validating what they feel. We need to take responsibility for the part we played in their alienation toward God, ask for their forgiveness, and assure them that no matter what, both we and

God will always love them. This is a time for us to let them do some serious venting about their disappointments with us (or the other set of parents), with the church they grew up in, or with God. It's a time for us to confess our sins of commission and omission and ultimately ask for their forgiveness.

Parents who raised their children in strident, legalistic environments often grow to realize just how graceless that kind of upbringing was for their kids. When we not only tell our kids that we see through the legalism but give them a track record of treating them with grace, we can actually see these situations turn around. But we can't expect their reluctance to expose their kids to our Christian faith to evaporate overnight just because we have an overdue and transparent discussion about it.

This is when we need to gracefully tell them that at our house we pray before meals and God holds a place of honor in our lives. We will not intentionally go against their directives, but our grandchildren won't be able to avoid seeing God in our hearts and our home. Continue to pray every day for their attitudes to soften. God will move in their hearts on His timetable. And He will honor our desire to be above reproach in our evangelistic efforts.

Crisis Intervention

Sometimes you have no choice but to intervene in the decisions that parents are making. Direct intervention may be necessary if your grandchildren are in peril as a result of their parents' being deadbeats, being in trouble with the law, or struggling with a drug or alcohol addiction. Often, these types of homes are hotbeds for abuse. God often calls grandparents into these scenarios to rescue the grandchildren. Some parents are in so much bondage to their behavioral problems that they can't get out without intervention. You might have to take over in the grandchildren's lives so the parents can get some professional help or until a time when they can step back up to their parenting responsibilities.

You can do this for the grandchildren without enabling your children to stay in their weakened state. When you intervene, you need to be sure the arrangement is in the best interests of all three generations involved. Sometimes you're the only hope these children have. But before you step in, think and pray long and hard about what you are going to do. Run your options by wise people who may have some experience in these types of family crises.

Matthew 18:15-17 provides some guidelines for intervening with a gracious but tough love as you strive to win a child back to righteousness and responsibility. "If your brother sins against you, go and show him his fault, just between the two of you. If he listens to you, you have won your brother over. But if he will not listen, take one or two others along, so that 'every matter may be established by the testimony of two or three witnesses.' If he refuses to listen to them, tell it to the church; and if he refuses to listen even to the church, treat him as you would a pagan or a tax collector."

In Jesus' day, *pagans* referred to people who not only embraced a belief system antithetical to the Jewish faith but also people who were often antagonistic to it. Tax collectors were most often members of the Jewish faith who worked for the Roman government. Because of the authority that went with their jobs, they were inclined to use their positions to exploit their fellow Jews. This caused them to be considered sellouts to the Romans. Sometimes the parents of our grandchildren fall into similar categories. They are either hostile to our faith, or they embrace our faith but compromise on its precepts for their own convenience. That's why we need to have other people to turn to for objective opinions about dealing with them.

Be proactive, and do your best to come up with a plan that will be the most beneficial to your grandchildren while leaving your sanity intact.

When it comes to childcare and financial arrangements, make sure the parameters are spelled out up front. Temporary crises have a bad habit of becoming permanent arrangements if we don't put a calendar on them. When you let your kids know what you're going to do for them, it's best to say, "This is what works for me . . ." Say it over and over again for each objection they throw at you until they understand what you are and aren't able to do.

As is the case when your grandchildren come to live with you on a long-term basis, you might want to talk with an attorney and see if there is a way you might—at least temporarily—get more legal control over your grandchildren's daily lives. You need to at least be able to make decisions regarding their schooling and have some authority regarding their medical care.

Taking an Honest Look at Ourselves

We need to acknowledge a painful truth here. If you were in the habit of rescuing your children when they were growing up in your home, they may have grown so accustomed to it that they expect you to continue to rescue them from foolish choices they are still making. Hopefully you realize that somewhere along the line they need to grow up and face the music. Now's as good a time as any, but it may still require that you at least make sure the grandchildren do not fall through the cracks.

We have seen enabling grandparents do irreparable harm to both their children and grandchildren by refusing to let their kids face the consequences of their poor choices. It is self-love when we do this. It pains us so much to see them suffer the consequences of their folly that we either cushion their fall or consistently bail them out of their foolishness. In doing this, we only set them up to do something worse. Unfortunately, when we enable our children to the point that our innocent grandchildren are harmed, we bear a great deal of the blame.

Helping Out in Special Circumstances

Rescuing your grandchildren from an abusive or neglectful home is not the only reason grandparents may need to intervene. One of the heartbreaking things that sometimes happens in families is having a child born with a mental, physical, or developmental problem demanding a huge amount of care. Often this special child requires more care than the parents can provide on their own. This is when we can come into the picture as a wonderful and indispensable part of the solution. Our children might be reluctant to accept our help, but ultimately, as we form a coalition, we can be used by God to bring not just help but hope to these folks who have been asked by God to lovingly raise this special child. God gives grandparents an uncanny ability to see these children as incredible gifts from Him and to treat them in a way that draws the best out of them.

Refereeing and Restoring

As grandparents, loving our grandchildren is easy; getting along with their parents is not always so easy. They no longer have "cute" going for them. Any family, whether it is functional or dysfunctional, is going to encounter the sticky situation of conflict within the ranks. It might be between individuals in different families, within your family network, or entire families pitted against each other.

Given that conflict is inevitable, we can choose only how we'll deal with it. Family conflict can result from acts of commission as well as acts of omission. Perhaps in-laws have become outlaws. Maybe harsh words have been spoken back and forth between different spouses without resolution. Maybe there is a blatant display of favoritism either on the part of a grandparent for a grandchild or for a particular set of parents. Perhaps there is a fundamental disagreement about parenting philosophy or theology. Maybe someone's birthday was overlooked or two members of the generations just don't get along. It falls to us, the senior statespersons in our families, to step up and do what we can to help resolve these conflicts.

Realizing that we are very capable of making mistakes, hurting someone's feelings, or being too opinionated and overbearing, we must be willing to admit our wrongs, seek forgiveness from all parties, and change our ways. When we are sure we have done all we can to obtain a solution, then we need to continue to speak the truth in love and call our children or grandchildren to a biblical standard of relationships. It is then up to them to respond in a spirit of humility and reconciliation. In the meantime, we continue to love them and do our best to be at peace with them. Truth, spoken in love in an atmosphere of forgiveness, gives grace a chance to work in people's hearts over time.

When we do have conflict, we need to use grace to guide us through to resolution.

The Grace-Based Rules for Resolving Conflict[2]

Focus on:	*Rather than:*
Facts	Assumptions
Single Issues	Many Issues
The Problem	The Person
Behavior	Character
Specifics	Generalizations
Unity	Victory

Jingle Bells, Christmas Smells

A lot of family conflict occurs when expectations are unmet and people get their feelings hurt. Much of this can be eliminated by dealing with some of the more common "danger zones." One of them has to do with how and where large family gatherings will take place. This especially becomes an issue when people can't agree on what their Thanksgiving and Christmas traditions will look like as the kids get married and start having children of their own.

We have seen these two holidays—celebrations that are supposed to represent the high-water mark of all that we value and believe—become the most dreaded times on a family calendar simply because of grandparents who insisted on maintaining past traditions at the expense of their kids' blossoming traditions. Some grandparents insist that the kids spend Thanksgiving and Christmas with them "just like when you were growing up." There are some extended families that are okay with this, but even if they aren't, they don't feel they could go another direction without paying a price. Some grandparents manipulate the kids into bringing the grandkids by for Christmas by refusing to go to their children's homes.

It's not surprising that the busiest month for therapists is January. People who make their living helping people process their frustrations know that Christmas is great for business.

Because we've seen how much joy can be lost and damage done, we have taken steps from the beginning to make sure each family member is free to do what they want during the holidays. When our children get married, we encourage them to establish their own traditions. We let them know when we are doing our celebrating and invite them to join us if it fits into their plans. They know they have the option to not come at all, show up when they're done with their other plans, or bring their in-laws along. If they'd rather we join them at their home, we do our best to comply with their wishes.

As grandparents, we need to be flexible and willing to recraft our traditions and celebrations to grow with our ever-changing family. This will eventually include our grandchildren's boyfriends and girlfriends and, if we live long enough, their spouses and children.

We should never be guilty of loving our traditions more than we love our kids. We had our chance to develop sweet Thanksgiving and Christmas traditions for our children. It's not our turn anymore. This is where that asset of *maturity* comes in handy.

Law & Order

Sometimes there are things that go on in families that go beyond conflict. They are crimes. How we respond in these situations not only determines if there can ultimately be healing within the family, but whether or not we can maintain an ongoing relationship with all parties involved.

We recently were third-party observers to a set of grandparents' taking a horrible problem and making it is almost unrecoverable. In a nutshell, a teenage grandson from one of their children's families committed a serious crime against a seven-year-old granddaughter in another one of their children's families. The police were called. There was an incredible amount of pain going back and forth between the siblings and spouses. The offender's parents were embarrassed, ashamed, and deeply sorry for what their teenage child did. The victim's parents were hurt and confused but desired to get through it with their love for this other couple and their teenage child intact. The sticky point had to do with the pressing of charges. A crime had been committed. One of the things that victims need in order to heal is a confidence that justice has been carried out on the people who harmed them. The little girl's parents wanted to make sure they did everything they were supposed to do to protect, defend, and empower their child to heal.

Along came Grandma. Because their family held a high position in their community, she was more concerned with the image of the family. She felt the legalities surrounding this crime could tarnish that image. The culprit's parents started to side with the grandmother, realizing this would make life much easier for their teenager. They agreed with the grandmother that this was better handled in-house.

But that put the parents of the victim in a fragile position. They felt they were being asked to choose between the family image and doing due diligence for their child who had been horribly violated.

The grandfather was in the best position to bring healing to this situation. He was the patriarch. He was respected. He was the one his children trusted to always do the right thing.

But he chose silence.

He did not intervene. He took the attitude that if he did nothing, it would eventually go away.

It hasn't gone away. It's just gotten worse. Image control and the silence of a patriarch have split a family in half. When it comes to conflict within a family, Robert Lewis's advice in his book *Raising a Modern-Day Knight* carries the day. He outlines the qualities of a true man, but they apply even more to the patriarch of the family.

- First, we must reject passivity as an option.
- Second, we must take responsibility. This means doing the right thing—not the comfortable thing—even though it will involve pain.
- Third, we must lead courageously. Courageous leaders lead from the front when a crisis occurs.
- Finally, we should trust God for a greater outcome.[3]

When we have to referee or intervene in a conflict between family members, there's always a price to pay. We might be rejected by one of the members. But if we do nothing, we could end up being rejected by everyone. In any conflict, even those that shock us, the goal is healing that runs deep enough to touch all hearts involved and a holiness that won't quit.

Helping with a Special-Needs Grandchild

1. Take your disappointment and pain to God. All children are gifts from God, and when you realize that although they may be different they are not less, your attitude and actions toward the special child and her parents will reflect that perspective. God will use your perspective to help shape your children's attitude toward their child and all the added responsibility she brings. No matter what challenges

your grandchild is dealing with, she is aware of how she is viewed. Your celebration of her as a special creation will help shape her view of herself.

2. Find out all you can about the challenges your special grandchild and her parents will face. In doing so, you'll become aware of her unique needs and ways you can come alongside her parents with help and encouragement. You may be able to lend an occasional hand in their home, give the parents some time off, be an extra set of wheels to run the other children to their activities, provide a special piece of equipment for the special child's care, or pay for a camp experience, special schooling, or even gift certificates for dinner for her parents every once in a while.

3. Have realistic expectations of what this grandchild can and cannot do. These will help you tailor your interaction with her and plan activities at which she can succeed and have fun. It will also help you choose appropriate gifts for her birthdays and Christmas.

4. Keep a positive, hopeful demeanor around the family of this special-needs child. Let them vent their frustrations and share their special joys. And share the hope you have from your heart of faith.

5. Though this grandchild may take more of your time or consideration, make sure your other grandchildren also get special times with you.

Nitty-Gritty Grandparenting

Grandparenting isn't always fun and games. But the fun can ultimately happen if we respond properly to the difficult parts of the grandparenting picture. We can't coast through these valuable years of our lives. God not only wants to do something for us, He wants to do something in us, and to us, and through us. And when we're willing to humble ourselves and take our cues from Him, He puts us in a position where He can use us in ways that will last forever. Now *that* sounds like fun!

For Further Thought and Discussion

> As God's chosen people, holy and dearly loved, clothe yourselves with compassion, kindness, humility, gentleness and patience. Bear with each other and forgive whatever grievances you may have against one another. Forgive as the Lord forgave you. And over all these virtues put on love, which binds them all together in perfect unity. Let the peace of Christ rule in your hearts, since as members of one body you were called to peace. And be thankful. (Colossians 3:12-15)

1. What are some circumstances that you feel would justify your intervention in your grandchildren's lives? What would you do first to make sure an intended action is the best approach?
2. Are there certain "hot spots" that seem to cause conflict in your family? What are some ways you can minimize these "hot spots" and allow the peace of Christ to rule in everyone's heart?
3. Is there something going on in your family that is undermining the unity and peace among your children and grandchildren? Realizing that you only have control of your own actions and attitudes, what can you do to reject passivity, take responsibility, lead courageously, and trust God for a greater good?

Heavenly Father,

Thank You that I can come to You for wisdom as I work to develop a plan for these challenging times. I need Your power and grace to be able to clothe myself with compassion, kindness, humility, gentleness, and patience. Help me to always be part of the solution rather than the problem. Please be with my grandchildren. Protect them from the effects of the shortcomings of others. I pray that I can represent an anchor for them in the midst of difficult situations. Most of all, I pray they will know Your love and peace in their lives. Amen.

15 Babysitting

Years ago, when we mentioned to a couple of our friends that we were going to be grandparents, these friends—who had already been inducted into this sacred club—told us it was going to be the best thing that ever happened to us. We had a hard time believing it could be that good—especially since we have had some absolutely wonderful life experiences, not the least of which are the four children God has blessed us with. But then the day came when we held our daughter's daughter in our arms, all seven pounds of her, just minutes after she was born.

It was love at first sight, and we've been smitten ever since. And along with our other grandparenting friends, we believe this is about as good as it gets. It's all the joy of parenting and less of the work. This is more like being able to lick the icing off the cake. Deuteronomy 14:2 expresses this same kind of love that God has for His children: "You are a people holy to the LORD your God. Out of all the peoples on the face of the earth, the LORD has chosen you to be his treasured possession." Because grandparents immediately fall under the spell of their grandchildren, they're willing to go to great lengths to accommodate and protect them.

We want to look at the best ways to accommodate and protect our grandchildren when they are in our care. Making the most of these opportunities can empower us to take the natural influence we have in their lives and turn it into something extraordinary. Our attention to the details not only communicates a deliberate love to our grandchildren, but also an amazing grace to their parents. There are some practical ways we can do this.

Keeping Them Safe

One way to protect our grandkids is by retrofitting our surroundings to make them safer. Sometimes it's not a bridge over troubled water but a fence *around* troubled water that is the issue. We live in Arizona. Because of the heat, backyard swimming pools are as standard a feature of homes in our neighborhood as are a garage and a kitchen. But a pool can be a death trap for little children. Arizona leads the nation in childhood drownings. When we hear the tragic news that another child has drowned, it isn't unusual to learn the child was at her grandparents' or relatives' house. When our children moved into their late teen and young-adult years, we took down the fence around our swimming pool. But once we knew we would have grandchildren in our lives, we immediately had another one installed. Regardless of the cost, a childproof pool fence is something you can't afford to omit from the safety features of your house. We've also got to keep medicines, cleaning solutions, insecticides, and scissors in cabinets and drawers that cannot be accessed by children.

The day you granddads put child-safety latches on all your cabinets and drawers may be one of the most miserable days you spend with a screw shooter, but it will be one of the best things you'll do for your younger grandkids.

It's also best to cover all electrical outlets with safety caps. Keep in mind, however, that it is hard to toddler-proof your house. Your young grandchild might appear to be playing very well by himself, and then you check on him only to find he's started a nice collection of these electrical safety caps from around the house. Even so, we've got to do our best to protect them.

If you have a set of stairs in your house as we do, you need to have sturdy safety gates at the top and the bottom. It may be a bother for you to open and close them every time you need to use the stairs, but it may well save your grandchild from breaking his neck. When our grandchildren were young and too small to manage the stairs, we had gates that we could put up when they came over and easily take down when they left. They are in storage now, ready for each new addition to our extended family photo.

And we've got to take every safety precaution when it comes to transporting them. Most states have gotten very specific and picky about car seats. We all need to know the proper way to restrain a child in his car seat as well as how to secure the seat in the car. When we were kids, the only restraint we had in the car was Granddad's arm coming across our chests when he slammed on the brakes. Today, that simply won't do.

Grandparents are the cheapest game on the block.

Obviously, firearms should be out of sight, out of reach, locked down, and inaccessible to children. This is especially true with older grandchildren who are more likely to get into closets and garages and discover things like this.

As much as you love that hot cup of coffee or tea, it has no place in your hand when you're holding one of your smaller grandchildren. And we have to be careful what kinds of plants we have around the house and where we keep them. Ditto on the kinds of pets we have and where we keep them. Dogs and cats that have staked their claims to our houses are notorious for feeling threatened when some grandchild starts moving around their territory. Until the grandkids are big enough to easily assume the alpha position in the presence of a pet, it's best if we keep the dog or cat in a pen, a room, the basement, or the garage. It they threaten or succeed in attacking the grandkids, it's probably time to find those pets a different home. If you want to know more on these kinds of safety issues, most maternity wards and pediatricians' offices have free booklets that will give you exhaustive lists of how you can make your house a safe place for your grandchildren.

Taking Care of Business

One of the standard responsibilities that grandparents take on in their grandchildren's lives is babysitting. We have a natural bond and a vested interest in their care. Our children are most familiar with our parenting skills, and they also know we are one babysitter who cares for their children as much as they do. Plus, the price is right. Grandparents are the cheapest game on the block.

When caring for grandchildren, it goes without saying that we should know their schedules, their individual needs, and the special ways our grandchildren like things to happen. For the younger grandchild, it is very helpful to have your children actually write out the grandchild's schedule and eating suggestions. Children are constantly growing and changing, and their needs, even from visit to visit, can change dramatically. One of our granddaughters has an allergy to certain foods, and it is very helpful to know what specific food items she can and cannot have. With that knowledge, we can make sure we have things she can eat and enjoy when she is at our house.

The older grandkids may have to practice a musical instrument at a certain time each day. If they are at our home on a regular basis or we are watching them for a prolonged period of time, we need to help them keep these practices consistent. The same thing goes for homework. Don't be surprised if they wear the ear buds to their iPods and stop every 15 minutes to text message a friend on their cell phones. Homework has become more complex since most of us were doing it.

Celebrating Their Uniqueness

Parents might explain some little quirk the child has about eating, or toys, or travel, or bedtime. We should pay close attention to these and work to accommodate them. Remember, quirks aren't wrong; they're just different. Some children come attached to blankets or plush toys. These are very special parts of their lives. It's best if we treat these items like they were appendages of our grandchildren. Disparaging the things that bring them so much comfort is the same as disparaging them.

Teenagers can show up adorned with numerous and oddly located piercings. Don't worry about them. They're nothing. The grandchildren are everything. It's silly to shame or embarrass them over things that in the long run have little or no bearing on how that grandchild is going to turn out. Let's not sacrifice our permanent spiritual impact on the altar of our immediate narrow-minded hang-ups. The best thing we can do is ignore the nonessentials and concentrate on what ultimately matters: that our grandchildren develop a secure love for Jesus, a significant purpose through Jesus, and a sufficient hope in Jesus.

We also need to show respect and reverence for some of their rituals. I heard a grandfather lamenting that his eight-year-old granddaughter was used to having whoever was putting her to bed shut out the light, leave, but come back in about five minutes, turn on the overhead light, and check to make sure she was all right. For some reason, this gave her a sense of security. Once she had that check-in, she would fall asleep. Her grandfather felt it was a stupid ritual, and it annoyed him that his children expected him to do it. This grandfather would probably be a lot more of an asset to his eight-year-old granddaughter if he'd just take a sip of grace, get over his annoyance, and check on his granddaughter the way the girl's parents asked him to.

Making Grandkids Mind Without Losing Yours

One of the big issues you have to deal with when you babysit your grandchildren is what to do when they disobey. This issue needs to be discussed and agreed upon with the parents as soon as the child starts to demonstrate he has a mind of his own. And the way you discipline him will have to be modified as he gets older. Corporal discipline is best left to the grandchild's parents. We grandparents have a special relationship with our grandchildren that we need to protect.

Leaving the serious discipline up to the parents becomes a little more difficult if we are the primary caregivers. There are many families where both parents work, and the grandparents serve as day care providers. Even if this is your arrangement, it's still best to see if you can work with the child's parents to come up with effective discipline that does not require you to be the heavy or pull out the heavy artillery. This may require you to be creative and consistent with noncorporal punishment when a child disobeys.

Don't put him in a stupor by giving him his candy fix for the week.

Some alternative forms of discipline include time-outs (set the timer), no TV, loss of a privilege, no treat after a meal, a chore or extra responsibility, and an eye-to-eye talk with Grandma or Grandpa. Once the discipline has been carried out, it is important to put the child on your lap or your arm around an older one and reassure the child that Nana and Papa are disciplining him because they love him and don't want him to grow up to be a bad person. If there is no additional punishment needed, and this is not a recurring infraction, this correction can be put behind her and does not have to be brought up when her parents pick her up. This communicates to the child that she has a clean slate. The child is much more likely to obey next time.

Be an Ally to Their Parents

Babysitting your grandchildren is not an opportunity to override any quirky parenting styles you don't agree with. If a child isn't allowed to watch television or a certain program at his house, unless you get special permission, he should not be watching it at your house. You might like your weekly dose of World Wrestling Entertainment *SmackDown* but if your grandson's parents say no, grace as well as common sense insist we should comply.

If his parents are trying to limit his sugar intake, don't put him into a stupor by giving him his candy fix for the week. If you still have your own children at home, make sure everyone is on the same page when it comes to protecting the young ones from inappropriate information (via movies, music, and friends who stop by). Actually it has been really good for our youngest child to have to defer to his nieces since he never had a baby brother or sister. Over the years, it has been fun seeing him interact with these new kids on the block and take on a protective responsibility for them.

You may differ from your children in the way you view life and freedoms. They may ask you not to drink, smoke, swear, or gamble around their children or expose them to any of your friends who do—even if their child is an older teenager. That doesn't sound unreasonable to us. If your friends have a problem with that, you might want to make new friends. If you have a problem with it, you might want to examine your definition of love again. It's the commitment of your will to your grandchildren's needs and best interests, regardless of the cost.

First Aid and CPR

When it comes to medical safety, we each need to keep a well-supplied first-aid kit at home, as well as current medical releases signed by our children and phone numbers for emergency services and the poison center. Always have a phone number where a parent can be reached in case of an emergency.

You may be surprised at how much undivided attention it takes to keep track of grandchildren—especially the little ones. Those little squirts can cover a lot of territory in a short amount of time. Because of this, limit your phone calls and TV time and even keep the door cracked open when using the bathroom. It is amazing how much trouble grandchildren can get into when unsupervised for just a few moments. It's also amazing how much danger they can get themselves into in the same amount of time.

You might need to take a refresher course on cardiopulmonary resuscitation (CPR). Infant CPR is different, so it wouldn't hurt to get some special instructions on that too. Don't place unnecessary temptation in front of your older grandchildren by having prescription drugs or alcohol out in plain sight.

Keeping Their Parents in First Position

This might be surprising, but it is not uncommon for jealousy to develop in your children's hearts toward you when it comes to caring for their children. The grandchildren might behave better for you than they do for their parents. You might have gotten to witness several "firsts" that their mother or father wished they had been there to see. They might be processing some guilt because they are both working or they went through a divorce. The responsibility for gracious behavior starts at the top. We need to refrain from saying things like, "He never does that when I take care of him." We should want our time with their children to enhance rather than undermine their relationship with their parents.

Setting Boundaries for Yourself

When it comes to babysitting the grandchildren, sometimes you have to tell your children no. It might stem from a conflict in your schedule, a lack of energy, or maybe you feel you are being taken advantage of. In these situations, clear, grace-filled communication is the key. Let them know as far in advance as possible when you have to cancel or are not going to be available.

It might be necessary to have a heart-to-heart with your children, out of earshot of your grandchildren, to let them know that as much as you love helping them with their children, you must also fulfill your other commitments to your spouse, your other children, your friends, and so forth. You may need to tell them how often and how long you are available to babysit and then let them decide how they want to schedule that time.

Using Time Wisely

When our grandchildren come to our home, it is important to plan ways to occupy them and have fun together. We're not implying you must have some wonderful and entertaining program scheduled each time they are with you. But it makes sense to plan things to do, so they will look forward to coming to your house. Often they just like hanging out with us. They may even find simple chores like splitting logs or reshingling the roof a ton of fun!

We're just kidding; those log-splitting machines can be dangerous. The point is, we need to put some forethought into what we're going to do when the grandchildren are coming over. When children are smaller, they adore just being with their grandmother and grandfather, regardless of what we're doing. They may want to tag along with us on errands or go with us to visit friends. But when we do this, we've got to remember that we're watching our grandchildren first, running errands and visiting with friends second. As we mentioned earlier, we must always use a properly installed car seat to transport a younger child and insist that everyone else wear a seat belt.

Mi Casa Es Su Casa

One way to communicate that our home has a special place for each grandchild is to set aside parts of it that are completely for them. If they stay over often, they might have a room of their own and a bed they are used to. It's smart to have a drawer or shelf that contains their favorite stuff (books, toys, art supplies, or movies). For our younger grandchildren, we have a drawer in the kitchen that holds some of their favorite toys. When we know they are coming over, it is fun to have a few new surprises in it for them to play with.

Our grandchildren need to be made to feel very much at home and sure of their space. Setting aside drawers, shelves, baskets, and closets that are just for them gives them a great sense of security, significance, and sufficiency. Younger children find connection in reading some of the same stories over and over again. I (Tim) can recite *Goodnight Moon* from memory. I've spent many hours reading Bible stories to our grandchildren. And for years when they were young, they couldn't leave to go home until I read them their favorite, *Bats at the Beach*.

If your grandchildren are staying with you for an entire day or perhaps a prolonged period of time, it's a good idea to have a special activity planned for those days. It gives them something to look forward to. As an example, when our grandkids were young, we made stick horses one day. They provided years of great rides for them.

Older grandchildren need to know what they have access to in your house. Let them have their own file on your computer, their own movies they can watch at their discretion, maybe an ongoing project in the garage or at the sewing machine, and definitely freedom to get a snack when the "hungries" hit.

And it's great to have a memory chest where we keep special memorabilia that remind them of great times we had together in the past (like programs, tickets, photos, seashells, and those goofy Mickey Mouse ears). Planning and preparation are keys to maximizing the time we spend with our grandchildren.

Keeping the Bigger Picture in Focus

As we're watching over our grandchildren, we need to keep our bigger roles in mind. It's easy to get so preoccupied with babysitting or entertaining them that we forget we are supposed to be giving them a sense of blessing that can put their hearts at ease, leaving them a legacy they can take into eternity, carrying a torch of grace and righteousness to light their way, and setting a standard for them to emulate. These informal times might look like babysitting to some people, but to grandparents they are opportunities to build into young lives the kind of love, mercy, and grace that can sustain them long after we are gone.

For Further Thought and Discussion

I lift up my eyes to the hills—
    where does my help come from?
My help comes from the LORD,
    the Maker of heaven and earth.

He will not let your foot slip—
    he who watches over you will not slumber. . . .

The LORD will keep you from all harm—
he will watch over your life;
the LORD will watch over your coming and going
both now and forevermore. (Psalm 121:1-3, 7-8)

1. In what practical ways have you made your home safer and more inviting for your grandchildren? Why do you think your home is a place that your grandchildren want to visit, or if they live with you, how have you made it home for them?
2. Are there any rules that your children have for your grandchildren that require you to adjust how you would handle the same issue? How are you doing at honoring their wishes?
3. What are some ways you can help care for your grandchildren but not feel taken advantage of? Have you effectively established this balance with your children? If not, how can you?

Heavenly Father,
Thank You for the safe haven You provide for our hearts.
I pray that my home will always be a place of safety, comfort,
and encouragement for my grandchildren. Help me as I seek
to honor my children's standards and enfold my grandchildren
deeper into my heart. Thank You for the opportunity to influence
these wonderful young people for Your kingdom. Please keep
them from harm, and help them always know that
You are watching over them. Amen.

16 Teenage Grandchildren

The title of this chapter may open a can of worms for some grandparents. Their reaction might come from the scars they still carry from the time they were teenagers. It also might have a close connection to some unfortunate things they had to endure when they were raising their own teenagers. The thought that they have to go round three over and over through the lives of each of their teenage grandchildren makes them wonder if their meds are up for the challenge.

But there are others of you who look at the title of this chapter and just smile. You are in the middle of one of the greatest relationships with your teenage grandson or granddaughter, and you wish you could make it stay just like it is indefinitely. Some of the greatest joys of a grandfather's life are the hours spent sitting in a boat next to his grandson talking about life and trying to catch some fish, or walking side by side with him around a golf course helping him trim a few strokes off his game. I (Tim) have hunted over the years with families where three generations are out in the woods together. Some of these grandfathers have long since stopped hearing the call of the wild. Their health and stamina aren't close to what they used to be. If it were just them, they'd sleep in and enjoy their memories. But they get up in the middle of the night and don their equipment for no other reason than to spend some great time hunting with their sons, daughters, grandsons, and granddaughters.

We are in the generation that should be the most patient with teenagers. We've been teenagers, and we've raised some. Though each generation of teenagers tries to play "Can you top this?" they are all struggling with the same pressures. As we mentioned earlier, many teenagers spend most of their time just trying to keep from being embarrassed. Overly self-conscious and unsure of themselves, they desperately need as many people as possible who love them unconditionally and believe in them relentlessly.

A Collision of Virtues

If you want to understand what it's like to be a teenager, find a globe of the world, spin it to where you can see the southern point of South America, and just stare at those waters right below it. There in that Strait of Magellan between those two great oceans—the Atlantic and the Pacific—waters churn, currents collide, and the seas are almost always in a state of turmoil. It's like the perfect storm all the time.

The thing that determined how easily a crew could endure their transfer through that hellish stretch of water was the unflappable confidence that they could read on their captain's face.

When our teenage grandchildren are navigating the turbulent waters between childhood and adulthood, they can weather this corridor of their lives much better when they look at the face of their grandfather or grandmother and see the calm, confident eyes of someone who's been there, has guided others through it, and knows how to get safely through to the other side. At this time in their lives, when virtues and values are colliding, teens need someone they can trust who believes in them.

Stumbling Blocks

We've learned that we have four roles as grandparents. We are to be giving an ongoing blessing to our grandchildren. We are to be leaving them a legacy they can guide their lives with after we are gone. We are to carry a torch for righteousness and grace to illuminate their path as they navigate the murky fog and dark shadows of their culture. We are to set a standard they can use as a benchmark for the challenges they face every day. Grandparenting our teenage grandchildren provides the perfect opportunity to play each one of these roles every time we see them. But that third role, of bearing a torch, is the one they need the most during this time in their lives. That's why, regardless of what we feel about this generation of teenagers, they need us now more than ever.

Unfortunately, the last thing a lot of grandparents want to do is willingly spend time with their teenage grandchildren. Perhaps it's because they find them annoying. And sometimes it's a two-way street; a lot of teenage grandchildren aren't that crazy about logging time with their grandparents either. The simple fact that we are many years older causes them to view us as irrelevant and out of touch with what they are interested in or going through.

Truth be told, sometimes we act in ways that reinforce this opinion. We do things that automatically shut off the ability to be that torchbearer who can benefit teen grandkids. In fact, we can think of *three mistakes* grandparents are notorious for making when it comes to helping their grandchildren process the unique features of their teenage lives. For over three decades we have been working with families where these three stumbling blocks undermine the ability to teach grandchildren discernment and how to make good choices.

Jesus weighed in on this in Matthew 18:5-7: "Whoever welcomes a little child like this in my name welcomes me. But if anyone causes one of these little ones who believe in me to sin, it would be better for him to have a large millstone hung around his neck and to be drowned in the depths of the sea. Woe to the world because of the things that cause people to sin!" As grandparents bearing a torch for this generation of teenagers, we need to avoid these damaging mistakes.

Mistake #1: Putting Them Down

The first mistake we make is putting them down. It's not so much that we put them down personally, but we put down the age group and culture they represent.

We've got to understand that when we put down their culture, we condemn *them* in the process. "How?" you might ask. Let us list some examples: We insult their music, the volume of their music, and the musicians who present their music. We make fun of their styles and fashion, their hair, and how they present themselves. We criticize their groups of friends and the prevailing thinking that comes from their generation. And we trivialize their interests—whether it's entertainment, technology, or a heavy preoccupation with their friends.

We are the generation that should be the most patient with teenagers.

This is ironic coming from *our* generation. Because if we are even minimal students of history, we of all people should know that for the second half of the past century, teenagers made some radical choices to draw distinctions between themselves and the adults around them. A lot of us who are now grandparents were value-programmed in the most bizarre decade of the last century: the 1960s. If anybody should understand the extreme nature of youth, we should. In fact, I think we could teach this present generation a thing or two about looking strange and acting weird.

When we put down our teenage grandchildren, we cause several things to happen, none of which are good. One thing we do is distance ourselves from them. We reinforce their opinion that we have no idea where they're coming from and that we are unwilling to do anything about it. They view us as irrelevant and unreliable when it comes to helping them sort out their world.

Another negative consequence is that we put them on the defensive regarding who they and their culture are. This may prompt them to embrace these things we put down even more just to drive home a point. They turn up their music, turn down their respect, and turn off their attention.

Which brings up the third reason that putting them down works against our ability to be torchbearers for them. Putting them down is exactly the opposite way Jesus would deal with their unique features and their culture. Listen to how Jesus engaged our culture: "For God did not send his Son into the world to condemn (put down) the world, but to save the world through him" (John 3:17, parenthesis added). No doubt Jesus was disturbed by things He saw in people's lives as He moved about at street level. But their problems weren't the focus of His attention. Instead, He zoomed in on their need for redemption. We might be disturbed by what we see or hear in our grandchildren's lives, but it is not our job to condemn them. Rather we are to hold our light high and show them the way through it all.

They'll see a torch of righteousness that is always lit.

What is interesting about that verse we just looked at is where it is located in the Bible. It follows one of the most quoted verses in the entire Bible, John 3:16: "For God so loved the world, that He gave His only begotten Son, that whoever believes in Him shall not perish, but have eternal life" (NASB). God loved us all so much that He sent His Son, not to put us down, but to help us up and ultimately give us eternal life. Earlier in the opening remarks of the Gospel of John, the writer is introducing Jesus to us. He says, "In him was life, and that life was the light of men. The light shines in the darkness, but the darkness has not understood it" (1:4-5). Then, after John makes some parenthetical remarks, he comes back to this theme and says, "Yet to all who received him, to those who believed in his name, he gave the right to become children of God" (1:12). Our grandchildren may not yet comprehend Jesus as the light of the world, but we can play a strategic role in helping that happen by holding up a light without putting them down. When we resist being known as an ongoing critic of their music, their styles, and their preoccupations, we give them a clear look at the heart of God.

Mistake #2: Ignoring Them

Another major mistake is ignoring our teenage grandchildren—beyond just wanting them to be seen and not heard. When we ignore them, they don't feel we want to see them either. Sometimes this feeling of being ignored comes simply from the way we prioritize our lives. We move far away from them, live out comfortable lives, and seldom make much more than token contact with them. When we do see them, it's often on our terms and at a superficial level.

This feeling of being ignored is compounded when they live close enough for us to visit just about whenever we want to. They can't help but interpret a lack of involvement in their lives as a statement of their unworthiness. "What is it about me that Grandma and Granddad don't like?"

Maybe our lack of attention isn't because we're so wrapped up in our own agendas. Sometimes it's because we're so annoyed by what they do and so disgusted by their culture that we simply write them off. We just don't have any desire to tolerate the extreme contrast between their generation and ours. And often we justify ourselves by moralizing the issue. As we mentioned earlier in this book, it's easy for grandparents to make the mistake of assuming that different is wrong and therefore sinful.

True, some choices our grandchildren make are sinful. Some of their music (maybe even most of it) is fairly unredemptive, and much of their style leans toward the immodest. Many teenage grandchildren have never put their faith in Jesus. In that regard, their choices are predictable. For others, they may have put their faith in Jesus but are struggling to find their way through the demands of their culture. They desperately need someone who is holding up a light for them to see where the right paths are. This is especially needed since this is the very time in their pilgrimage when they are most likely to make a final decision as to who is going to be the master of their lives.

What was true for our grandparents is still true today. To be an effective grandparent, you've got to have a high gag threshold. Grandchildren love to challenge the comfort level of their parents and grandparents. It's their job. Just like the generations of teenagers past, kids today are *different.* Different can include: weird, bizarre, strange, goofy, and quirky. If we want to be grandparents who hold God's torch high, then there's got to be plenty of room in our hearts for weird, bizarre, strange, goofy, and quirky grandchildren. It's called *grace.*

Mistake #3: Trying to Imitate Them

In addition to putting them down and ignoring them, trying to imitate them puts a stumbling block in their path to figuring out life. The questions that come to mind after decades of working with grandparents are: What is a groovy grandmother anyway? What is a cool grandfather? Do they spike and spray paint what little hair they have left, jump into the mosh pit with their grandchildren at the rock concert, hang out at the mall, and get their belly buttons pierced . . . that is, if they can find their belly buttons?

All I (Darcy) have to say about that last comment is, "Speak for yourself!" This whole issue of imitating our grandchildren is not just a problem of trying to *look* like them or *act* like them, but trying to *reason* or *think* like them. They are the children; we are supposed to be the mature adults, seasoned with wisdom from decades of living on the front lines of life. The last thing they need is grandparents who are ruled by their emotions and take the easy way out in life. That's what children are known for. Our turn for childish behavior has come and gone. We've circled the block enough that our grandchildren should be able to count on us to act like adults. When we do, we get to be torch-bearers for responsible living they so desperately need to see.

We've seen grandparents, unflinching stalwarts of the faith, revert to the irresponsible thinking of youth when it came to advising their grandchildren. We've heard a grandfather encourage his football-playing grandson to intentionally try to hurt a player on the other team. We've heard a Christian grandmother tell her Christian granddaughter to go after the nonbelieving suitor, saying, "He's so cute! There might be a future for you two. *That's* the kind of stuff you want to wake up next to each morning." We've heard several grandparents encourage their older teenagers to move in with a boyfriend or girlfriend.

If we've walked in the light of God's truth longer than everyone else in the family picture, we should be the ones who have the most unflinching and uncompromising confidence in it. Our grandchildren have all kinds of irresponsible people influencing them. They need to have confidence that when they are around us, they'll see a torch of righteousness that is always lit, always bright, and always held high.

Clearing the Path

Rather than being stumbling blocks for our teenage grandchildren, we have a wonderful opportunity to stay out ahead of them and clear the path for them. For the remainder of this chapter, we want to look at ways to make it easier for them to navigate the troubled straits of adolescence.

We mentioned earlier that it is easy to become irrelevant in the eyes of our teenage grandchildren if we don't adapt our perspective to the persons they are becoming. Remember, we are the ones who can see both the Atlantic and the Pacific from our vantage point. We can see the childhoods they are leaving behind and the adult world they are anxious to reach. This should keep us from overreacting to different things they try out during this turbulent period of time in their lives.

They might show up at our doorstep looking rather weathered during these years. This is a great time for us to focus on their hearts, not their hair—on their character, not their clothing. We need to be committed to maintaining a connection to their spirits during this fragile and exciting time in their development.

And there is some painful truth we need to face. There comes a time when some of those chubby-cheeked cherubs who thought we hung the moon turn into indifferent, prepubescent young people who would rather go over to a total stranger's house and be completely bored than come over to spend time with Grandma or Granddad. As they enter adolescence, our status may change from being adored by them to being tolerated. We need to anticipate that these sweet little angels will grow up to have whiskers and tattoos and belly-button rings. After years of being number one on their list, there's a chance we will be replaced with friends named Spike and Airhead. Still, this is a season when we need to make time for them. We need to *pursue* them, and *call* them, and *invite* them to activities with us, and show up at their events to cheer them on. This is a time to spend more resources on them, take them fishing or shopping, drive their cheerleading squad or athletic team to an event, and let them use your backyard for a youth-group gathering.

We know some great folks who have a dozen grandchildren. They've had the honor of having most of them live close-by since they were born. When the kids started going to school, both Grandma and Granddad asked permission of the parents for a back-to-school shopping day with each of them. They would spend the day buying them new clothes and school supplies. The day always included lunch at a nice restaurant, where the grandchildren could talk about their anticipations and fears as they moved into this next chapter of their lives. This tradition became crucial to the grandchildren when they became teenagers. Our friends thought the grandkids would want this tradition to fade away as they moved into adolescence. It was just the opposite. The kids had grown to rely on this tradition that marked the start of the school year. It represented more than clothes, supplies, and food. There was something stabilizing about it that they knew they needed. They were starting their new school year with people who embodied the four roles of grandparenthood in everything they did. These grandparents represented a blessing, a legacy, a bright light, and an uncompromising standard upon which these grandchildren could rely. This is just one thing these wonderful grandparents have done to secure the ongoing platform for their involvement in their teenage grandchildren's lives.

Speaking of food, eating has always been a wonderful gateway to the heart of an adolescent. Because of this, the teenage years are a great time to establish the habit of taking our grandchildren out to lunch or dinner to do some serious talking about life. These are meals where we listen, they talk, and we pick up the tab. These could well be the best moments you will ever experience with your grandchildren. It may be a time in their lives when they are struggling in their relationship with their parents and just need a sounding board.

We know one dear lady who started taking her grandchildren out to lunch and kept it up until she died. By then, her grandchildren were well into their forties. She told us, "You know you've passed the baton to them when *they* start picking up the check."

Taking the Initiative

When grandchildren are younger, they are excited to do just about anything with their grandparents. We've known little ones who were satisfied just to sit next to their grandmother and watch the *QVC* shopping network or next to their grandfather and watch the Weather Channel. This wasn't happening in our house, mind you, but in our research we learned that is wasn't uncommon in other grandparents' homes. Teenagers aren't nearly as accommodating. We grandparents shouldn't be surprised that our teenage grandchildren can become easily bored at our homes. It's part of that perception that we don't have as much in common. This is why building the relationship with them when they are younger is so important. It bridges the gap and assures them that regardless of what you do together, you are close to their hearts and know how to have fun. As we spend time with our grandchildren and listen carefully, we can find out what they are most interested in. Is it things that go fast? Take them to car shows, boat shows, motorcycle races, or a tractor pull.

We realize that some of you grandfathers reading this just got a little misty-eyed thinking about being down at the Civic Arena with one of your grandsons cheering on some guy in a Peterbilt with no mufflers. Some of your grandchildren would probably get misty-eyed too. They love it when grandparents go out of their way to make things happen that these young hearts enjoy.

Whether it's music, sports, trains, volunteering, collecting certain things, hunting, target shooting, fishing, cooking, sewing, or painting, the options are endless. But we need to be deliberate. This is also an opportune time to get them together with gifted people in areas of their interest. My (Darcy's) stepfather has really had an impact on our son Cody. He gave him a medal he earned for sinking a record number of enemy submarines in World War II. On another occasion, Cody had read the story of the famous ship *Endurance* that got stranded in the ice pack in the Antarctic early in the twentieth century. My stepfather happened to be quite familiar with that ship as he had become friends with one of the surviving crew members from that perilous voyage. That man had given my stepfather a set of wooden matches from that ship. He really made Cody's day when he passed these treasures on to him for safekeeping.

During their teenage years, our grandchildren experience wide swings in their emotions. Their hormones are off the chart; they're facing severe sexual temptation. They need someone who is a safe harbor for their inner worries. They're used to most of the adults in their lives either lecturing them or overreacting to the struggles they are having. It's amazing how much emotional ballast we can supply to them as they are trying to maneuver through the troubled seas of teenage confusion.

Through Thick and Thin

During their teenage years, some of our grandchildren get into serious trouble. The power of a grandparent who is praying for them, refusing to reject them, and challenging them to a higher standard is often the catalyst that ultimately turns them around. If we have been deliberate in cultivating a close relationship over the years, then we have a much greater opportunity to influence them and help them when they sometimes lose their way.

For some of our grandchildren, their journey through adolescence truly is "the perfect storm." Life doesn't necessarily add up. Parents don't make sense. The things of the Spirit are often confused by the many conflicting voices they hear. Their sexual urges are awakening. Their fears take center stage. What they need is a seasoned veteran—a captain who has weathered many adventures through similar seas—whom they can turn to and know that everything is going to be okay.

We grandfathers and grandmothers represent those veterans of life's stormy seas. We are the very people these tender young ones so desperately need. We hope your time spent in this chapter will inspire you to rise above the tendency to put them down, ignore them, or imitate them, and instead make yourself available to be a steady light held high that can guide them safely through to the deep and open waters of their future adult lives.

For Further Thought and Discussion

> Don't let anyone look down on you because you are young, but set an example for the believers in speech, in life, in love, in faith and in purity. (1 Timothy 4:12)

1. Of the three stumbling blocks mentioned that we can be guilty of (putting them down, ignoring them, or imitating them), which one do you find hardest not to do?
2. Why do you think grandparents might feel less confident or connected with a teenage grandchild? What can you do to retrofit your relationship with a teenage grandchild so that you will continue to have a close relationship?
3. How are you doing at remaining relevant in the eyes of your children and grandchildren? What are some things you can do to keep up with the culture in which your grandchildren are growing up?

Heavenly Father,

Thank You for these grandchildren of mine who are growing into adulthood. Let me surrender those areas in my life that are stumbling blocks to my grandchildren. My greatest prayer for them is that their hearts are committed to You and that they are living their lives to honor You. Please draw my grandchildren to You on Your timetable, and until then, protect them from themselves and forces of evil around them. Help me to be creative in fitting into their lives and connecting to their hearts. Use me to show them the way to You by how I live and how I love others. Amen.

17 Long-Distance Grandparenting

Earlier in this book we weighed in on the issue of retirement. Until lately, this season in older people's lives looked too much like the dictionary definition of the word. To retire means: to withdraw to a place of seclusion, to go away to a place of privacy, to remove oneself from active service. Families have suffered because too many of the senior members of their family tree took these words literally.

Fortunately, there's a new generation of retirees moving into position who don't have much interest in a plan that doesn't allow them to play an ongoing part in the rhythm and harmony of their extended families. There will always be some folks who pull away. Many of these represent the parents whose experience raising their children netted out to a major disappointment. For them, they are just looking forward to a relief from the pressure. But for the major share of the baby-boomer grandparents, that plan doesn't fit their philosophy of family, let alone life. These millions of people who are just now beginning to reconfigure their lives around the payouts of their pensions and 401(k)s are folks who see this new era of their lives as a time to take new ground and live greater adventures. The idea of removing themselves from active service only to relocate in a cloistered community committed to active self-service rings hollow to them. They want to play an engaging and gracious role in their grandchildren's lives.

Obviously, you can tell by what you've read so far that we're not advocating grandparents' living in tight communal configurations with their children and grandchildren—even though most families outside of North America do live lke this. These can be healthy arrangements where three of four generations have daily interaction and growth. But if there is dysfunction, these same configurations can breed enmeshed, codependent relationships that have very little upside to them. Sometimes economics or circumstances leave multigenerational families with no choice. But the ideal, however, is when we can live independent lives that allow us ample time to do the things we personally want to do while still being actively involved in the lives and dreams of our greater families.

But here is the problem: Even if you're committed to prioritizing your twilight years around your grandchildren's lives, just about every grandparent will have some of their grandchildren living far away from them. It's not necessarily that we move away from them; they move away from us.

Though your physical contact may be limited to vacations you spend with them or special times you bring them to your home, you can still maintain a regular presence in their lives. So, how do we stay close to our grandchildren when they've been scattered to the wind?

Help for the Distant Grandparent

There is good news! We live in one of the most fortunate times for grandparents who want to stay connected to grandchildren who may be time zones away. Technology provides us with numerous yet affordable ways to maintain close and meaningful relationships with these people who mean so much to us. But we've got to be deliberate. When we are, it is possible to forge paths of communication and closeness that can make the times we do see each other a comfortable continuation of an already-close relationship.

Most of us carry the best tool for staying close in our pockets or purses. Cell phones with unlimited long-distance plans can put us instantly and frequently in touch with our grandchildren. If you plan on calling often, it might be a good idea to set an agreed-upon time or ask when you reach them if this is a good time for them to talk. When children are very small, it may be a one-sided conversation with a few giggles and coos on the other end. Don't be discouraged. A baby can very quickly remember your voice and sense your love when you call. There have been many times when the sound of a gramma's voice has distracted and soothed a fussy baby into becoming a contented little child.

As your grandchildren grow and learn to talk, be prepared to ask some age-appropriate questions to keep the conversation moving. Some grandchildren are naturally chatty, and others never will be. In order for them to look forward to talking to you on the phone, the conversation needs to be fun, interesting, and comfortable for them. You might need to speak to the parent first and find out about the latest DVD a grandchild has watched, the outcome of his ball game the night before, or a major milestone like getting his training wheels removed from his bike or losing his first tooth. Armed with this inside information, you can ask relevant questions about something that is fresh, meaningful, and fun. You can be your grandchild's number one fan from a distance, using this outlet to communicate how proud you are of him and how much you love him.

A grandson who gets these kinds of messages knows he's on the mind of his grandparents.

As a grandchild gets older and enters the adolescent and early adult years, a grandparent must be more in tune to the signals a child sends through the phone lines. Ask if she has a minute to chat. If not, don't allow your disappointment to make her feel bad, but instead set up another time to call back. Also make a commitment to keep your conversation short and focusing mainly on her. You can give her a one-minute report on yourself and answer any questions that may follow, but your call should be primarily about her. Once again, it is smart to call armed with some current information about what is going on in her life. You can ask about school, sports, friends, trips, camps, and special occasions. But don't limit your conversation to what the grandchild is doing. Spend some time finding out what she's thinking and feeling about these events in her life.

Perhaps you find out he's enamored with a certain video game he's been playing. A quick search online or a few questions to the high-school geek working the video-game aisle at your local electronics store can give you a lot of insight. Obviously, this isn't to fake like you know all about the game. You don't. And unless you play it, you won't. But a grandmother or grandfather can show incredible interest in a young grandson by saying, "A neat guy over at CompUSA was showing me that game you love to play on your computer. I see why you like it. Next time I'm at you're house, I want to watch you play it." When he knows you are going out of your way to maintain a current-events relationship with him, it makes it easier for him to open up to you.

Because of the relationship you have built with your grandchild, she may feel safe to talk with you about some of her feelings and frustrations. This is where your relationship comes to a fork in the road. You have the opportunity to hear her out and leave her feeling as if she has been understood and loved, or you can jump in with advice and stories about when you were her age. If you do, she may not want to share her feelings with you often. Here are a few tips for being a good telephone sounding board to your older grandchildren:

- Listen as she describes a problem or feeling.
- Give the child time to talk it out.
- Don't interrupt.
- When you do speak, express understanding for what your grandchild is going through.

- Do not try to fix the problem or give advice unless you're specifically asked.
- If you do give advice, keep it short and to the point.
- Though you may not agree with a grandchild's lifestyle or choices, avoid preaching. Rather, affirm your love and availability. Grandchildren know what you believe and most likely know what you think of their poor choices. What they most need to know is that they have in you a safe harbor for their hearts and a place to repent when they finally come around. In the meantime, you can be praying for them.
- Avoid criticizing the people a grandchild is mad at or disappointed in—especially the parents, stepparents, siblings, or other grandparents.

The other great way to use the cell phone to maintain a connection to your grandchildren is through text messaging. We are aware that some people feel they are too old to learn new technology. That is an attitude that a conscientious grandparent can't afford to embrace. If we have cell phones and they have the capacity to send text messages, we hold in our hands a powerful tool for staying close to our grandchildren. If you don't know how to send a text message, just ask one of your grandchildren. Like so many other things we've learned to do, after you do it a couple of times, it will seem as if you were doing it all your life.

Let's say you have a grandson in college. You are tracking with his life and know his academic schedule through contact with him and his parents. You could send him short-and-sweet text messages that speak straight to his soul. Two or three of these a month will not only keep your hearts close, but they can also be a huge encouragement to him. For this example, your grandson is named Mark.

- Hi Mark. I'm praying for your history final today.
  Granddad
- Mark. I made a cinnamon apple pie today. Your favorite.
  I wish you were here to help us eat it. Grandma

- Hey Mark. I went to the Cubs game today. Wish you had been sitting next to me. They lost. Granddad
- Mark. I know you are discouraged because of all that has been happening lately. I'm praying for you. Love, Grandma
- Mark. Your grandma and I celebrated our 43rd anniversary last night. Took her out dancing. I'm a lucky man. You're a lucky grandson. GDad
- Mark. Look what I caught this morning. (He sends him a picture of a nice trout with the camera on his cell phone.) You'll get yours when you're here next summer. Granddad
- Hi Mark. I can't wait to see you at Thanksgiving. Let's ditch everyone and go to breakfast Friday morning, just you and me. I love you. Grandma

A grandson who gets these kinds of messages several times a month knows he's on the mind of his grandparents. Furthermore, they are simple ways to tell him how much he's loved, how much he is missed, and how concerned you are about his life. In the process, you can subtly teach him the priority of family, faith, and even marriage.

A friend who works with teenagers told me (Tim) about a teenage girl who lived with her single mom. The only man in her life was her grandfather, but he lived in another state. This girl had hit an all-time low. She had no social life. Boys simply hadn't been interested in her. She was convinced it was because she wasn't attractive. In desperation for recognition she talked with a boy in her class at school and agreed she would have sex with him that night. She was scared, lonely, and loathing her decision but was determined to carry it out. She felt it was her only way to find any acceptance with the guys. Just as she got in her car, her cell phone vibrated. And on that tiny screen she read these words.

"You need to know something. You are one of the most beautiful girls in the world. I'm so proud of you. Grampa."

Her plans for the evening immediately changed.

Please, Mr. Postman

Though the art of letter writing seems to be on its way out, it's still thrilling for a child to find a personal letter or postcard in the stack of bills and junk mail. Whenever we travel for an extended period of time, we always mail postcards to our grandchildren. A picture of the local wildlife or a scenic attraction is fun for a grandchild to receive. They love reading about their Nana and Papa being in a new place. A card on their birthdays or Valentine's Day is pretty standard, but cards that come for no reason at all communicate that you were thinking of them and took the time to write. Even teenagers like to get silly postcards that bring a smile and a shaking of the head that their "crazy" grandma or grandpa would send a funny card like that.

One grandfather told us that he wrote a letter to each of his grandchildren every year on his or her birthday telling each how proud he was of them, how he had seen the child mature that year, and how he would be praying for him or her during the upcoming year. Those letters, while special to receive, will become an even greater treasure as the child grows into adulthood.

Another way to connect with your grandchildren and really communicate that they are important to you, regardless of the distance that separates you, is to send them a thoughtful or funny gift. They expect them on their birthdays or Christmas, but it's fun when they get one out of the blue. These gifts don't need to be expensive or large. But they can communicate a lot of concern.

When children are small, they love getting something delivered to their house just for them. A book, a couple of special uninflated balloons, even a pack of gum (with their mom's permission), accompanied by a note saying how you were thinking about them, can make their day.

I (Darcy) was a houseguest at some friends' home and happened to be in their kitchen when the mail was being opened. One of the letters was for their six-year-old son. When he saw it was from his grandma, his eyes lit up, and he quickly opened the envelope to find one of the special-issue quarters with the state of Kentucky featured. His grandma and he were building his collection of all 50 of these new quarters. They kept track by email of those he had, and his grandma carried a list of those he was still missing. She kept a lookout for the quarters he still needed and sent them along with a note that often included an experience she had in that state represented on the quarter.

God can use our prayers to bless them on our behalf.

As children get older, it helps to stay current with their interests and send an occasional gift that hits a passion of theirs. A grandpa who lives in Phoenix goes to the spring-training games of his grandson's favorite baseball team. He does his best to get an autographed program and occasionally a signed baseball. They communicate a lot about this common interest through email and instant messaging (two other great ways to stay connected), and those occasional gifts are special ways of saying "I wish you were here. I'm thinking of you."

When our children were younger, my (Darcy's) mom, who lives in Florida, often sent a word-search puzzle from the local paper to our daughter with a note: "I saw this and thought of you. Have fun." It wasn't a big deal, but she loved that her grandmother was thinking of her.

Reach Out and Touch Them

It's hard to beat face time when it comes to staying close to our grandchildren. The Internet provides an inexpensive way to talk face-to-face by using a camera installed on your computer monitor. This is already a standard feature on some computers. But it can easily be added. Stop by your local computer store to get a crash course in what kind of hardware you need. You'll be amazed how inexpensive it is and how easy it is to set up.

Jet travel is increasingly affordable. Many of our grandparent friends structure their annual calendars around trips to see the grandchildren and trips the grandchildren make to their house. The standard times most people choose are around the holidays. However, these are not only the most hectic times to be traveling, but are also the weeks when it's harder to get the lowest prices on airline tickets. Picking alternative times that don't involve as much pressure on the family often grants you the chance to make better memories with the grandkids. Times like just after the first of the year, the week before they start back to school, or the first week after they get out of school make it a lot easier to plan and create ample one-on-one time.

As we bring this discussion to a close, we have yet to mention the two best ways you can keep grandkids close to your heart. The first is checking in with their parents on a regular basis in order to keep informed about all that is happening in their lives. The second is to use that information to pray for their specific needs *every day.* They have things they are excited about, worried or disappointed over, and hoping for. When we make it our aim to take these things that mean so much to them to the God to Whom they mean so much, they become closer to our hearts. We may not be on their minds as much as they are on ours, but God can use our prayers to bless them on our behalf.

Surrogate Grandchildren

Just because our grandchildren don't live close to us doesn't mean we can't have grandchildren in our daily lives. There are families all around us who have children who could use some older, wiser people crossing their paths. Our churches and communities have single moms who are carrying an enormous load. Divorces often take grandparents out of the picture for their children. You could play a huge role in helping to provide a "grandparent" for these children. A private discussion with your pastor or a sensitivity to single-parent families in your community is probably all you'd need to connect with one of these moms.

Being a volunteer reader to children at the library or helping coach a basketball or football team in a distressed community allows you to have a spiritual and moral influence on kids and teenagers who really need it. You'll be sharpening your skills for those times when the phone rings or there's a knock at the front door and you hear "Hi, Grandma!" or "Hi, Grandpa!"

Making the Most of Long-Distance Grandparenthood

1. Write a letter or send a note or card often.
2. Keep your mental picture of them up to date so you don't send or say something way too babyish.
3. Get on the computer and email them.
4. Set up an instant-messaging time each week.
5. Participate in a family Web page.
6. Exchange digital photos.
7. Call them on the phone often, and follow up on any major events, such as games, performances, and big tests.
8. Plan to be a part of their family vacations as often as asked. Make a photo album of these special times.
9. Invite them to come and spend a week with you for some individual fun time.
10. Do your best to be with them for the celebrations and milestones in their lives, such as births, recitals, holidays, baptisms, graduations, and weddings.

For Further Thought and Discussion

For this reason, since the day we heard about you, we have not stopped praying for you and asking God to fill you with the knowledge of his will through all spiritual wisdom and understanding. And we pray this in order that you may live a life worthy of the Lord and may please him in every way: bearing fruit in every good work, growing in the knowledge of God. (Colossians 1:9-10)

1. What are some creative ways you have heard of or used to stay connected to grandchildren who live far away? What might you have to do to get "tech savvy" in order to communicate with your grandchildren?
2. What are some of the reasons grandchildren live far away? What are some reasons that might encourage you to move closer to your grandchildren, or are there reasons that may take you farther away in the future? What will your children and grandchildren think of these reasons?
3. Is there a child in your life right now, not including your own, who may need a grandparent? What can you do to fill that void?

Heavenly Father,
Thank You that Your love knows no bounds and that prayer knows no limits. Please keep my grandchildren who live far away in the forefront of my mind and heart. Help me to stay current with them and communicate my love and interest in who they are and what they are doing. Please use me, in spite of the miles, to meet their needs for security, significance, and strength. Use my life as a testimony to them that ultimately they may find all they need in You. Amen.

part four

A GRAND IMPRESSION

18 Rock-'n'-Roll Grandparents

Who would have thought that these two concepts—*rock 'n' roll* and *grandparents*—could be used in the same sentence? It's called "extreme grandparenting." It represents the baby boomers coming full circle. What consumed so much of our attention as young people is now a prefix to our new role as grandparents.

We are part of the new generation of grandparents who aren't likely to be known for our rocking chairs. We're a high-tech, high-touch collection of grandmothers and grandfathers who have traveled more, read more, seen more, and done more than the generation that created us. If rocking chairs illustrated our parents' generation, then rock 'n' roll illustrates ours.

Bridges over Troubled Water

Rock-'n'-roll grandparents? It fits. In fact, I (Tim) saw exactly what we're talking about played out right before my eyes . . . in church of all places. It was Easter Sunday morning, a day when churches welcome a lot of folks from their communities who don't usually attend. Our church had prepared for the extra guests by offering services at two different locations on our campus on that Sunday morning. Our daughter, the mother of our first grandchild, was in one of the choirs and was going to be singing a solo in a couple of the services. Her husband was overseeing the technical aspects of the services. They called on us to see if we could give them a hand with the baby that morning.

We love those kinds of requests. There's nothing like trying to get yourself and an infant ready for church on time to remind you of how much you need a Savior. We actually did better than we thought we would. We enjoyed a great breakfast with our three children who were still at home at that time and even managed to pull into the church parking lot early. That's when we had a brief tug-of-war over our granddaughter in her car seat.

We are a bridge between the past and future.

She had drifted to sleep on the way to church. I (Tim) was going to drop the family off close to the sanctuary and then go park the car. Darcy reached to take the baby with her so she could put her in the nursery, but I wanted to do it. I think we were both looking forward to the joy of carrying her across the church campus to the "oohs" and "aahs" of our friends.

The fact that no one would actually notice either one of us carrying her was more the reality, but Darcy was kind enough to agree to let me do it after I peeled her fingers, one at a time, off the handle of the infant car seat. Actually, it wasn't quite that bad, but she could see I was looking forward to being left in charge of my granddaughter.

I didn't have to look long for a parking spot. But just as I pulled into it, a crisis occurred. Simon and Garfunkel's ballad "Bridge Over Troubled Water" came on. I *love* that song. And I hadn't heard it in a long time.

I wondered what I should do. I needed to get my granddaughter to the nursery. But, as I said, I hadn't heard the song in a long time.

I looked at my watch. I peeked at the backseat and saw she was deep in sleep. And then it hit me: *This song is like a lullaby; a sweet and quiet melody that will wash over her before I drop her off in a room of screaming babies.* I decided to let her savor the moment. And to add to her listening enjoyment, I joined Simon and Garfunkel with some nice harmony.

But God wanted to point something out to me in the music's gentle strains and peacefulness of the moment. Before I mention what it was, I probably need to let you in on something I've learned about God. I believe that when you let the Holy Spirit into every part of your life and every moment of your day, He can use just about anything—even an old Simon and Garfunkel ballad—to teach you His truth.

As I sat there in the car with my granddaughter asleep in her car seat, I couldn't get over how much the words to that familiar song define our role as grandparents. When they are worn out and feeling overwhelmed, we will help dry their tears. When they feel all alone in difficult times, we'll be there to give them support. We want to promise them that no matter what, "like a bridge over troubled water, I will lay me down . . ."[1]

I couldn't help but think of the troubled water the little girl sleeping in the backseat of my car would encounter in the future. She would need some way to ford those streams. Fortunately, God had blessed her with great parents, but there would be times when even they would look at the rushing waters before them and wonder what they should do.

God reminded me through that ballad that He had a very important role for Darcy and me to play in this little child's life and in the lives of all the other grandchildren who would join her in our family tree. When the song ended, I carefully unbelted her from the car seat, put her diaper bag over my shoulder, and carried her to the nursery—careful not to wake her. But the lesson wasn't over.

Savvy Grandparents

When I opened the door to the nursery, I was surprised and pleased to see three sets of grandparents waiting to take her off my hands. I knew two of these couples very well. They were a little older than Darcy and I. Each had raised two sons and a daughter and had done a phenomenal job. These were rock-'n'-roll grandparents—people who had seen Elvis and the Beatles in concert—but who were now sitting in the church nursery comforting a new generation of infants. I thought of how fortunate my granddaughter was that people like these waited in the wings, ready to offer her a helping hand. These folks had given their hearts to Jesus as young people. They had raised their children through some of the toughest chapters in our nation's history. They hadn't cloistered their hearts or hidden their faith from the world around them. They had boldly lived out their beliefs in the middle of their rock-'n'-roll culture and managed to raise wonderful children in the process. It's not that difficult to do when you make Jesus your life, rather than a compartment in it.

I was leaving my granddaughter in expert care . . . and savoring the moment as I walked over to the church service. But the lesson still wasn't over.

Once I joined Darcy and our children in church, I was reminded why any of us has even a remote chance of being a bridge over the challenges our children and grandchildren face. It is because God first sent His Son to build a bridge between time and eternity for us. The most troubled water any of us ever faces is a river that has its source in our sinful and lost hearts. But it is Jesus who built a bridge over the raging water separating us from God, and He did it with a cross.

We have been given a chance to represent something sure, steady, and reliable to our grandchildren. We are a bridge between the past and the future, a bridge that spans the troubled water of the present with calm and confidence.

CliffsNotes for the Epic Story of Life

Our grandchildren are watching us and quietly taking notes. Hopefully they will take their cues for living meaningful lives from what they learn. God has given them parents, teachers, and coaches—good people from whom they will learn much. But it is to us, *their grandparents,* He has given the task of showing them whether a life of faith can carry people through to the end and ultimately enable them to finish strong.

We've tried to outline for you the ingredients for a clear mission statement for grandparenthood. Grandparenthood is a deeply relational way to use our lives to make an earthly and eternal difference in the lives of those we will someday leave behind. We've talked about four roles we have and three needs our grandchildren have. This has been a study about making an impact on lives we love more than our own. It's been about living lives that matter beyond this life. Our grandchildren are longing for people in their lives who truly believe that God *is,* and that He is a rewarder of those who diligently seek Him (see Hebrews 11:6).

Many of you reading this book are young. As we said at the beginning, the average age of a first-time grandparent is 47. You have the luxury of being actively involved in your grandchildren's lives. Inevitably, your bodies will start to deteriorate, and your disabilities will hinder you from playing the kinds of active roles you'd prefer. Yet you can still have an extreme impact on them. How you are living as grandparents now, while you're young and energetic, will play a significant role in how you are viewed when your physical limitations finally have their way. Your passionate commitment to being godly and gracious grandparents *now* will become the symbolic persona your grandchildren will attach to you *then.*

Being a grandparent is a reminder that, though we may have a lot of years left on earth, the years ahead are likely fewer than those behind us. What do you want your life to count for? What is your mission going to be for the rest of your life? Do you want it to be leisure? Do you want it to be the accumulation of more material possessions you have to leave behind? Or do you want to use these last semesters of your life to make an eternal difference? Your role as a grandparent offers you one of the most significant opportunities to leave a legacy that never dies.

Finding Us Faithful

Singer Steve Green captured the power of a good legacy in a song he recorded several years back called "Find Us Faithful." It's a song written by Jon Mohr, whose poetry both hounds us and haunts us to be diligent about the kind of legacy we are leaving. We want to share the last verse and the chorus of this song with you as we bring this discussion of grandparenthood to a close:

> After all our hopes and dreams have come and gone
> And our children sift through all we've left behind
> May the clues that they discover and the memories they uncover
> Become the light that leads them to the road we each must find
> Oh may all who come behind us find us faithful
> May the fire of our devotion light their way
> May the footprints that we leave
> lead them to believe
> And the lives we live inspire them to obey
> Oh may all who come behind us find us faithful.[2]

We grandparents are lights, we're standards, we're blessings, we're legacies, and we're bridges over troubled water for a young and fragile generation. We're all making choices. Time will prove, and eternity will tell, whether or not our choices add up.

When our lives here on earth are finally over, our true epitaphs will not be carved in stone. They will be carved on the souls and in the memories of our children, our grandsons, and granddaughters. Regardless of what someone someday chooses to write about us on our tombstones, those words can never overwrite what we were. God gives the last word on our lives to those we leave behind. We are all writing the epitaphs of our lives on the hearts of our children and grandchildren. They will sum up our significance someday. And that sum total will have a deep and abiding effect on the lives that they end up leading. We are not curators of the dead; we are stewards of the living. The children and grandchildren who must move into tomorrow surround us. Someday we will stand before the God who bought our eternal souls on a cross. Now we are leaving a legacy. Then we will give an account. Between now and then is all the time we have. Let's make good use of it.

What is your mission going to be for the rest of your life?

Since my youth, O God, you have taught me,
 and to this day I declare your marvelous deeds.
Even when I am old and gray,
 do not forsake me, O God,
 till I declare your power to the next generation,
 your might to all who are to come. (Psalm 71:17-18)

For Further Thought and Discussion

I pray that out of his glorious riches he may strengthen you with power through his Spirit in your inner being, so that Christ may dwell in your hearts through faith. And I pray that you, being rooted and established in love, may have power, together with all the saints, to grasp how wide and long and high and deep is the love of Christ, and to know this love that surpasses knowledge—that you may be filled to the measure of all the fullness of God. (Ephesians 3:16-19)

1. How would you say your mission statement for your life as a grandparent has changed after reading this book? How will your children and grandchildren benefit?
2. What are some ways God can use you to be a bridge over troubled water for your grandchildren?
3. What are two things you are putting into practice that were discussed in this book? What are some additional things you need to change in order to become a more effective grandparent?
4. Along the lines of Paul's prayer in Ephesians 3:16-19, write out a prayer for the lives of your grandchildren.

Thank you for reading *Extreme Grandparenting: The Ride of Your Life!* Why not share this book with a friend, neighbor, or your pastor? One of the ways you can make a difference in the lives of many grandchildren and grandparents is to organize a group to go through this book as a study. Here are some ideas for formats:

- A grandparents' Sunday-school class
- A grandparents' retreat
- A weekly breakfast or luncheon series
- A home-fellowship study
- A Sunday-evening series

We also recommend the *Extreme Grandparenting: The Ride of Your Life!* DVD study for you or your group. Call 800-467-4596 or go to www.grandparenthood.net for more information.

We invite you to close this book with the Grandparents' Prayer:

Dear Heavenly Father, thank You for creating families, and thank You especially for the gift of our grandchildren. I pray that You would protect and prepare them morally, physically, emotionally, intellectually, and spiritually. I offer myself to be used by You in the lives of my grandchildren to bless them, to light their way, to be a good example, and to leave a legacy through them that lasts forever. Amen.

notes

Chapter 1

1. For more information on the *Extreme Grandparenting: The Ride of Your Life!* DVD Series, go to www.grandparenthood.net.
2. Peggy Noonan
3. Kathryn and Allan Zullo, adapted from *The Nanas and the Papas* (Kansas City: Andrews McMeel, 1998), 11–12.

Chapter 2

1. Tim Kimmel, *Raising Kids for True Greatness* (Nashville: Nelson, 2006).
2. Tim and Darcy Kimmel, *Extreme Grandparenting: The Ride of Your Life!* DVD curriculum (Scottsdale: Family Matters, 2004). For more information, go to www.grandparenthood.net.

Chapter 3

1. Melody Warnick, "Your Family Next Door," *Better Homes and Gardens* September, 2006.

Chapter 4

1. Tim Kimmel, *Grace-Based Parenting* (Nashville: W Publishing Group, 2004). To learn more about this book go to www.family matters.net.

Chapter 6

1. Arthur Kornhaber, *The Grandparent Guide* (New York: McGraw Hill, 2002), 165.

Chapter 11

1. Bob Moos, "Grandparents Face Challenges Raising Another Generation," *Dallas Morning News*, September 7, 2004.

2. Alvin Powell, "Grandkids Can Make You Sick," *Harvard University Gazette,* December 4, 2003.
3. Powell, "Grandkids Can Make You Sick."
4. If you aren't familiar with this Bible story it is definitely worth your time to check it out. Just look up the book of Esther in the front of your Bible. It only takes up about seven pages in the average Bible, but it's an incredible story of trusting God to face a huge challenge. It's a tremendous encouragement for grandparents who find themselves raising their grandchildren.

Chapter 14

1. Tim Kimmel, *The High Cost of High Control* (Scottsdale, AZ: Family Matters, 2005). Available at www.familymatters.net.
2. "Resolving Conflict," adapted from the *Weekend to Remember* Conference Manual (Little Rock, AR: Family Life, 2006), 179.
3. Robert Lewis, *Raising a Modern-Day Knight* (Colorado Springs: Focus on the Family, 2005).

Chapter 18

1. Paul Simon, "Bridge Over Troubled Water," copyright © 1970, Columbia Records.
2. "Find Us Faithful" words and music by Jon Mohr. Copyright © 1987 Jonathan Mark Music, Birdwing Music. All rights reserved. Used by permission.